The Madwoman in the Rabbi's Attic

Rereading the Women of the Talmud

מגיד
MAGGID

Pardes | פרדס
Institute of Jewish Studies

Gila Fine

The Madwoman in the Rabbi's Attic

Rereading the Women of the Talmud

Pardes Institute of Jewish Studies
Maggid Books

The Madwoman in the Rabbi's Attic
Rereading the Women of the Talmud

First Edition, 2024

Maggid Books
An imprint of Koren Publishers Jerusalem Ltd.

POB 8531, New Milford, CT 06776-8531, USA
& POB 4044, Jerusalem 9104001, Israel
www.maggidbooks.com

The publication of this book was made possible
through the generous support of *The Jewish Book Trust.*
and the Pardes Institute of Jewish Studies.

ISBN 978-1-59264-687-6, *hardcover*

Printed and bound in Israel

In loving memory of our parents

Belda Kaufman Lindenbaum

בילה שרה בת זאב דב ורבקה ז״ל

Marcel Lindenbaum

מרדכי בן נתן נטע ודבורה גיטל ז״ל

Joseph Appleman

יוסף בן הלל ובינה ז״ל

Florence Appleman

פרדל עליזה בת יצחק יעקב וחנה מלכה ז״ל

Shari & Nathan J. Lindenbaum

Contents

Beruria said to him, "Fool! Cast your eyes to the end of the verse."
(Berakhot 10a)

Revision – the act of looking back, of seeing with fresh eyes,
of entering an old text from a new critical direction –
is for us more than a chapter in cultural history:
it is an act of survival.
(Adrienne Rich)

Introduction

This book begins three days before my twelfth birthday. I was on a family visit to my grandparents in London; everyone had gone out for the day, and I was left behind with a pile of my grandfather's books and strict instructions to write my bat mitzva speech. Not knowing much about, well, anything, I reached for the first book on the pile: *The Book of Legends* – a collection of stories from the Talmud and other rabbinic works, organized according to theme. I opened to the theme of "woman," which seemed appropriate to the occasion, and started to read. Three stories in, I felt a little uneasy; by the tenth, I was in tears, sobbing as only a nearly-twelve-year-old can. I was so hurt, so deeply offended that the rabbis, the architects of my religion and heroes of my childhood, could have such a low opinion of me and my kind. The women in their stories were weak. They were irrational. They were greedy and petty and promiscuous and vain. "When woman was created, the Devil was created with her," one of the sources read (Genesis Rabba 17:7). Woman was the mother of all vice.

I ended up cobbling together some quotes for my speech (thankfully, there were enough sources from which to cherry-pick), but everything changed for me that day. The simple faith, the unquestioning devotion of my childhood were gone, and in their place were confusion and pain and doubt. I fought to make peace with a religion I so loved, knowing that its founding fathers felt about me the way they did. I spent many years questioning, searching, reading everything in sight. After high school and national service, I went to a seminary to study Talmud (a subject forbidden to me growing up[1]). But it wasn't until I went to university to study literature that I began to find the answers I was looking for. Learning how to read talmudic stories as talmudic stories ought to be read, I discovered that they are not at all as they first seem; that there is a great deal more to the heroines of the Talmud than initially meets the eye; and that the rabbis had some surprising – so as not to say, proto-feminist – ideas of marriage, childbirth, female sexuality, and what it means to be a woman in the world. After many years of intense religious struggle, the stories of the Talmud, which had so upset me at twelve, became my constant study and my greatest joy. This book is the result of that struggle.

Seeing with Fresh Eyes: Rereading the Women of the Talmud

Women in the Talmud are notoriously nameless. It's not that they do not appear at all – they do (though, as a work composed by rabbis for rabbis, the Talmud features women as often as it features non-rabbinic men, which is to say, not terribly often). But when they do, they are generally marginal and almost always anonymous, named after the important rabbi in their life; they are mothers of, daughters of, sisters of, wives of. In all of rabbinic literature, there are just fifty-two named women, as opposed to over a thousand named men.[2] Of these fifty-two, only half a dozen are heroines of their own talmudic narrative: Yalta, Ḥoma, Marta, Ḥeruta, Beruria, and Ima Shalom.[3]

1. On the historical exclusion of women from the study of Talmud, see Chapter 5.
2. Tal Ilan, *Mine and Yours Are Hers: Retrieving Women's History from Rabbinic Literature*, 278–79. Ilan's count is limited to rabbinic (and pre-rabbinic) women, and does not include references to biblical women.
3. One notable absence from this list is Rabbi Akiva's wife, popularly known as Raḥel. This name, however, is only given to her in the later work of Avot DeRabbi Natan (6); the Talmud, as is its wont, refers to her just as "Kalba Savua's daughter" or "Rabbi Akiva's wife" (Y Shabbat 6:1, Ketubot 62b–63a, Nedarim 50b).

Other than having their very own name, and their very own story, there seems to be little to connect these heroines. Three of them live in Israel during the late Second Temple and early rabbinic periods, three live in Babylonia during the later rabbinic period. Four are married, two are widowed. One is beautiful, one is rich, at least three are highly knowledgeable. Four are tragic figures, one is comedic, one features in a drama. All, however, have this in common: Every one of these heroines seems, at first reading, to embody an anti-feminine archetype, a derisive caricature of a "bad woman"; Yalta is a shrew, Ḥoma a femme fatale, Marta a prima donna, Ḥeruta a madonna/whore, Beruria an overreacherix, and Ima Shalom a (fallen) angel in the house. And yet, with practically every one of them we will find, upon second reading, that this is not at all the case; once the heroine's story is reread, more closely and in context, her archetype systematically breaks down, and in its place emerges the character of a complex, extraordinary woman, as misunderstood by her own world as by generations of readers.

We will therefore read the story of each heroine twice: once, to determine its primary meaning, and a second time, to uncover the deeper truth that lies hidden between its lines. The rereading of a text in order to try and see it in a new, redemptive light is what 20th-century poet Adrienne Rich describes as "revisioning": "Revision – the act of looking back, of seeing with fresh eyes, of entering an old text from a new critical direction – is for us more than a chapter in cultural history: It is an act of survival."[4]

In revisioning the stories of the women of the Talmud, there is a great deal we stand to learn, both about how to read a text, and about how to regard an Other. Women, for the rabbis, are the paradigmatic Other, "a people unto themselves" (Shabbat 62a).[5] When the Talmud tells a tale of a woman, nine times out of ten it tells a tale of an Other,

---

4. Adrienne Rich, "When We Dead Awaken: Writing as Re-Vision," 18.

5. The statement is attributed to Ulla, whose views on women will be discussed in the following chapter. Rabbinic literature, says Judith Wegner, "treats the male as the norm and the female, by definition, as an anomaly, a deviation from the norm. Woman as 'Other' automatically occupies a different category from man… she is both 'like' and 'not like' man." Judith R. Wegner, *Chattel or Person? The Status of Women in the Mishnah*, 5.

imparting moral lessons about how to treat the Others in our midst. In this respect, the rabbis, far more than they may be said to be feminists, are, fundamentally, moralists.

Now, I do not wish to imply that everything in the Talmud is proto-feminist. Far from it; the Talmud is a product of Late Antiquity, and much of it, we shall see, is steeped in patriarchal thought (there was a reason I cried that day). Women throughout the ancient world were repressed and restricted, financially dependent and politically dispossessed, deprived of basic social and legal rights – and the women of the Talmud were no different.[6] But every now and then, the text transcends its historical context, as the Talmud tells a story that critiques patriarchal culture, portrays a powerful woman, or offers a feminine point of view. It is to these moments that this book is dedicated.

Negotiating Our Differences: Reading as Relationship

The relationship with the Other is one of the central themes of rabbinic narrative. Indeed, it's been suggested that the stories of the Talmud all fall into one of two categories: those that show that the gap between man and God is smaller than we think, and those that show that the gap between man and man is greater than we imagine.[7] The tales of the heroines of the Talmud belong to this second group.

6. "Classical rabbinic Judaism has always been… a male dominated culture, whose virtuosi and authorities are males, whose paragon of normality in all legal discussions is the adult Jewish male, whose legal rulings in many areas of life (notably marriage and ritual observance) accord men greater privilege than women, and whose values define public communal space as male space. Within this culture, women are unable to initiate a marriage or a divorce, are obligated to dress modestly in public and to segregate themselves behind a partition in synagogue, and are excluded from the regimen of prayer and Torah study that characterizes, and in the rabbinic perspective sanctifies, the life of Jewish men…. In this culture, women are socially and legally inferior to men." Shaye J.D. Cohen, *Why Aren't Jewish Women Circumcised? Gender and Covenant in Judaism*, 135–36.
7. Ari Elon, "The Symbolization of the Plot Components in the Talmudic Story," 107.

But relationships are not just a main concern of rabbinic stories; reading these stories is itself a relationship. The ways we respond to the talmudic text are not unlike the ways we respond to an Other, particularly when the Talmud – like the Other – doesn't see things exactly as we do.

The first type of response is rejection. You and I are too different, we might say to the Other, we disagree on far too much; this relationship can never be. Such is the response made by many readers throughout Jewish history, as we have moved further and further away from the rabbinic period, and the gaps between our views and those expressed in the Talmud – scientific, theological, ethical, political – have grown ever wider. No longer reflecting what they believe in, the Talmud, for these readers, has ceased to be a source of religious authority, cultural heritage, or moral wisdom. They have simply walked away.

A second possible response is accommodation. We're clearly very different, we would say to the divergent Other, but I want this relationship so badly, I will change everything about myself to make it work. This is a response often found on the right, where readers, faced with the inevitable dissonance between the Talmud's opinions and their own, alter the latter to accommodate the former. Such readers sacrifice their identity to the text.

A third response is subjection. You and I are different, so if you want to have this relationship, you are going to have to change everything about yourself. This response is typically found on the left, where readers eliminate the gap between themselves and the Talmud by misinterpreting it (whether deliberately or not), subjecting its meaning to contemporary thought. The text loses its integrity so that the readers may maintain theirs.

A fourth response, the one this book strives to adopt, is negotiation. We're very different, you and I, and there's much we disagree on, but this relationship is something we both want. So I will come to it with all of my opinions, and you will do the same, and we'll negotiate to make it work. This is not only the healthiest way to manage a relationship, it is also the best way to read a text. We must bring our whole selves to the encounter with the talmudic text, as we must allow the Talmud to bring its full self to its encounter with us. We must give full voice to our beliefs and our biases, and let the Talmud speak its own (for we are no less conditioned by the 21st century than the Talmud is by Antiquity).[8] We must negotiate our differences, and dialogue where we disagree. It is only when we are who we are, and accept the Talmud for what it is, that a true relationship, a real act of reading – where we learn and evolve and grow – can occur.

The Laughing Face of God: A History of Aggada

The rabbis were, as mentioned, the founding fathers of the Jewish religion, and the rabbinic period (c. 1st–7th century) is roundly considered to be the classical era of Judaism. It was during this time, following the Destruction of the Second Temple (70 CE) and consequent upheaval of Jewish life, that Judaism acquired the character and creed it has to this day.[9]

The first work of rabbinic culture was the Mishna (c. 200 CE), a compendium of legal traditions which had been passed down orally from one generation to the next (and which were attributed to the Oral Torah revealed at Sinai as a companion to the Written Torah). After the Destruction, the rabbis, fearful for the survival of these traditions, organized and codified them into the sixty-three tractates of the Mishna, each tractate dedicated to a different area of Jewish life: Berakhot (blessings), Kiddushin (marriages), Avoda Zara (idolatry), etc. Shortly after there appeared the Tosefta (c. 230 CE), a supplementary work to the Mishna

8. This is what Daniel Boyarin terms "generous critique" – a critique of a text from the reader's perspective, without diminishing either the former's then and there or the latter's here and now. Daniel Boyarin, *Carnal Israel: Reading Sex in Talmudic Culture*, 21.
9. See Chapter 3. It is not for nothing that the Judaism practiced for the past two thousand years is known as *rabbinic* Judaism. What follows is a very broad overview of rabbinic history and works; for a more comprehensive introduction, see Charlotte E. Fonrobert and Martin S. Jaffee, eds., *The Cambridge Companion to the Talmud and Rabbinic Literature*, 1–9; Hermann L. Strack and Günter Stemberger, *Introduction to the Talmud and Midrash*, 1–350; Barry S. Wimpfheimer, *The Talmud: A Biography*, 15–40.

which followed the same structure and contained many traditions not included in the latter.

Another set of works produced during this early rabbinic period were the halakhic midrashim (c. 3rd century) – collections of legal statements ordered, not by theme as in the Mishna and Tosefta, but by the biblical verses on whose interpretation they hinge (midrash being the rabbis' unique mode of biblical exegesis). There are three main works of halakhic midrashim: the Mekhilta (on Exodus), the Sifra (on Leviticus), and the Sifrei (on Numbers and Deuteronomy).

As rabbinic history progressed, the rabbis turned their interpretive skills from biblical law to biblical narrative, composing numerous aggadic midrashim (c. 4th century on) – works devoted to close and creative readings of the stories of the Bible. Best known among these are the ten volumes of Midrash Rabba on the Torah and the Five Scrolls, in addition to such later works as Midrash Mishlei, Pirkei DeRabbi Eliezer, and the Tanḥuma.

Finally, of course, there is the Talmud, the crowning achievement of rabbinic culture. After its completion, the Mishna became the central text of the rabbinic study hall (or beit midrash), where its finer points were parsed, debated, and developed so that a large body of commentaries was formed around it. These commentaries were orally transmitted through the generations until they, too, were collected and redacted, and so was the Talmud born. Or, more accurately, Talmuds, for there are two such compositions: the Jerusalem Talmud (or Yerushalmi, c. 400 CE), edited – contrary to its name – in the north of Israel, and the Babylonian Talmud (or Bavli, c. 650 CE), edited in the Babylonian yeshivas of Sura and Pumbedita. It is the Bavli that became the cornerstone of Jewish life and learning, the one we refer to when we say, simply, "the Talmud."

Because the Babylonian rabbis, unlike their Israelite counterparts, did not create independent works of midrash (the primary halakhic and aggadic midrashim all originated in Israel), the Bavli became the single repository for all of Jewish wisdom at the time: legal conversations surrounding the Mishna, midrashic interpretations of the Bible, legends concerning the rabbis, sermons made in the synagogues, philosophical discussions of God and the universe, principles of Jewish faith and particulars of Jewish practice, ethical epigrams on the good life and the just society, biological theories and astrological teachings, folk remedies for brain tumors and kidney stones and toothache. All this, and more, is the Talmud – an immense, encyclopedic, kaleidoscopic treasure trove of Jewish knowledge.

The vast rabbinic corpus is traditionally divided into two meta-genres: halakha – the legal debates, and aggada – the narratives. The rabbis themselves describe aggada as a distinct discourse on several occasions. "Do you wish to know the Creator of the world?" asks the midrash, and rhetorically replies, "Then learn aggada, for through it you will come to know God and cleave to His ways" (Sifrei Deuteronomy 49); while halakha deals with the fine detail of the law, aggada is concerned with the big questions of God and religion and morality. Elsewhere, the rabbis play on the two possible roots of "aggada" – *H-G-D* (lit., to tell) or *N-G-D* (lit., to draw) – when they describe it as "words which draw one's heart like a tale" (Shabbat 87a), alluding to the compelling nature of narrative. In yet another instance, the rabbis list aggada among the different parts of the Oral Torah revealed by God at Sinai: "God appeared… with an angry face for Bible, a moderate face for Mishna, a friendly face for Talmud, a laughing face for aggada" (Pesikta DeRav Kahana 12:25); as opposed to the other elements of the rabbinic curriculum, aggada is playful, whimsical, subversive – the laughing face of God.

The beauty of these rabbinic descriptions notwithstanding, the real working definition of aggada was coined years later, in the geonic period (directly following the rabbinic period, c. 7th–11th century): "Aggada is every interpretation that appears in the Talmud about any matter that is not a commandment."[10] Simply put, aggada is everything in the Talmud (and, by extension, rabbinic literature) that is not halakha. Under this broad negative definition there is a whole range of aggadic sub-genres: midrash and rabbinic legends and philosophical inquiry and parables and sermons and folktales and epigrams and jokes.[11] But it is

10. Rabbi Shmuel ben Hofni Gaon, *Introduction to the Science of the Mishna and Talmud*.
11. Hayim Nahman Bialik, Israel's national poet and the editor of the aforementioned *Book of Legends*, aptly captures the richness and variety of aggada in the book's introduction: "Aggada is… a classic expression of the spirit of our nation…. Practically all

not just a multiplicity of form that defines aggada, it is also a multiplicity of content: from the lofty discussions of metaphysics and theology to small, everyday tales of friendship and family, food and money, study and sex. Herein is the profound humanism of the rabbis; nothing is deemed too trivial or mundane to be the subject of a rabbinic story. In aggada, everything is included because everything is important, everything is meaningful, everything carries a lesson to be learned.[12]

Thus was aggada immortalized within rabbinic literature in general, and the Talmud in particular (where it constitutes one-third of the text[13]). The geonim, who succeeded the rabbis as leaders of the Babylonian Jewish community, were the first to recognize the foundational significance of their forebears and canonize their writings. The Talmud assumed its rightful place at the heart of the beit midrash and as the basis of Jewish law.

Not all parts of the Talmud, however, were considered equal. The study of aggada, as opposed to that of halakha, had no immediate practical implications. The stories often seemed silly and inconsequential. Above all, cultural changes between the rabbinic and post-rabbinic periods rendered aggada more than a little problematic: The worldwide turn, inspired by Greek philosophy, from mythos (narrative) to logos (reason) called into question many of the rabbis' more fantastical tales; and the Talmud's newfound canonical status made its subversive

literary genres that were prevalent in Israel at the time made their way into aggada.... Whoever wishes to know the nation of Israel in all of its different dimensions, let him learn aggada." H.N. Bialik and Y.N. Ravnitzky, eds., *The Book of Legends*, 1.

12. "Classical Judaism produced a literature which looks at first sight like someone's grandmother's attic in which endless quantities of curious things which 'might someday come in handy' have been passed down like so many balls of string lovingly collected over the years and piled on top of each other without apparent concern for distinctions between weighty and trivial matters.... This apparent jumble of piety and trivia is the medium of the rabbinic message which is the effort to penetrate every corner of ordinary life with God's presence.... The rabbis think nothing of making their most profound comments on the nature of God in the midst of discussing the uses of cheese!" Rosemary Radford Ruether, "Judaism and Christianity: Two Fourth-Century Religions," 7–8.
13. J.H. Weiss, *Dor Dor VeDorshav*, 9.

stories – accounts of bad rabbinic behavior, composed by rabbis for rabbis and not meant for public consumption – a matter of deep discomfort.

The geonim, as we saw, responded to these cultural challenges by formally contrasting halakha and aggada – and invalidating the latter. "We do not rely on aggada," they repeatedly stated;[14] whereas halakha is authoritative and binding, aggada should only be heeded when it accords with reason. Another response, formulated in the geonic period and popularized by talmudic commentators in the Middle Ages, was to rationalize aggada, usually by interpreting it allegorically, "as a riddle [or] a parable"[15] (so that even the most trivial of tales became a vehicle for deep esoteric wisdom). A third response, equally popular among medieval talmudists, and surviving well into the modern era, was to remove the subversive sting from the stories by providing them with apologetic explanations. The most prevalent response, however, was marginalization; the stories of the Talmud were consistently ignored, glossed over in traditional yeshiva study, and disregarded by the majority of commentaries.

The modern resurgence of aggada began in the 19th century, when Jewish historians turned to it as a window into the rabbinic period. Here was, after all, the classical era of Judaism, and practically the only historical records they had of it were the works of the rabbis themselves. Historical records which, all told, weren't terribly historical: The glaring contradictions between key facts and figures of Antiquity and their representation in rabbinic literature, the internal inconsistencies between different rabbinic descriptions of the same event, the stories' emphasis on spiritual or moral (rather than geopolitical) causality, their featuring of mythical creatures and supernatural occurrences, and most importantly, their literary elegance and structural artistry – all these point to the obviously fictional nature of aggada.[16] Nineteenth-century historians, however, held fast to the premise that the stories of rabbinic literature

14. See, for example, B.M. Levin, ed., *Otzar HaGeonim*, Berakhot:91, Ḥagiga:59–60.

15. Maimonides, *Commentary on the Mishna*, Sanhedrin:10:1.

16. This claim was not, strictly speaking, new; even traditional commentators were forced in some cases to admit that "our rabbis' story… never happened in this manner." Rabbi Azaria de Rossi, *Meor Einayim*, 16:299.

contained a kernel of historical truth, and devoted much of their efforts to trying to identify these kernels and piece them together into a full account of rabbinic history. The rabbinic chronologies created in this process were not only methodologically flawed (the result of imposing a modern view of history onto pre-modern texts that didn't share the same view) but also highly speculative, no less fictional than the fictional chaff the historians sought to eliminate.

It was only in the late 20th century that aggada became the province of those best suited to analyze it: literary scholars. Aggada is literature, these scholars asserted; this is how it was authored, and this is how it ought to be read. The rabbis, in telling their stories, did not seek to chronicle history. Rather, they used the literary devices and rhetorical ploys of narrative, those *words which draw one's heart like a tale,* to convey certain religious or ethical teachings. The turn toward aggada-as-literature was nothing short of revolutionary. It shifted scholarly attention from the stories' content to their form, so that their literary properties, once an obstacle to interpretation, now became its object. It also considerably expanded the field, opening it up to the many different schools of literary criticism. Above all, it made aggada not less historically valuable, but more: If a rabbinic story actually happened, as previous historians had assumed, it is an account of one thing that occurred to one person (or, at most, a small group of people) at one time. But if, as scholars were now arguing, the story didn't happen exactly as told, if it was authored, transmitted, and edited by successive generations of rabbis – then it can shed light on the intellectual and spiritual lives of all of those rabbinic authors, transmitters, and editors. Aggada, turns out, *is* a window into the rabbinic period, but not in the way 19th-century historians had meant; it is a historical record, not of the stories' characters, but of their creators.[17]

17. Jacob Neusner, who, together with Jonah Fraenkel, laid the groundwork for the shift in the study of aggada away from history and toward literature, maintained that "talmudic literature simply cannot be converted into historical narrative.... No passage can be treated as an eye-witness account. None can be supposed to tell 'just how things were'.... The question, Did these things 'really' happen? is not important. What is important is the question, What view of reality shaped the minds of the men who told these stories, lived by these laws, believed these myths?" Jacob Neusner,

After a millennium and a half on the sidelines of the beit midrash, aggada, in the 21st century, has risen to unprecedented heights of popularity. Today, the stories of rabbinic literature are some of the most beloved texts of Judaism, studied in traditional yeshivas and secular universities, synagogues and schools, organizations and communities across the Jewish world. The aggada-as-literature movement has revealed these stories to be literary masterpieces. They may read like simple folktales, but scratch the surface of these texts and worlds and worlds of drama, of conflict, of passion and emotion burst forth from between the lines. The rabbis' storytelling genius, and their repeated rounds of editing through the generations, ensured that by the time the stories assumed their final form they were intricately structured and elaborately stylized. Unpacking a piece of aggada is therefore uniquely challenging and (when done successfully) extremely rewarding.

Another reason for the current popularity of aggada is its accessibility. The halakhic sections of the Talmud – long, complex, and laden with jargon – require years of study to master; whereas the stories, short and seemingly straightforward, can be read and understood (at least on some level) by anyone.[18] Similarly, while halakha includes many arcane and obsolete laws that have no bearing on life as we know it, aggada deals with themes that feel remarkably close to home. It tells of people contending with difficult parents and disobedient children, treacherous friends and insensitive spouses, financial insecurity and failing health, ethical dilemmas and spiritual crises, loneliness and death. They may be hundreds of years old, but the stories of the Talmud are as existentially relevant to us today as they were to the rabbis of 7th-century Babylonia.

Finally, aggada seems particularly compatible with the spirit of our age. Halakha, a general system designed for the general good, cannot but infringe upon those who do not fit the norm (as does any code of law). The rabbis knew this, so alongside halakha they gave us aggada, stories which critique their own legal system, acknowledge

---

Development of a Legend: Studies on the Traditions Concerning Yohanan ben Zakkai, 300–1.

18. I say "at least on some level" since, as we'll see, there is a major gap between the narratives' apparent and actual meaning.

its limitations, and give voice to those it inadvertently hurts.[19] Hence the aforementioned interest of aggada in the treatment of the Other, who often takes center stage in these stories: We have tales of simple folk criticizing rabbis, of non-Jews putting Jews to shame, and – most notably for our purpose – of women showing up men.[20] There is something about this rabbinic self-critique that is especially appealing to our 21st-century sensibilities. Aggada's *laughing face of God,* the subversiveness that made it so problematic for so long, is precisely what makes it so popular today.[21]

Cast Your Eyes to the End: How to Read Aggada

One of the hallmarks of rabbinic storytelling is the false front. Aggada, as noted, is deceptive; the simple understanding one comes away with after the first reading is frequently at odds with the deeper meaning that emerges after the second.[22] This is particularly true in the case of

19. "One of the more interesting theories in aggadic studies posits that the narratives of the Talmud are a critical tool through which the rabbis examine themselves and criticize their halakhic creation. The stories constitute a reflection on the talmudic work, which is why they often diverge from the halakhic ethos and even oppose it." Ishay Rosen-Zvi, "The Evil Inclination, Sexuality, and Forbidden Cohabitations: A Chapter in Talmudic Anthropology," 69–70.
20. As Shulamit Valler demonstrates, rabbinic stories "present explicitly feminine positions, or at the very least positions of thoughtfulness and sensitivity toward the feminine view, positions which do not correspond with, and perhaps even contradict, what is said or inferred from the halakha." Shulamit Valler, *Women and Womanhood in the Stories of the Babylonian Talmud,* 19. That said, it cannot be denied that even within aggada there are numerous expressions of rabbinic prejudice against women, non-Jews, and unlearned men; the rabbis were no more consistent in their egalitarian tendencies than they were in their feminism. Yet it is specifically in their stories that the rabbis recognize the humanity, at times even superiority, of the non-rabbinic Other (it is, for example, no coincidence that the remarkable women of this book all exist in the realm of aggada).
21. Indeed, this is probably the first time in Jewish history that rabbinic narrative can be read with the same subversive mindset with which it was composed.
22. According to Jeffrey Rubenstein, the realization "of the true nature of things as opposed to their surface appearance… comprises the didactic or ideological point of the [rabbinic] story." The rabbis, he argues, envisioned an "implied audience of…

rabbinic legend (the aggadic sub-genre explored in this book[23]). With their literary sophistication and moral complexity masked by their short, folktale-like appearance, these legends can never just be read – they must always be reread.

And not only reread; there are specific rules that must be applied to our rereading. If we are to break through the stories' false front and expose their true significance, we must zoom in and do a close reading of the text, and zoom out and examine the context.

Zoom In: Close Reading

Since aggada is literature and ought to be read as such, we must treat it as we would any other novel, short story, or play. This last genre is perhaps the most apposite, as rabbinic legends are fundamentally scenic; they present their plot directly through dialogue and deed, unmediated by lengthy descriptions of scenery or characters, thereby giving the reader the impression of watching a drama enacted on a stage.

We begin, then, with a close reading, breaking the narrative down into its literary building blocks:

(1) Structure

Our first step is to map the story's structure, dividing it into acts (and, when relevant, the acts into scenes). Rabbinic legends, we will find, tend toward the three-act drama.

(2) Setting

Next, we must determine when and where each act takes place. Rabbinic legends are generally set in condensed time and space, lending the drama an air of immediacy and intensity.

---

like-minded sages" who were sophisticated and knowledgeable enough to unpack their stories and uncover their hidden meaning. Jeffrey L. Rubenstein, *Talmudic Stories: Narrative Art, Composition, and Culture*, 9, 21.

23. Despite its generic diversity, aggada's two primary forms are midrash – the stories the rabbis told about the Bible, and rabbinic legend – the stories the rabbis told about themselves. The narratives of this book, all concerning rabbinic (and pre-rabbinic) women, belong to the latter category.

(3) Characters

The third element to analyze is the story's dramatis personae – their views, personality traits, and relationships to one another. Rabbinic legends usually feature a limited cast of characters, who interchange from one act to the next, as a chamber play of sorts.

(4) Plot

The next step is to follow the storyline through, identifying its important parallels, turning points, and climaxes. Like the setting and characters, the plot of rabbinic legends is compressed, taut, and thus highly dramatic.

(5) Themes, Motifs, Symbols

Finally, we must search the narrative for underlying themes, repeated words, and elements of symbolic significance. This is the surest way to get past the story's façade, go from text to subtext, and discover the deeper message that lies beneath.

Zoom Out: Contextual Reading

Yet zooming in is not enough. The Talmud features several instances of close readings of the Bible which are met with "Fool! Cast your eyes to the end of the verse";[24] no reading, no matter how close, can be quite accurate if it fails to take the context into account. Aggada, specifically, comes to us embedded in numerous levels of context, and we must zoom out and consider them each in turn:

(1) Immediate Context

The stories of the Talmud do not appear in isolation, but within a unit of talmudic discussion (or sugya). They frequently come on the heels of a halakhic debate, clarifying, illustrating, or – as mentioned – subverting it. Other times, they follow a narrative, as part of a cluster of tales on a single theme.[25] The framing of the story, whether by law or by narrative,

24. See, for example, Berakhot 10a (discussed in Chapter 5), Eiruvin 101a, Ḥullin 87a.

25. "A great number of the narratives in the Talmuds and midrash do not appear discretely, but in cycles of stories which follow one another… unified by… a common subject and structure." Eli Yassif, *The Hebrew Folktale: History, Genre, Meaning*, 232–38.

is typically the result of the rabbis' deliberate editorial decision, and has direct ramifications for the way the story should be read.[26]

(2) Broad Context
Zooming out further, we must explore the story within the broad context of the Talmud in particular, and rabbinic literature in general. Breaking the story down into its literary components can only get us so far; we must understand what these components mean to the rabbis, the role they play in the rabbinic imagination. To this end, we must search for other appearances of every setting, character, plot device, motif, and symbol we identified in our close reading, so that we may determine their full literary significance. This is especially relevant in the case of rabbinic legend, where stories of a specific character often presuppose knowledge of other stories about the same character.[27]

(3) Historical Context
Although the stories of the Talmud are not historical, they are nonetheless set in a historical reality – a reality from which we are removed by a good millennium and a half.[28] We can never assume that the historical circumstances depicted in these stories are in any way like our own. To

26. "The literary contexts created by the rabbinic redactors suggest the influence of the context on the narrative it frames, and on the worldview it presents." Ofra Meir, "The Influence of the Redactional Process on the Worldview of Aggadic Stories," 83.

27. While rabbinic legends are not connected by historical truth – they regularly contradict one another, and almost always fail to fit neatly onto one timeline – they are usually linked through conceptual consistency; the biographical details may differ, but the character's basic personality, worldview, and life trajectory remain largely the same. Hence it is consistency, rather than history, that justifies the reading of rabbinic legends in light of one another. "Rabbinic sources cannot be used at face value to reconstruct history. The relinquishing of the biographical program, though, has brought with it a tendency not to pay attention to the construction of particular sages within rabbinic literature as figures with distinctive personalities, dispositions, ideological stances, and perhaps even life stories.... The appearance of one of these sages within a given agada... must be read with a consciousness of other agadot about this sage." Devora Steinmetz, "Agada Unbound: Inter-Agadic Characterization of the Sages in the Bavli and Implications for Reading Agada," 293–310.

28. As noted, the historical reality reflected in these narratives is less the characters' reality than that of the creators, from 7th-century Babylonia.

avoid the all-too-common mistake of projecting our reality onto that of the rabbis, we must zoom out even further and explore the social conventions, political climate, cultural mores, economic structures, scientific knowledge, and material objects of the rabbinic world.[29]

For this purpose, in addition to the texts of the rabbis themselves, we also have recourse to works from the surrounding cultures, in which the rabbis operated and by which they were deeply influenced – Greco-Roman (to the west), Persian (to the east), and Christian.

Reading Hypotheses

To our two planes of reading – close and contextual – we must add three reading hypotheses:

(1) Omnisignificance

The stories of the Talmud, as mentioned, are terse and compact, whole worlds of drama held together in a few short lines. This minimalism (shaped, primarily, by the oral nature of the stories' transmission and the need to commit them to memory) requires that we look closely at each and every sentence, clause, and word. Not unlike the way we read biblical narrative, we must assume that every detail is there for a reason; nothing in these carefully crafted stories is redundant.[30]

(2) Interiority

Because rabbinic legends are scenic, they tell us what characters say and do, rarely what they think or feel. It is therefore up to us to get into the head and heart of every character (for, like in a play, there are as many points of view as there are speaking parts), teasing out the unstated

---

29. "To understand the past in the present, one must know the past and the present and be able to distinguish between them.... Any scholarly study of an ancient text requires an in-depth familiarity with generations past (including different cultural eras of the past), primarily in order to differentiate the past from the present.... We must go back to rabbinic times... to be sure that we have interpreted the past as the past." Jonah Fraenkel, "Hermeneutic Problems in the Study of the Aggadic Narrative," 12–14.

30. "The extreme brevity of Babylonian Talmud stories [gave rise to] the need to invest as much meaning as possible in every word." Rubenstein, *Talmudic Stories*, 247.

thoughts and feelings. The bulk of these stories' drama, we shall see, is often in the emotional subtext.[31]

(3) The Moral of the Story

Just because a rabbinic legend didn't happen, it doesn't mean it isn't true. There is a profound truth to these stories, but it is ethical, religious, philosophical – not historical. The rabbis told their tales not to record history, but to teach us how *to know God and cleave to His ways.* Hence the final question we must ask ourselves when reading a piece of aggada is: Why are the rabbis telling us this? What is the lesson they would like us to learn?[32]

Archetypal Criticism

So far, this section has outlined three sets of fairly standard reading rules for aggada. There is, however, a fourth methodology I'd like to add, one which is rather more unique to this book: archetypal criticism. According to archetypal critics, if certain literary elements – character types, plotlines, motifs – appear in stories from different times and different places (where no cross-cultural influence can be discerned), it is because their origin is not cultural, but psychological. The recurrence of an archetype in narratives throughout history and across cultures indicates that the archetype is rooted deep within the human psyche. The stories we tell, from ancient mythology to medieval folklore to modern fiction, are all

31. "Since [talmudic] stories do not center on the internal world of their characters, but reveal it through the characters' actions, they leave whole spheres blank, unnarrated.... The psychological experience resonates beneath the text's mute surface... thoughts, feelings, views, motives, and intentions, which the reader is called upon to articulate." Inbar Raveh, *Fragments of Being: Stories of the Sages – Literary Structures and Worldview*, 31–41.

32. "Historiography was of no interest to the rabbis. They saw no point in describing events and characters just as they were. Undoubtedly they believed that one ought to learn from the lessons of the past... but did not see any difference as to whether the lessons... are learned from actual historical reality or from moral literary fiction. In fact, the rabbis seemed to prefer fiction and recognize its advantages. In this respect, they were not unlike the great moral authors of history." Moshe David Herr, "The Conception of History Among the Sages," 139.

essentially the same, since they are all trying to work through the same primal fears and fantasies.[33]

Thus, when an archetypal critic looks at a literary text, it is in order, first, to identify its archetypal elements (the elements it has in common with works of other cultures), and second, to trace those elements back to the unconscious forces whence they derive.[34] The value of archetypal criticism to our understanding of literature has been repeatedly demonstrated by contemporary critics. In the study of aggada, it hasn't been used quite as much – although, I submit, it has the power of casting these stories in an entirely new light.

Reading the Text, Regarding the Other: The Program for the Book

Our reading of the stories of the heroines of the Talmud begins, accordingly, with an archetype. Each chapter opens with a cross-cultural exploration of an anti-feminine archetype, sketching it through prominent examples from the Bible, rabbinic literature, classical myths, medieval folktales, modern novels, poems, and plays, and 20th-century film.[35] In

---

33. Archetypal criticism developed out of the psychoanalytic thought of Sigmund Freud and Carl Gustav Jung. The latter describes the theory as follows: "When, for instance, one examines the world of fairytales, one can hardly avoid the impression that one is meeting certain figures again and again, albeit in altered guise.... The psychologist of the unconscious proceeds no differently in regard to the psychic figures which appear in dreams, fantasies, visions, and manic ideas, as in legends, fairytales, myth, and religion. Over the whole of this psychic realm there reign certain motifs, certain typical figures which we can follow far back into history, and even into prehistory, and which may therefore legitimately be described as 'archetypes.' They seem to me to be built into the very structure of man's unconscious, for in no other way can I explain why it is that they occur universally and in identical form." Carl Gustav Jung, "Fundamental Questions of Psychotherapy," 16:254.
34. "The archetype is synchronous.... The extent of the archetypal critic's interest in drawing attention to the similarities between a later work of art and an earlier one should be in demonstrating that an archetype is in operation... [as] a constant in our psyches that we share with humans of all times and places." Evelyn J. Heinz and John J. Teunissen, "Culture and the Humanities: The Archetypal Approach," 194.
35. I must confess to a Western bias here: The majority of examples are taken from the Western canon, with which the reader is most likely to be familiar; I have, however,

the course of this survey, the archetype is defined: her character traits, relationships with those around her, and key moments in her story.

Next, we will conduct a primary reading of our talmudic heroine, whose narrative, we will find, features all of the elements previously delineated. The Talmud's portrayal of its heroine, at first reading, perfectly conforms to the archetype at hand.

We will then proceed to a revisioning of the story, beginning with an analysis of the unconscious forces that gave rise to the archetype in the first place. With this archetypal critique in mind, we will reread the story, subjecting it to aggada's three sets of reading rules: (1) Close reading – mapping the text's structure, setting, and characters; zooming into the twists and turns of the plot; and identifying the motifs, symbols, and underlying themes. (2) Contextual reading – zooming out to the surrounding sugya; examining other rabbinic references to the story's characters, plot details, and motifs; and highlighting relevant historical facts about the rabbinic world. (3) Reading hypotheses – looking closely at each and every word; trying to get into the characters' heads and hearts; and ultimately, attempting to articulate the moral of the story.

Finally, we will go back and revisit our primary reading, in light of what we have gone on to learn. With the story's false front completely deconstructed, and its deeper truth now plain to see, we can recognize how grossly we had misread our heroine, and by extension, how often we misinterpret the Other. The moral of the story is born of the gap between its apparent and actual meaning; the way we read the characters in the text becomes the way we must regard the people in our lives.

Having charted what the book will do, a few words on what it won't. This is by no means a general survey of rabbinic attitudes toward women. Over the past few decades, several such studies have been undertaken, arriving at very different conclusions – from claims of the rabbis' essential

---

included a handful of well-known non-Western examples where relevant. I must also issue a general spoiler alert: In many cases, I discuss how the stories end, so let the reader proceed with caution.

patriarchy and subjugation of women,[36] through attempts to nuance and qualify their patriarchal positions,[37] to arguments in defense of rabbinic proto-feminism.[38] This book, by contrast, has the far more humble goal of reading six stories of named talmudic women; any broader conclusions regarding the rabbinic view of women will be drawn directly, and exclusively, from these readings.[39]

Nor am I claiming that the readings proposed are the only readings possible. My sole objective is to apply the reading rules of aggada to the stories of the six talmudic heroines in an effort to understand them as best I can. There are many aspects of each legend I do not touch upon, since I find them less relevant to this purpose. Similarly, I do not analyze the stories' manuscript variants, compare them to parallel

---

36. Judith Baskin, for instance, explores several aggadic traditions concerning women, demonstrating that "the rabbis' justifications of the patriarchy they themselves maintained and fostered relied on establishing the secondary nature of females… and the inferior nature of their abilities and qualities." Judith R. Baskin, *Midrashic Women: Formations of the Feminine in Rabbinic Literature*, 2–12.

37. Shulamit Valler, as mentioned (n. 20), posits a difference between rabbinic law, which tends to overlook the female perspective, and rabbinic narrative, where the rabbis display a far greater sensitivity to women and their sometimes difficult circumstances. Judith Wegner, for her part, identifies a rabbinic distinction between women whose reproductive function belongs to a man, who were consequently regarded as property, and women to whom no man lays claim, who were accorded "a measure of personhood… many rights, powers, and duties corresponding to those of men." Wegner, *Chattel or Person?*, 174.

38. Daniel Boyarin, reading rabbinic culture alongside Hellenistic and Christian cultures, finds that the former's affirmation of sexuality made it significantly less misogynistic than its contemporaries, and that "on the margins of [the rabbis'] dominant and hegemonic discourse, there was… a dissident proto-feminist voice." Boyarin, *Carnal Israel*, 242. Judith Hauptman, comparing rabbinic law to biblical law, which the rabbis inherited and by which they were bound, shows that while "the rabbis upheld patriarchy as the preordained mode of social organization, as dictated by the Torah," they simultaneously "broke new ground, granting women benefits that they never had before… in almost every key area of law affecting women." Judith Hauptman, *Rereading the Rabbis: A Woman's Voice*, 4.

39. It must be owned, though, that the abovementioned studies are also all limited in scope (Wegner confines her research to the Mishna, Baskin to aggadic literature, and Hauptman to halakhic literature; Boyarin focuses on texts dealing with sexuality and the body; and Valler looks at five sugyot concerning women). Rabbinic literature is vast and multivocal by nature, and any attempt to analyze it is bound to be selective.

versions elsewhere in rabbinic literature, or try to identify their historical kernels; I address such questions only inasmuch as they impact the literary reading of the text.

I have elected, throughout the book, to let rabbinic texts speak for themselves, so that explanations always come after the texts, never before. I have also chosen to keep bibliographical references to a minimum; the reader can find the full range of works that have informed each chapter, and the book as a whole, in the bibliography. As is customary, "Talmud" alone refers to the Babylonian Talmud. I have largely followed the Steinsaltz English translation, but have modified it in places, and have regularly replaced pronouns with proper names, for the sake of clarity. Citations of tractates preceded by (M) are to the Mishna, (T) to the Tosefta, and (Y) to the Jerusalem Talmud; when they are unpreceded, they are to the Babylonian Talmud. The book uses "rabbi," "ben," and "beit midrash" when discussing stories set in an Israelite context, and "rav," "bar," and "yeshiva" when discussing stories in Babylonia. Because of the impossibility of distinguishing talmudic authors from editors in the multigenerational process of oral transmission, I shall refer to them collectively, simply as "the rabbis."[40] Since rabbinic stories tell more of their creators than of their characters, this book is primarily about them.

The Talmud is a prime example of a collective act of creation. Yet every act of creation is, in its way, collective. This book, specifically, would never have been written were it not for the help of many, many others.

I am grateful, first and foremost, to God. For charting the course of my life directly to aggada (in a manner so random it could have only been providential); for leaving me no choice but to walk away from everything and write; for giving me life, sustaining me, and bringing me to this day.

40. "As producers of literary works, the sages of Late Antiquity imagine themselves at most as shapers of what already exists in tradition. They are not authors... they do not invent, they merely transmit." Martin S. Jaffee, "Rabbinic Authorship as a Collective Enterprise," 1–24. Note also that I speak of "readers," although the original audience of the stories would have heard them communicated orally, rather than in writing.

Second, to my parents, Dina and Philip Fine. For supporting my terribly irresponsible decision to go off and write a book; for encouraging me every step of the way; for believing in me when I didn't believe in myself.

Third, my students. The people I've been privileged to teach at the Pardes Institute of Jewish Studies, the Nachshon Project, Amudim Seminary, the Tikvah Scholars Program, the Bronfman Fellowship, the London School of Jewish Studies, the Community Scholars Program, WebYeshiva, and Limmud conferences, communities, and campuses across the Jewish world. It was your insightful questions and comments that sharpened my thinking about these stories, your enthusiasm that inspired me to turn my teachings into a book, and your faces that stood before me when I did.

Fourth, Professor Jeffrey Rubenstein. For introducing me, through his writings, to the wonderful world of aggada, and years later (as no good deed goes unpunished) for agreeing to mentor me through this book project. Though he knew nothing about me and owed me even less, Professor Rubenstein gave generously of his time and expertise. If there is any merit in what follows, it is due to everything I've learned from him. Likewise, this book has benefitted from the close and careful attentions of Dr. Adam Cohen, Ilana Kurshan, and Rabbi Shoshana Boyd Gelfand. Each of these readers, in their own way, improved the book tremendously, and I am so grateful for their wisdom and their kindness. I am also indebted to the following scholars, whose brains I have, at one point or another, picked: Professor Galit Hasan-Rokem, Dr. Inbar Raveh, Professor Shuli Barzilai, and Professor Tal Ilan.

Fifth, my profound thanks to Shari and Nathan J. Lindenbaum, who have done so much for the world of Torah in general, and for women's Torah in particular. This book owes its existence to them, in more ways than one. I am honored by their friendship and humbled by their generosity. I am also grateful to Jackie Frankel and Joel Weiss of the Pardes Institute of Jewish Studies; after providing me with a happy teaching home for the past decade, I'm thrilled that Pardes has taken on the role of co-publisher of this book. Finally, to the Sefaria Word-by-Word Fellowship which, under the leadership of Dr. Erica Brown and Sara Wolkenfeld, has made it its mission to advance female Torah scholarship, a cause particularly close to my heart.

Sixth, to the talented individuals who, time and again, have saved me from myself. After many years of editing other people's books, I was so fortunate to team up with former colleagues who agreed to take on the thankless task of editing an editor (and a fastidious, opinionated editor at that): my outstanding editor Deena Glickman, who lovingly turned over every word, endured my Britishisms, and let me have my way with semicolons; and my equally excellent copyeditor Tali Simon, who combed through the manuscript with painstaking thoroughness and eagle-eyed precision. Thanks are also owed to my research assistant Claire Abramovitz, whose research was so entertainingly compiled, it kept me reading through hundreds of pages of findings; my editorial assistant Emma Richter, who dotted all my i's and crossed all my t's with a proficiency well beyond her years; and my accountability partner Joel Haber, whose annoying punctuality in meeting his deadlines shamed me into not completely missing mine. Lastly, it is a pleasure to return to Maggid Books, the imprint I helped build from infancy. My thanks to Matthew Miller, who believed in this book when it was still a twinkle in its mother's eye; to Dr. Yoel Finkelman, who shepherded it through the publishing process with professionalism and skill; to Tomi Mager, for her typesetting flair; to Ruth Pepperman, for her proofreading prowess; and to Tani Bayer, for expressing so perfectly in image what I tried to capture in words.

Seventh, to friends. Far too many to mention, but you know who you are. You who let me prattle on about my heroines, who listened as I complained about the difficulties of writing, who talked me off the ledge more times than I care to remember. I can't list you all, but there are a number who cannot go unmentioned: Eleanor Zinkin, Eliyahu Misgav, Jeffrey Saks, Liron Niego, Miriam Loberbaum, Rachel Harris, Rebecca Zeffert, Roni Zahavi, Sefi Kraut, Tamar Marcus, Yehoshua Engelman, Ayelet and Adi Libson, Batya and Herzl Hefter, Carol and Johnny Arkush, Miriam and Harris Lorie, Sally Berkovic and Jonathan Fishburn, Simi Hinden and Louis Sachs, Suzi and Elie Holzer, Tamra Wright and Ian Gamse, and Tilla and Ben Crowne.

Three women inspired this book, three women who are my personal heroines:

My Savta Judith Felsenstein (née Freilich), who, together with Saba Arnold, bought me my first classics, took me to my first plays, and introduced me to the world of arts and letters. It is to them that I owe my love of all things literature.

My Grandma Pearl Fine (née Rubinstein), who, together with Grandpa Morris, taught me the meaning of true heroism, how to face life with fortitude and with grace. I miss them both every day.

My mentor Maureen Kendler, who guided me through my first steps in the world of Jewish education, quelled my anxieties, celebrated my successes, and constantly reminded me to "never threaten to leave, always threaten to stay." This, precisely, is what the heroines of the Talmud do. In writing about their stories, it's what I have tried to do, as well.

Yalta
The Shrew

The Archetype: Hell Hath No Fury Like a Woman Scorned

> Shrew: A mouse of which the bite is generally supposed venomous, and to which tradition assigns such malignity, that she is said to lame the foot over which she runs.... Our ancestors looked on her with such terror, that they are supposed to have given her name to a scolding woman, whom for her venom they call a shrew.[1]

Far from the quarrelsome, ill-tempered woman she is today, "shrew" was originally the zoological term for a small, mouse-like creature. In the late Middle Ages, however, the malignant mouse, known for its aggressive nature and venomous bite, became a malicious wife, known for her aggressive temper and venomous tongue. Her name might have emerged only in the 13th century, but the archetype itself did not; shrews may be found much earlier, snarling and scolding their way throughout world literature.

1. Samuel Johnson, ed., *Dictionary of the English Language*, 4:213.

Queen Vashti Refuses to Obey Ahasuerus' Command, Gustave Doré

"It is better to dwell in the wilderness than with a contentious and angry woman," the Bible cautions its readers (Prov. 21:19). A number of books later, it provides an example of such a contentious woman in the character of Queen Vashti, who disobeys her husband's order to appear at the royal banquet (Est. 1:12).

Moving from biblical to rabbinic literature, we find in the Talmud an entire story cycle devoted to the subject of shrews. Prefaced by a distinction between good and bad wives – "If he is lucky, she is a helpmate to him; if not, she strikes him" – the cycle tells of three hapless rabbis and the shrewish women to whom they are married:

> Rav was constantly tormented by his wife. If he told her, "Prepare me lentils," she would prepare him peas; if he asked for peas, she would prepare him lentils. When his son Ḥiyya grew up he reversed his father's requests to her. Rav said to him, "Your mother has improved." Ḥiyya replied, "It was I who reversed your requests to her"....
>
> Rabbi Ḥiyya was constantly tormented by his wife. Nevertheless, whenever he would find anything suitable, he would wrap it up in his shawl and bring it to her. Said Rav to him, "But surely she is tormenting the master?" He replied, "It is sufficient for us that they rear up our children and deliver us from sin."
>
> Rav Yehuda was reading his son Rav Yitzḥak the verse "And I find more bitter than death the woman" (Eccl. 7:26). His son asked, "Who, for instance?" His father replied, "For instance, your mother." (Yevamot 63a–b)[2]

2. It must be noted that following his response (one of history's first ever *yo-mama* jokes), Rav Yehuda admits to being quite happy with his wife, who "was indeed hostile, but

The women of this shrew trilogy are all contrary and aggressive (or passive-aggressive, in the case of Rav's wife, who expresses her resentment indirectly, in a series of petty disobediences[3]). They are also, significantly, all absent. An entire shrew story cycle, with not one shrew to be found. All we have are the husbands – the poor, tormented rabbis suffering patiently at the hands of their shrewish wives. Shrew tales, in general, are told from the point of view of the husband; rarely do we get the perspective of the shrew herself.

Strikingly similar to these rabbinic shrews are the classical depictions of Xanthippe, the disagreeable wife of the great Greek philosopher Socrates:

> Of Xanthippe, who first scolded Socrates and later drenched him with water, he said, "Did I not say that Xanthippe's thunder would end in rain?" When Alcibiades said that Xanthippe's scolding was intolerable, he said, "But I am used to it, exactly as if I were constantly hearing the clattering of pulleys. And… Xanthippe provides me with children."[4]

Xantippe Dousing Socrates, Otto van Veen

> Alcibiades sent to Socrates a large and beautifully made cake. Xanthippe, who was rather jealous of the giver, took it out of

could be easily appeased" (ibid.). Such a quick-to-anger, quick-to-forgive disposition is not uncommon in shrews, whose behavior, we shall see, is often irrational and erratic.

3. This point is reiterated in a brief epilogue to the trilogy, which returns to the opening definition of a bad wife: "Abaye said: She prepares a table for him and prepares her mouth for him…. Rava said: She prepares a table for him and then turns her back to him" (ibid.); the shrew may fulfill her household duties, but is bitter and belligerent in doing so.
4. Diogenes Laertius, *Lives of Eminent Philosophers*, 2:36.

> the basket and stamped upon it. Socrates only smiled, and said, "Now, my dear, you will not get a slice of it any more than I."[5]

Like the shrews of the Talmud, Xanthippe is vexatious and spiteful. So spiteful, in fact, she becomes self-destructive; as Socrates points out, her furious trampling of the cake ruins it for them both. Socrates himself, like the husbands of the Talmud, endures his wife's behavior with equanimity, explaining (as Rabbi Ḥiyya had) that he puts up with the abuse because she is the mother of his children.

Going further down history to the Middle Ages, the thousand and one stories of *Arabian Nights* feature a couple of memorable shrews, though none so notorious as Fatimeh, wife of the cobbler Marouf. The woman, we are told, "ruled her husband and used to revile him and curse him a thousand times a day; and he feared her malice and dreaded her mischief."[6] When Marouf, attempting to placate his implacable wife, brings home a honey cake (more costly than he could afford, but not quite as extravagant as the one she had demanded), Fatimeh flies into a fit, throws it in his face, and knocks out one of his teeth. Herein is the popular portrayal of the shrew as mad – in the double sense of the word; the shrew as mad-woman is both angry and crazy, raging and deranged.

Geoffrey Chaucer's *Canterbury Tales* is similarly peopled with shrews. From the malicious bride – "the worst one that can be" – of the unhappy Merchant, through the "babbling shrew" the Host wishes he had never married, to the irrepressible Wife of Bath, who admits to having made the lives of her five husbands a misery: "For God knows that I nagged them mercilessly… stubborn I was as is a lioness, and with my tongue a very jay, I guess."[7]

---

5. Aelian, *Various History*, 11:12. There is little evidence that the historical Xanthippe was actually the shrew Greco-Roman sources proclaim her to be. My interest, however, is in literary representation, not historical fact; the less historically accurate an example, the more culturally valuable it is, as it readily demonstrates the archetype a culture imposes on its women.
6. "Marouf the Cobbler and His Wife Fatimeh," *Arabian Nights*, 9:180.
7. Geoffrey Chaucer, "The Merchant's Tale," 6, 1216; "The Wife of Bath's Tale," 229–30, 643–44. Interestingly, the Wife of Bath goes on to explain the pervasiveness of shrew tales by observing that they are all, as mentioned, told by men. If the difficulties of marriage were related by women, she claims, we would have some very different

The biblically themed mystery plays cast Noah's wife (about whom the Bible tells us next to nothing) in the role of the belligerent shrew. To the delight of medieval English audiences, Noah's wife taunts, curses, pummels, and cuffs her poor husband, refusing to heed his warnings about the Flood until she is finally dragged, kicking and screaming, aboard the ark.[8]

The Taming of the Shrew, The Globe Theater (Alastair Muir)

The most famous shrew in Western literature comes to us courtesy of William Shakespeare. Katherine Minola, the eponymous heroine of *The Taming of the Shrew*, is dreaded throughout Padua for being "stark mad… [a] fiend from Hell." When Petruchio boldly tries to win her hand – and dowry – in marriage, Katherine responds with her quick fists and even quicker tongue:

> Katherine: Asses are made to bear, and so are you.
> Petruchio: Women are made to bear, and so are you.
> Katherine: No such jade as you, if me you mean…
> Petruchio: Come, come, you wasp; i'faith, you are too angry.
> Katherine: If I be waspish, best beware my sting…
> Petruchio: Who knows not where a wasp does wear his sting? In his tail.
> Katherine: In his tongue.
> Petruchio: Whose tongue?
> Katherine: Yours, if you talk of tails: and so farewell.
> Petruchio: What, with my tongue in your tail? Nay, come again, good Kate; I am a gentleman.
> Katherine: That I'll try. [*She strikes him*][9]

---

stories: "By God, if women had but written… they would have written of men more wickedness, than all the race of Adam could redress." Ibid., 699–703.

8. See, for example, "Noah and His Wife, the Flood and Its Waning," *The York Plays*; "Noah and the Ark," *The Towneley Plays*; and "The Deluge," *The Chester Plays*.

9. William Shakespeare, *The Taming of the Shrew*, 1.1.69–88, 2.1.190–210.

Writing a hundred years later, William Congreve echoes Shakespeare's description of the shrew as mad when he coins the catchphrase for shrews everywhere: "Hell hath no fury like a woman scorned."[10]

Nineteenth-century literature makes regular use of the archetype, often as a troublesome secondary character the hero has to overcome. Dame Van Winkle, the "termagant wife" of the legendary Rip, rants and raves against her henpecked husband; indeed, it is Rip's desire to escape "the fiery furnace of domestic tribulation" that leads him to his great time-traveling adventure.[11] Mrs. Joe Gargery, another scold, looms large over the opening scenes of *Great Expectations*, her prickly self covered by a prickly apron bristling with pins and needles. Using a cane to hit her brother, and sometimes her brother to hit her husband, Mrs. Joe terrorizes her menfolk, boxing ears, knocking heads.[12]

Rip Van Winkle, N.C. Wyeth

She may not be funny to the men in her life, but for the reader, the shrew is a humorous character, and her genre is typically comedic. Humor, as a rule, is a product of incongruity, the bringing together of disparate elements into an unexpected, and therefore humorous, whole: a baby wearing a suit, say, or a cat playing the piano.[13] A violent woman, in this respect, is like a piano-playing cat – incongruous, and therefore funny. There is something inherently comedic about a woman who hits and kicks and curses (and, no less so, about a man who cowers helplessly before her).

Yet the final shrew I'd like to consider, before proceeding to our talmudic heroine, comes to us in a tragic, rather than comic, setting: Bertha Mason, from the 19th-century classic *Jane Eyre*. Bertha is a shrew of such "violent and unreasonable temper," she has to be locked away

10. The precise (and often paraphrased) quote is "Heav'n has no rage, like love to hatred turn'd; nor Hell a fury, like a woman scorn'd." William Congreve, *The Mourning Bride*, 3:8.
11. Washington Irving, "Rip Van Winkle," *The Sketch Book of Geoffrey Crayon, Gent.*
12. Charles Dickens, *Great Expectations*, ch. 2.
13. James Beattie, "Essay on Laughter and Ludicrous Composition," 304.

in the household attic. This is the archetype taken to a mad and murderous extreme, as Bertha repeatedly tries to kill her husband and burn the house down:

> In the deep shade, at the farther end of the room, a figure ran backward and forward. What it was, whether beast or human being, one could not, at first sight, tell: it groveled, seemingly, on all fours: it snatched and growled like some strange wild animal: but it was covered with clothing; and a quantity of dark, grizzled hair, wild as a mane, hid its head and face…. Mr. Rochester flung me behind him; the lunatic sprang and grappled his throat viciously, and laid her teeth to his cheek: they struggled. She was a big woman, in stature almost equaling her husband, and corpulent besides: she showed virile force in the contest – more than once she almost throttled him.[14]

Bertha Mason, F.H. Townsend

This, then, is the shrew: a madwoman, ill-tempered and irrational, who flies into fits and attacks those around her; wife of a timid and terrorized husband, who suffers through her antics and does his best to appease her temper; a comedic character, whose tale (told from the point of view of said suffering husband) includes scenes of verbal abuse or physical violence, oftentimes both.

With this image in mind, let us turn to the great shrew of the Talmud – Yalta.

Primary Reading: The Madwoman in the Rabbi's Attic

Mentioned no fewer than seven times, Yalta (whose name is the Aramaic version of the Hebrew Yael) is the most frequently named woman of the

14. Charlotte Bronte, *Jane Eyre*, chs. 26–27.

Talmud.[15] She is generally identified as the daughter of the exilarch (the leader of the Babylonian Jewish diaspora) and the wife of Rav Naḥman, head of the Nehardea yeshiva.[16]

Yet of all her talmudic appearances, this is the story for which Yalta is perhaps best known:

> Ulla was once at the house of Rav Naḥman.
> He had a meal, said the Grace after Meals, and handed the cup of blessing to Rav Naḥman.
> Rav Naḥman said to him, "Master, please send the cup of blessing to Yalta."
> Ulla responded, "So said Rabbi Yoḥanan: The fruit of a woman's body is blessed only from the fruit of a man's body, as it is written, 'He will bless the fruit of your body' (Deut. 7:13). It does not say the fruit of her body, but the fruit of your body"....
> Meanwhile Yalta heard, and she got up in a passion and went to the wine storehouse and broke four hundred jars of wine.
> Rav Naḥman said to him, "Let the master send her another cup."
> He sent it to her with a message, "All that wine can be counted as a blessing."
> She returned answer, "Gossip comes from peddlers and lice from rags." (Berakhot 51b)

Ulla, a prominent Israelite scholar, *was once at the house of Rav Naḥman.* During the 3rd century, when our story takes place, the rabbinic centers of Israel and Babylonia communicated through messengers who would travel between the two centers, conveying words of Torah from one to

15. Ilan, *Mine and Yours*, 121.
16. This identification, accepted by the majority of scholars, is based on the numerous mentions of Yalta together with Rav Naḥman – who, per Ḥullin 124a, was the exilarch's son-in-law – in what seem to be domestic or intimate settings (for a few of these mentions, see below, pp. 14–16). It should be noted, though, that Yalta is never explicitly called Rav Naḥman's wife (as is commonly the case with talmudic women; four of the five other heroines of this book, for example, are referred to as "the wife of").

the other.[17] Ulla, who made his living as a merchant and was often in Babylonia on business, acted as such a messenger.[18] On one of his many trips through Babylonia, we are told, Ulla is hosted by his rabbinic colleague and friend, Rav Naḥman.

He had a meal, said the Grace after Meals, and handed the cup of blessing to Rav Naḥman. As the guest, Ulla is given the honor of leading *Birkat HaMazon*, the blessing at the end of the meal, customarily recited over a cup of wine. Once the Grace after Meals is said and the two men drink, Rav Naḥman requests that the cup be sent to Yalta, so that she may partake of its blessing (the use of the verb "send," *lishadar*, implies that Yalta, though close by, is not seated at the table with the men). Rabbinic messenger that he is, Ulla seizes upon the opportunity to teach his Babylonian host some words of Israelite Torah: *"So said Rabbi Yoḥanan,"* he intones, quoting the leading rabbi back in Israel, *"The fruit of a woman's body is blessed only from the fruit of a man's body, as it is written, 'He will bless the fruit of your body.' It does not say the fruit of her body, but the fruit of your body."*[19] Women do not drink from the cup of the Grace after Meals, since the blessing of the cup, traditionally

17. "Since Rav immigrated to Babylonia at the beginning of the 3rd century, bringing the Mishna of Israel to the scholars of Babylonia, the current of wisdom and learning that flowed between the two communities was considerably expanded. Its central agents were the scholars who traveled from Babylonia to Israel and back, relaying legal traditions and sayings from Israel to Babylonia, and from Babylonia to Israel." Paul Mandel, "Tales of the Destruction of the Temple: Between the Land of Israel and Babylonia," 141.
18. "Our colleagues who descended from the Land of Israel, and who are these? – Ulla" (Berakhot 38b). The Talmud abounds with references to Ulla's teaching of Israelite law to Babylonian rabbis in general, and to Rav Naḥman in particular (see, for the latter, Shabbat 108b, Gittin 67a, and Ḥullin 76b, 124a).
19. Rabbi Yoḥanan's argument is based on the selective reading of the Deuteronomy verse "He will bless the fruit of your body (*vitnekha*)" in the male, rather than gender-neutral, tense (which in Hebrew are one and the same); such masculinized readings, according to Tal Ilan, are typical of rabbinic literature, whose default assumption is that biblical texts "refer to men only. This generalization was adopted by the rabbis themselves in their interpretation of seemingly inclusive language in the Pentateuch, which they interpreted as exclusively male." Ilan, *Mine and Yours*, 222–23.

understood to be the blessing of childbirth, is transmitted to the woman through her husband. It is enough that he drink and be blessed.[20]

Meanwhile Yalta overhears the men's discussion, and flies into a rage. She storms up to the wine storehouse and – madwoman in the attic that she is – smashes *four hundred jars of wine.*[21] So passionate is her temper, so violent and vindictive, she doesn't care that the wine she is destroying (much like Xanthippe's and Fatimeh's cakes) is her own. If she can't have the wine, no one will.

Rav Naḥman said to him, "Let the master send her another cup." Poor Rav Naḥman! Yalta has just broken four hundred jars of wine, and all he can do is beg Ulla to send her a second cup, please, before she breaks anything else. Cowering helplessly before the wrath of his wife, Rav Naḥman is thoroughly, comically, henpecked.

Ulla accedes, sending Yalta a second cup, together with another wine-related teaching and some not-so-subtle criticism. *"All that wine can be counted as a blessing,"* he says; once a cup is blessed, all the wine-filled vessels in the vicinity become a cup of blessing.[22] Had Yalta been less halakhically ignorant, had she known this law, she would have realized that she could have drunk from any cup, and that there was no call for this violent outburst. She has unreasonably, wildly overreacted.

"Gossip comes from peddlers and lice from rags," Yalta snaps back, incensed. Infuriated by this rabbinic messenger and his Israelite ways, she responds by throwing Ulla's gesture, together with as many insults as she possibly can, back in his face: "You, Ulla, are nothing but a gossiping, rag-wearing, lice-infested peddler!"[23]

---

20. For more on this classic patriarchal argument, by which women ought to receive, take part, or be represented through the proxy of their husbands, see pp. 165–67.

21. "In some of the homes of the more wealthy Babylonian rabbis, the wine flowed with abundance." Moshe Beer, *The Babylonian Amoraim: Aspects of Economic Life*, 321. Four hundred, specifically, is a standard number of rabbinic hyperbole (see Berakhot 5b and Bava Metzia 83a for other mentions of four hundred wine jars, as well as the more general use of the number in Gittin 57b–58a, and Kiddushin 70b, 76b).

22. "After he recites the Grace after Meals, he recites the blessing on the wine and drinks, and then others drink .... He does not need to pour from his cup to the cups of others." Rabbi Yosef Karo, *Shulḥan Arukh, Oraḥ Ḥayim*:190:1.

23. "Yalta mocks [Ulla] .... His offer of wine ... is like a beggar offering his lice, a worthless and repulsive gift from a giver with nothing to give." Rachel Adler, *Engendering*

Thus far the story of Yalta. At first reading, we seem to have before us a classic shrew tale: We have the comedic undertones; the violence, both verbal and physical; the pitiable and placating husband; and most importantly, the bad-tempered madwoman, who feels herself scorned and unleashes her fury at everyone, and everything, in her path.

But is this the story the Talmud is telling?

Deconstructing the Vessels: Yalta Revisioned

Our revisioning of Yalta begins with another moment of literary revisioning, a rereading of the story of the other madwoman in the attic: *Jane Eyre*'s Bertha Mason. A century after the novel was first published, British-Dominican writer Jean Rhys posited that we know nothing about Bertha Mason, save the fact that she is a madwoman in an attic. But no madwoman in an attic is a madwoman in an attic born. So Rhys decided to write her story.[24] The result is the profoundly poignant *Wide Sargasso Sea*, a prequel to *Jane Eyre*, recounting the events that led to Bertha's mental breakdown. The book opens with the scene of Bertha's childhood, as the daughter of a slave-owner in the British colony of Jamaica. After the Emancipation Act of 1833, the locals turn on Bertha and her family, burn her house down, and send her mother spiraling into madness:

> As I knew they would be, they were waiting for me under the sandbox tree. There were two of them, a boy and a girl.... They looked so harmless and quiet, no one would have noticed the glint in the boy's eyes. Then the girl grinned and began to crack the knuckles of her fingers. At each crack I jumped and my hands began to sweat.

Judaism: An Inclusive Theology and Ethics, 55–56.

24. "When I was in London last year," Rhys wrote a friend, "it 'clicked in my head' that I had material for the story of Mr. Rochester's first wife. The real story – as it might have been.... She's necessary to the plot, but always she shrieks, howls, laughs horribly, attacks all and sundry – off stage. For me she must be right on stage. She must be at least plausible with a past, the reason why... she goes mad." Jean Rhys, "Selected Letters," *Wide Sargasso Sea*, 135–36.

> I was holding some school books in my right hand and I shifted them to under my arm, but it was too late, there was a mark on the palm of my hand and a stain on the cover of the book.... They closed in on me and started talking. The girl said, "Look the crazy girl, you crazy like your mother. Your aunt frightened to have you in the house. She send you for the nuns to lock up. Your mother walk about with no shoes and stockings on her feet... she try to kill her husband and she try to kill you too that day you go to see her. She have eyes like zombi and you have eyes like zombi too.... You don't want to look at me, eh, I make you look at me." She pushed me and the books I was carrying fell to the ground.[25]

This, according to Rhys, is what drives Bertha Mason to insanity. "You crazy like your mother." Treat someone as if they are mad often enough, and they will eventually become so.

A similar point is made by Susi Kaplow in a 1973 essay "Getting Angry," which discusses the fraught relationship between women and anger. When men get angry, claims Kaplow, they are indignant; when women get angry, they are irrational. This, too, is a self-fulfilling prophecy. Dismiss a woman as irrational, ill-tempered, and shrewish, and she will become irrational, ill-tempered, and shrewish:

> A woman in our society is denied the forthright expression of her healthy anger. Her attempts at physical confrontation seem ridiculous; "ladies" do a slow burn, letting out their anger indirectly in catty little phrases, often directed against a third party, especially children. A woman has learned to hold back her anger: It's unseemly, aesthetically displeasing, and against the sweet, pliant feminine image to be angry. And the woman fears her own anger: She the great conciliator, the steadier of rocked boats, moves, out of her fear, to quiet not only others' anger but also her own. Small wonder that when the vacuum-sealed lid bursts off, the angry woman seems like a freaked-out nut.... Her frenzy is intensified by the shakiness of her commitment to her own anger.

25. Ibid., 29–31.

> What if she's really wrong? What if the other person is right? – Or worse (and this is the greatest fear) hits back with, "You're crazy, I don't know what you're so mad about."[26]

Thus, argues Kaplow, does the shrew go from angry to crazy, raging to deranged. A woman who is mad is so easily turned into a madwoman; all it takes is for someone to treat her as such.

"You're crazy, I don't know what you're so mad about." Precisely the response Ulla gives Yalta after she smashes all those jars of wine. Ulla dismisses Yalta as a mad shrew. But is that really who she is? Let us review the evidence.

Broad Context: Yalta

As mentioned, Yalta appears several times in the Talmud. Let's zoom out and look at some of these other passages, and see whether Yalta is the shrew she is accused of being.

(i)

> Yalta once brought some blood to Rabba bar bar Ḥana, who informed her that it was impure. She then took it to Rav Yitzḥak son of Rav Yehuda, who told her that it was pure. But how could he act in this manner, seeing that it was taught: If a rabbi declared anything impure another rabbi may not declare it pure? … At first he informed her that it was indeed impure. However, when she told him that every time she brings this kind of blood to Rabba bar bar Ḥana he declares it pure, but that on the last occasion he had a pain in his eye, Rav Yitzḥak gave her his ruling that it was pure. (Niddah 20b)

This passage, in Tractate Niddah (lit., menstruation), is part of a lengthy discussion on the types of bloodstains that render a woman a menstruant and impure (thereby forbidden from engaging in marital relations). Yalta presents a bloodstain of questionable nature to Rabba bar bar

26. Susi Kaplow, "Getting Angry," 37.

Ḥana, who rules that it is indeed menstrual blood. Dissatisfied with this answer, Yalta makes the audacious and highly unusual decision to seek a second halakhic opinion. She takes the stain to Rav Yitzḥak, who overturns the original ruling after Yalta explains that Rabba bar bar Ḥana was suffering from an eye ailment and was consequently incapable of issuing a valid judgment.[27]

Contrary to Ulla's charge, Yalta is portrayed in this story as halakhically knowledgeable.[28] She is also highly rational, able to argue cogently in favor of her position. And she is eminently reasonable, responding to adversity in an assertive yet self-possessed manner; hardly your typical shrew.

(ii)

> Yalta said to Rav Naḥman, "Everything that the Torah prohibited, it permitted a corresponding thing. It prohibited blood – it permitted liver, a menstruating woman – pure blood, the fat of domesticated animals – the fat of wild animals, pork – the brain of a carp, a marsh-hen – the tongue of a fish, a married woman – a divorcee in her husband's lifetime, a brother's wife – a levirate bride, a Samaritan woman – a beautiful captive woman. I would like to eat milk and meat." Rav Naḥman told the cooks, "Roast her an udder." (Ḥullin 109b)

Here too, Yalta is described as having a deep understanding of halakha and its workings. For every law, she tells Rav Naḥman, there is a loophole: We may not be allowed to eat blood, cattle fat, pork, or marsh-hen – but we can have liver, beast fat, carp brain, and fish tongue (which, respectively,

27. According to the Mishna, halakhic diagnoses of this kind cannot be made by one who is in any way visually impaired: "A priest who is blind in one eye, or the light of whose eyes is dim, should not inspect leprous lesions, for it says, 'As far as appears in the eyes of the priest' (Lev. 13:12)" (M Negaim 2:3).

28. Her allusion to the aforementioned Mishna, says Charlotte Fonrobert, "catapults Yalta rhetorically into an argumentative position in which she is familiar with mishnaic halakha… can replicate rabbinic knowledge… [and is able to make] a creative halakhic argument, which is strong enough to convince Rav Yitzhak." Charlotte Fonrobert, *Menstrual Purity: Rabbinic and Christian Reconstructions of Biblical Gender*, 121.

are believed to have the same flavor); a man cannot have intercourse with a menstruating woman, a married woman, a non-Jewish woman, or a sister-in-law – but he can have relations with a woman whose discharge is non-menstrual (such as after birth), a divorcee, a brother's widow, and a war bride. There must therefore be an exception to the rule against eating milk and meat. Rav Naḥman concurs, and orders the cooks to prepare his wife an udder.[29] In addition to erudite and intelligent, the story depicts Yalta as a strict adherent of the halakhic system, within which she is careful to remain (even when pushing against its boundaries). It also suggests that her marriage to Rav Naḥman was amicable, based on mutual respect.

(iii)

> When the household of the exilarch would afflict Rav Amram the Pious, they made him lie down in the snow.... Yalta heard and took him into the bathhouse, and bathed him till the water of the bathhouse turned the color of blood and his flesh was covered with bright spots. (Gittin 67b)

After the exilarch's servants torment Rav Amram to the point of hypothermia, Yalta arranges for him to be taken to the bathhouse and gently nursed back to health.[30] Far from a malicious shrew, the Yalta of this account is kind and compassionate. And she is once again shown to be pushing against authority, defying the most powerful institution of the Babylonian Jewish community.

---

29. Earlier on the page, the Talmud states: "If the udder was cooked with its milk it is permitted" (ibid.). For another instance when Rav Naḥman finds a legal loophole to accommodate Yalta's wishes, see Beitza 25b.
30. We're not told what Rav Amram had done to provoke this aggression, though the leading talmudic commentator Rashi claims that, in his piety, Rav Amram would impose upon the servants unwanted halakhic stringencies (for other examples of the aggressive nature of the exilarch's "household," generally understood to mean his servants and courtiers, see Shabbat 121b, Avoda Zara 38b).

(iv)

> Rav Naḥman said to Rav Yehuda, "Let Donag come and pour us drinks."[31] Rav Yehuda replied, "Shmuel said: One should not make use of a woman." Rav Naḥman said, "She is a minor." Rav Yehuda replied, "Shmuel explicitly said: One should not make use of a woman at all, whether adult or minor." Rav Naḥman said, "Would the master send a greeting to Yalta?" Rav Yehuda replied, "Shmuel said: A woman's voice is considered indecent." Rav Naḥman said, "Through a messenger." Rav Yehuda replied, "Shmuel said: One should not send greetings to a woman." Rav Naḥman said, "Through her husband." Rav Yehuda replied, "Shmuel said: One should not send greetings to a woman at all." His wife sent Rav Naḥman a message, "Conclude his business and let him go, lest he make you as an ignoramus." (Kiddushin 70a–b)

This story is part of a longer incident in which Rav Yehuda, a leading rabbi from Pumbedita, is summoned by Rav Naḥman to stand trial before him. Upon arrival, Rav Yehuda expresses his indignation with Rav Naḥman by finding copious fault with his conduct (which, he keeps pointing out, contradicts the teachings of their rabbi, Shmuel). The passage bears a striking resemblance to our story: In both cases, a guest arrives at Rav Naḥman and Yalta's home; in both cases, Rav Naḥman requests that the lady of the house be acknowledged; and in both cases, the guest, citing a greater halakhic authority (with more exclusionary views of women), refuses. Two very similar situations, two completely opposite responses. Here, Yalta doesn't throw a tantrum or hurl insults or break any household goods; rather, she sends a discreet message to Rav Naḥman to let the matter – and the guest – go, and spare himself any further embarrassment. Yalta seems far more concerned with her husband's honor than with her own, and is tactful and even-tempered in defending it.

Taken together, these sources present Yalta as rational and intelligent, self-possessed and kind, and deeply solicitous of her husband's honor – nothing like the shrew of our primary reading.

---

31. Following Rashi, Donag is widely believed to be Rav Naḥman's daughter.

Immediate Context: The Cup of Blessing

Next, we must examine the sugya in which our story is situated. The legend of Yalta follows a detailed halakhic discussion in Tractate Berakhot (lit., blessings) concerning the cup over which the Grace after Meals is recited and the ceremonial way it must be handled:

> Ten things have been said in connection with the cup of blessing. It needs to be rinsed and washed, undiluted and full, it requires adorning and wrapping, he takes it up with both hands and places it in the right hand, and he raises it a handbreadth from the ground, and fixes his eyes on it. Some add that he sends it round to the members of his household.... He sends it round to the members of his household, so that his wife may be blessed. (Berakhot 51a–b)

The Talmud enumerates ten rules for the cup of blessing, capping its list with an additional eleventh requirement: After drinking, the cup should be passed round to the rest of the household.[32] Later in the sugya, the Talmud offers a reason for this requirement – *so that his wife may be blessed* – and immediately proceeds to tell the story of Yalta. In framing the narrative with this precept, the talmudic editors place themselves squarely on Yalta's side; sharing the cup of blessing with other family members, and one's wife in particular, is standard practice according to the Talmud, and Yalta was absolutely right to expect it.[33] A second indication of where the rabbis stand is in the story's final line; although

32. The Talmud, incidentally, provides an alternative list by the Israelite Rabbi Yoḥanan (the same Rabbi Yoḥanan cited by Ulla). This list includes just four rules, and makes no mention of sending the cup round to other members of the household ("We only know of four: rinsing, washing, undiluted, and full"; Berakhot 51a). The difference in rules may be ascribed to the cultural gap between Israel, where women did not drink of the cup of blessing, and Babylonia, where they did. Tamara Or, ed., *Massekhet Betsah: A Feminist Commentary on the Babylonian Talmud*, 129–31.
33. Another prooftext for the prevalence of this practice is in the Bavli's interpretation of the angels' visit to Abraham: "'And they said unto him: Where is your wife Sarah? And he replied: There, in the tent' (Gen. 18:9).... The ministering angels knew that Sarah was in the tent, rather... [they asked] in order to send her the cup of blessing" (Bava Metzia 87a). The practice became codified in later halakhic sources; see, for example, Karo, *Shulḥan Arukh, Oraḥ Ḥayim*:183:4.

the men do all the talking throughout the narrative, it is Yalta, significantly, who is given the last word.

Close Reading

In light of what we've learned of Yalta, and of the rabbinic attitude toward her, let us now zoom in and attempt a second, closer reading of her story – this time, from the perspective of Yalta herself. We begin, as we must, with an initial mapping of the story's structure, setting, and characters:

Act 1

> Ulla was once at the house of Rav Naḥman.
> He had a meal, said the Grace after Meals, and handed the cup of blessing to Rav Naḥman.
> Rav Naḥman said to him, "Master, please send the cup of blessing to Yalta."
> Ulla responded, "So said Rabbi Yoḥanan: The fruit of a woman's body is blessed only from the fruit of a man's body, as it is written, 'He will bless the fruit of your body.' It does not say the fruit of her body, but the fruit of your body"….

Act 2

> Meanwhile Yalta heard, and she got up in a passion and went to the wine storehouse and broke four hundred jars of wine.

Act 3

> Rav Naḥman said to him, "Let the master send her another cup."
> He sent it to her with a message, "All that wine can be counted as a blessing."
> She returned answer, "Gossip comes from peddlers and lice from rags."

Act 1 – The Cup Denied	*Home*	*Rav Naḥman, Ulla*
Act 2 – Four Hundred Broken Jars	*Wine Store*	*Yalta*
Act 3 – Another Cup	*Home*	*Rav Naḥman, Ulla, Yalta*

Act 1 – The Cup Denied

As the curtain rises, we find Rav Naḥman and Ulla together at the table. Having eaten and drunk and said the Grace after Meals, Rav Naḥman, wishing to honor his wife, asks that she be sent the cup of blessing (as is the local custom). Ulla demurs, quoting Rabbi Yoḥanan's opinion by which a woman receives the blessing of childbirth, not independently, but through her husband. This is not, as some feminist readers maintain, a sexist argument for the exclusion of women from the cup of blessing. This, according to the ancient view of reproduction, is a basic biological fact.

Historical Context: Reproduction in Antiquity

For much of the ancient world, the power of procreation belonged exclusively to man. It was man who produced life through the generative force of his seed, whereas woman merely carried that life inside her. "She who is called the mother is not her offspring's parent, but nurse to the newly sown embryo," declared the Greek tragedian Aeschylus. "The male, who mounts, begets. The female, a stranger, guards."[34] Writing a century later, and rather more scientifically, Aristotle explained that the source of reproduction was man's active seed, passively incubated within the woman's womb.[35] The womb itself was likened by Greco-Roman biologists to a jar, lying upside-down inside the woman's body, hollow, waiting to be filled.

Such theories influenced the rabbinic understanding of women's anatomy.[36] The Talmud says that man fashions woman into a "vessel" through the act of intercourse (Sanhedrin 22b); elsewhere, the rabbis describe woman as having "more store-room than the man [i.e., a womb], wider at the bottom and narrower at the top, so that it could receive

34. Aeschylus, *The Eumenides*, 658–61.

35. "Male is that which is able to concoct, to cause to take shape, and to discharge, semen possessing the 'principle' of the 'form'.... Female is that which receives the semen, but is unable to cause semen to take shape or to discharge it." Aristotle, *On the Generation of Animals*, 765b10–19.

36. "The contemporaneity of the flourishing Greco-Roman gynecological literature with the burgeoning discourse on women's bodies and rabbinic culture needs to be taken into consideration as a possible cultural context for the rabbis to develop their own medical language." Fonrobert, *Menstrual Purity*, 42.

embryos" (Genesis Rabba 18:3[37]). For the rabbis, like the classical biologists, the woman's body was little more than an inverted jar, a receptacle to hold man's seed.[38]

Hence Ulla's insistence on the futility of sending Yalta the cup. *"He will bless the fruit of your body." It does not say the fruit of her body, but the fruit of your body.* Man is the primary agent of childbirth, and he alone should be blessed for it. Woman is ancillary at best, and will receive the blessing when she receives man's seed into the vessel of her womb.[39]

Act 2 – Four Hundred Broken Jars

Hearing the reason for denying her the cup, Yalta gets up, goes to the wine store, and breaks four hundred jars of wine. Not, I'd like to claim, in a fit of rage, but as a very clever, very sophisticated response to Ulla's biological argument. "Vessels are unimportant, are they?" she asks, as she sends jar after jar crashing to the ground. "Alright: Let's see how you do without them. I'm not going to touch the wine. I'm just going to deconstruct the vessels. If vessels are so unimportant, it shouldn't make any difference, now should it?"

37. See also Leviticus Rabba 14:3.
38. That said, rabbinic literature (in this as in all subjects) is far from monolithic, and gives voice to alternative biological views as well; see Joshua Levinson, "Cultural Androgyny in Rabbinic Literature," 123–25.
39. "Cultures lacking biological knowledge naturally perceived childbirth as resulting from a man's planting his seed in a woman, much as he ploughs and sows his field… reinforc[ing] man's dominance over woman in the very aspect of human activity that is most peculiarly her own." Judith R. Wegner, "The Image and Status of Women in Classical Rabbinic Judaism," 82–83. The male appropriation of the reproductive function (born, according to psychoanalysts, of womb envy) is perhaps best expressed in various couvade rituals found across the ancient world, and to this day in certain tribal cultures, in which "the father, on the birth of his child, makes a ceremonial pretense of being the mother," mimicking the symptoms and behaviors of the birthing process. Edward B. Tylor, "On a Method of Investigating the Development of Institutions, Applied to Laws of Marriage and Descent," 254.

Act 3 – Another Cup

With the ground beneath them running red with wine, Ulla sends Yalta another cup, together with the message, *"All that wine can be counted as a blessing."* The wine is all blessed; Yalta did not need to drink from that particular cup. Like Yalta's breaking of the vessels, this message, too, is far more complex than it seems (had Ulla simply believed this to be the law, he would have cited it the first time Rav Naḥman asked him to send Yalta the cup). Ulla understands perfectly well what Yalta has just tried to tell him, and he responds in kind. If wine symbolizes man's seed, and the vessel (in this case, the cup) represents woman's womb, Ulla's reproach to Yalta that she could have drunk from any cup is an effective doubling down: Vessels – that is, wombs – are incidental and therefore interchangeable; the only important thing is what is inside the vessel – that is, wine – that is, man's seed. Therefore procreation is, fundamentally, a male act.

The story's biological subtext thus decoded, we may now understand the final line, not as a torrent of abuse, but as Yalta's staking her claim to the blessing of childbirth. *"Gossip comes from peddlers and lice from rags"*; lice, according to ancient biology, did not reproduce, but rather spontaneously generated.[40] Take women out of the reproductive equation, says Yalta to Ulla, and you might be able to reproduce lice, you might be able to generate gossip. But for any real act of procreation, both woman and man, vessel and seed, are necessary. Women might be vessels, but they are no less essential to the creation of life.

The Moral of the Story: The Danger of Dismissal

Having revisioned the legend of Yalta, we find that it is radically different to how it was first read. Not a petty fight over a cup of wine, but a

40. Aristotle wrote that certain animals "grow spontaneously" and that lice, specifically, "are generated out of the flesh of animals." Aristotle, *The History of Animals*, 539a18–556b25. Here, too, we may discern the influence of classical biology on rabbinic thought, as the Talmud decrees that lice, contrary to all other living creatures, may be killed on Shabbat since they "do not procreate" (Shabbat 107b).

principled debate about the power of procreation. Not an outburst of physical and verbal violence, but a highly intelligent argument in favor of women's reproductive worth (and their right to its blessing). Not a shrew storming off in a tantrum, but a rational, self-possessed woman who stays and fights the system from within.

This final point, for me, is Yalta at her most remarkable. At no stage does she say, "I am not a vessel." The dominant tradition of her day held that women were vessels, and Yalta accepts that. But within that tradition, she tries to carve out a space for herself. She may be a vessel, but vessels are critically important. As such, Yalta is an ideal reader, and it's her strategy I'd like to adopt as we make our way through the stories of the heroines of the Talmud. Not every text we come across will sit well with our 21st-century feminist sensibilities. Some may strike us as difficult or (forgive the pun) jarring. We must not reject these traditions but, like Yalta, accept them as our own, and try and create a space for ourselves within them. We might just find, like we did with Yalta, that these traditions, once revisioned, are not so far from what we believe in after all.

Yet the ultimate lesson of the story of Yalta is, I submit, an ethical one. Ulla dismisses Yalta for being a raging shrew. So do generations of readers after him, who never bother to look at the story more closely, or from her point of view. And dismissal, we've seen, is the worst kind of self-fulfilling prophecy. Katharine says, "If I be waspish, best beware my sting"; treat me like a snarling, scratching, biting shrew, and I will be a snarling, scratching, biting shrew. Shylock, another famous Shakespearean Other, exclaims, "Thou calledst me dog before thou hadst a cause. But since I am a dog, beware my fangs";[41] accuse me of being a vicious Jew-monster, and I will be a vicious Jew-monster, and demand my pound of flesh. Bertha Mason is mocked for being crazy, until she is eventually driven mad. And returning once again to the Talmud, we find Timna, the Horite princess who wanted to convert to Judaism, but was rejected by Abraham, Isaac, and Jacob; so Timna went off and gave birth to Amalek, archenemy of the Jewish people (Sanhedrin 99b). Dismiss the Other as irrational, or wicked, or unworthy, and they will become the very thing you dismiss them for. It is a moral error few of

41. William Shakespeare, *The Merchant of Venice*, 3.3.6–7.

us avoid. Men, in their depictions of the shrew, often dismiss women; adults dismiss children all the time; we dismiss people from the wrong culture, political camp, religious affiliation – anyone, really, who doesn't see things exactly as we do. So before you next dismiss the Other (and we all, inevitably, do), pause, and think of Yalta, of how unfairly she was dismissed, and try to see things from their perspective. You don't have to adopt it, you may never agree, but at least you will not have created another madwoman in the attic.

Ḥoma
The Femme Fatale

The Archetype: Desire Like a Serpent's Poison

> The dark lady, the black widow, the evil seductress who tempts man and brings about his destruction is among the oldest themes of art, literature, mythology, and religion.... She is as old as Eve, and as current as today's movies, comic books, and dime novels.[1]

Dark, deadly, and dangerously beautiful, the femme fatale haunts the pages of Western literature, ensnaring its heroes in her irresistible web. Saints have succumbed to her charms, warriors fallen at her feet. Fairest and most fatal of villains, she is lovely and malevolent, the subject of fantasies and the stuff of nightmares.

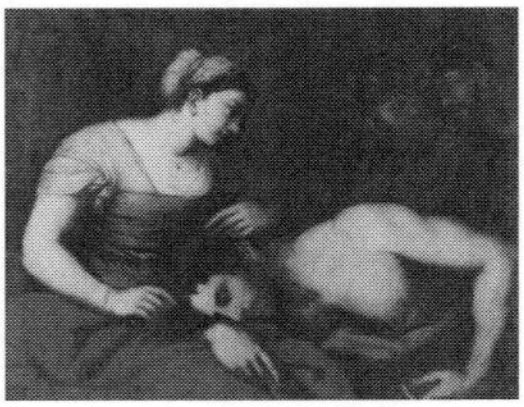

Samson and Delilah, Follower of Luca Giordano

Some of the earliest and most striking femmes fatales are found in the books of the Bible: the Daughters of Moab, who entice the Israelites to harlotry and idolatry, bringing

1. Janey Place, "Women in Film Noir," 47.

about a divine plague that causes the death of thousands (Num. 25:1–9); Delilah (whose name has become synonymous with the archetype), who lures Samson into betraying the secret of his strength and delivers him, shorn of his hair and virility, into the hands of the Philistines (Judges 16:4–21); the Daughters of Zion, who "walk with outstretched necks and wanton eyes, strutting along with swaying hips," their promiscuity leading to the downfall of Jerusalem (Is. 3:16); and, perhaps most sinister of all, the Crafty Harlot of Proverbs, who seduces and destroys many an unsuspecting youth:

> He was walking through the marketplace… and there the woman met him, with the attire of a harlot, and a crafty heart. She was wild and rebellious; her feet would not stay at home…. So she caught him and kissed him, with an impudent face she said… "Come, let us take our fill of love until morning, let us delight ourselves with love. For my husband is not at home"…. With her fair speech she caused him to yield, with her flattering lips she seduced him. Immediately he went after her… as a bird hurrying to the snare. He did not know it would cost his life. (Prov. 7:8–23)

These biblical femmes fatales become even more brazen in the midrashic interpretations of their stories. The Daughters of Moab are reimagined as prostitutes who came before the Israelites naked (Sanhedrin 106a); Delilah used sexual teasing to wrangle Samson's secret out of him (Y Ketubot 5:8); and the Daughters of Zion would cavort in the marketplace, painted and perfumed, sending their scent toward the young men of Jerusalem and "instilling in them a passionate desire like a serpent's poison" (Shabbat 62b).

Moving from midrash to rabbinic legend, the Talmud features a remarkable number of seduction narratives, many of them cautionary tales about how even the greatest of sages can be overcome by passion at the sight of a beautiful woman:

> Captive women were brought to Nehardea. They were taken up to the house of Rav Amram the Pious, and the ladder was removed from under them. When one of them passed by, light fell

across the opening. Rav Amram seized the ladder, which ten men together could not raise, and began climbing. When he got halfway up the ladder, he stayed his feet and cried, "Fire in Amram's house!" The rabbis came. They said to him, "You have shamed us." Rav Amram said to them, "Better to be shamed in this world than to be shamed in the next." (Kiddushin 81a)

So pious is Rav Amram, he is entrusted with an attic full of sexually vulnerable women.[2] Yet even he cannot contain his desire when the beauty of one of them shines out.[3] This story, like most rabbinic seduction narratives, is told from the perspective of the seduced man, not the seducing women.[4] As a rule, tales of femmes fatales (like those of shrews) center on the experience of the male victim; the femme fatale's point of view is hardly ever there.

The Odyssey, Homer's Greek epic, provides us with more femmes fatales per capita than perhaps any other work in the Western canon. Practically every female character Odysseus encounters on his long journey home is a temptress bent on preventing him from reaching his destination: Calypso, the "lovely nymph" who keeps Odysseus by her side for seven years, making him "l[ie] with her each night"; Circe, the beautiful sorceress who charms Odysseus into her bed, and turns his men into pigs; and the Sirens (who, like Delilah, lend their

The Sirens Imploring Ulysses to Stay, Unknown

2. "Captivity usually entailed sexual violence toward the captive woman.... The captive woman who was redeemed back into the Jewish community found herself in a sorry state... subject to a heightened risk of sexual violence.... Placing such women under protection was meant to ward off potential attackers." Sagit Mor, "The Status of Female Captives on Their Return to the Jewish Community in the Talmudic Literature," 108–12.
3. The emitting of light from a beautiful body – male or female – is a standard rabbinic motif (see Genesis Rabba 40:5, Berakhot 5b, Megilla 14b).
4. See, for example, the seduction story cycles of Kiddushin 39b–40a and 80b–81b (the latter discussed at length in Chapter 4).

name to the archetype) whose melodies "bewitch men casting by... sing[ing their] mind[s] away on their sweet meadow lolling. There are bones of dead men rotting in a pile beside them, and flayed skins shrivel around the spot."[5]

Christianity gives us the Great Whore of Babylon, the diabolical seductress whose lechery knows no bounds:

> The great whore who sits upon many waters, with whom the kings of the earth have committed fornication, and the inhabitants of the earth have been made drunk with the wine of her fornication.... The woman was arrayed in purple and scarlet color, and bedecked with gold and precious stones and pearls, having a golden cup in her hand full of abominations and filthiness of her fornication; and upon her forehead was a name written: Mystery, Babylon the Great, Mother of Harlots and Abominations of the Earth.[6]

Like the rabbis of the Talmud, the knights of medieval chivalric romance are frequently faced with temptation, often in the form of a femme fatale deployed to test their virtue. Sir Gawain is thrice trapped in his bed by Lady Bertilak, who (under the orders of Morgan le Fay, herself a notorious femme fatale) tries to "allure him to love-making." Though he never fully succumbs, Sir Gawain does indulge in the fair lady's advances and is ultimately punished for it, prompting him to cry out against "the wiles of women" everywhere:

> For even so Adam by one on earth was beguiled, and Solomon by several, and to Samson moreover his doom by Delilah was dealt; and David was after blinded by Bathsheba, and he bitterly suffered.... All of them were betrayed by women that they knew.[7]

5. Homer, *The Odyssey*, 5:90–163, 12:43–49.
6. Revelations 17:1–4.
7. *Sir Gawain and the Green Knight*, 1550; 2415–26. Note that Eve, included in Sir Gawain's list, is not portrayed as a typical femme fatale in the Bible itself. She does, however, come to be regarded as one in classical Christian works, which accuse her of introducing sin into the world through her temptation of Adam (Tertullian, for

Acrasia, John Melhuish Strudwick

Acrasia, the evil enchantress of *The Faerie Queene*, lulls knights away from their quests, entrapping them "in chains of lust and lewd desires." True to her name (lit., intemperance), Acrasia robs her victims of their self-control, sucks their spirit with her kisses, and turns them into beasts once she's had her fill of them.[8]

With the advent of Modernity, the femme fatale becomes more manipulative and sexually aggressive than ever. The unscrupulous Marquise de Merteuil, who confesses to "turning the formidable male into the plaything of [her] whims and fancies," seduces and discards a series of lovers, ruining the lives of everyone in her sphere.[9] John Keats's La Belle Dame sans Merci captivates strong and valiant men with her beauty, drains them of their power, and leaves them to die a lovesick death:

> I met a lady in the meads, / Full beautiful, a fairy's child;
> Her hair was long, her foot was light, / And her eyes were wild...
> And there she lulled me asleep, / And there I dreamed – Ah! woe betide! –
> The latest dream I ever dreamt / On the cold hill side.
> I saw pale kings and princes too, / Pale warriors, death-pale were they all;
> They cried – "La Belle Dame sans Merci / Hath thee in thrall!"[10]

example, describes her as the source "of the first sin... the Devil's gateway... the first deserter of the divine law, she who persuaded him whom the Devil was not valiant enough to attack." Tertullian, *On the Apparel of Women*, 1:1).

8. Edmund Spenser, *The Faerie Queene*, 2:1:54. The magical transformation of men into animals, common to both Circe and Acrasia, symbolizes the loss of autonomy that is the lot of the femme fatale's victim.
9. Pierre Choderlos de Laclos, *Dangerous Liaisons*, letter 81.
10. John Keats, "La Belle Dame sans Merci." We find a similar emasculating effect with the Sirens and Delilah, the latter so called because "she weakened (*dildela*) [Samson's] strength" (Sotah 9b).

Carmen

The fiery gypsy Carmen bewitches the men of Seville with her charisma and her castanets. When the honest José comes under her spell, abandoning his military duties and fiancée Micaëla to join Carmen's life of crime, Micaëla makes a desperate attempt to save him from the "woman whose evil wiles have finished by making a criminal of the man I once loved."[11] But José refuses to let Carmen go, his mad desire ultimately destroying them both. Micaëla is no match for Carmen, any more than the wretched widow Amavia is for Acrasia, or the naïve Cécile for the Marquise de Merteuil. The betrayed woman, an important antithetical character to the femme fatale, is respectable, modest, and the rightful partner (wife or fiancée) of the male victim – everything the femme fatale is not.[12] Caught in a deadly love triangle with the man she loves and the woman who's lured him away, the betrayed woman fights in vain to save her man, watching helplessly as he falls into the seductress's "demon clutches."[13]

Oscar Wilde's play *Salomé* (inspired by the Christian tradition of Salome the Temptress) depicts the titular character as a provocative princess who, having been spurned by John the Baptist, turns her charms onto her stepfather, King Herod. Like the naked Daughters of Moab and the hip-swaying Carmen, Salomé uses her body as an instrument of seduction; performing the sensual dance of the seven veils, she sheds one veil after another, until the lust-crazed Herod agrees to grant her the head of John the Baptist (whose dead lips she proceeds to kiss).

Yet the height of the femme fatale's stardom comes in the 20th century, with the popular film noir genre of the '40s and '50s. Films such as *Double Indemnity, The Killers,* and *The Postman Always Rings Twice* feature treacherous women who drag the hero down to the underworld, enticing him to steal, cheat, and murder on their behalf. Often, it's their

11. Henri Meilhac and Ludovic Halévy, "Carmen," 3:21.
12. A parallel antithesis, that of the madonna/whore, will be explored in Chapter 4.
13. Meilhac and Halévy, "Carmen," 1:6.

own husbands these would-be black widows want killed, as they convince the infatuated hero to pull the trigger for them. Here too, courtesy of the cinematic close-up, we find extensive use of the femme fatale's body. The eponymous Gilda, for instance, taunts her former lover (and present husband's assistant) with the iconic "Put the Blame on Mame" striptease, suggestively peeling off her satin gloves to a song about the dangers of female sexuality.

Gilda, Columbia Pictures

Hence the femme fatale is, quite simply, a fatal woman; a temptress who is as deadly as she is beautiful; whose victim, no matter how virtuous or strong, falls captive to her irresistible sexual power; and whose tale (rarely told from her own point of view) features a seduction, sometimes by manipulation, often through the baring of the body, and always ending in destruction.

The archetype thus defined, we now turn to the great femme fatale of the Talmud – Ḥoma.

Primary Reading: The Black Widow of Meḥoza

To fully understand the story of Ḥoma, we must begin with the sugya that precedes it:

> If someone maintains his wife through a trustee, he must give her no less than two kabs of wheat or four kabs of barley [a week] .... He must also give her half a kab of legumes, and half a log of oil, and a kab of dried figs or a maneh of pressed figs, and if he has no such fruits, he must supply her a corresponding quantity of other fruit. He must also give her a bed, a mattress, and a rush mat. He must also give her a cap for her head, and a belt for her waist, and new shoes each festival, and garments of the value of fifty dinars each year. (M Ketubot 5:8)

At the heart of the Jewish marriage contract are the husband's obligations toward his wife, defined in the Torah as "her food, her garments, and her conjugal relations" (Ex. 21:10). Our Mishna, in Tractate Ketubot (lit., marriage contracts), unpacks the first two categories of this biblical formula,[14] listing the elementary items of food, clothing, and furniture a husband must provide his wife with if he wishes to set her up in a separate household.[15] Wheat and oil, fruit and legumes, basic bedroom fixtures, and a fifty-dinar wardrobe are the bare necessities every woman – whether she lives with her husband or not – has a right to expect.

Wine, note the rabbis of the Talmud, is conspicuously absent from the Mishna's list, prompting the following debate:

> No allowance for wine is made for a woman.... An objection was raised: If a woman is accustomed to drink, she is given an allowance of wine. Where she is accustomed to drink the case is different.... Abaye said:... If she was accustomed to drink two cups in the presence of her husband, she is given one cup in his absence; if she was accustomed to drink only one cup in the presence of her husband, she is given none at all in his absence.... It was taught: One cup is becoming to a woman; two are degrading; if she has three, she solicits [sexual relations] publicly; and if she has four, she solicits even a donkey in the marketplace and cares not. Rava said: This was taught only with regard to a woman whose husband is not with her; but if her husband is with her, the objection does not arise. (Ketubot 65a)

Opening the talmudic discussion is the premise that *no allowance for wine is made for a woman.*[16] Unless, that is, the woman in question is

14. For the third category, see p. 100 n. 27.
15. In rabbinic times, it was not uncommon for a husband and wife to live under different roofs, either because of the husband's lengthy absence from home (to work or study) or because he had multiple wives housed in different locations. For women's historical dependence on their husbands for their financial needs, see pp. 60–61.
16. It is perhaps no coincidence that wine appears both in Yalta's story and in this one. Signifying irrationality on the one hand and sexuality on the other, wine is a common

accustomed to drink, in which case she is given a wine allowance – but only if she is an especially seasoned drinker, and only for half the amount to which she is accustomed. This is because wine, in a woman, causes promiscuity and sexual impropriety.[17] *One cup is becoming to a woman; two are degrading; if she has three, she solicits publicly; and if she has four, she solicits even a donkey in the marketplace and cares not.*[18] Such danger of licentiousness, says Rava, exists only in the case of a woman drinking alone; if, however, there is a husband present, she may drink as much as she likes.

Which takes us back to the femme fatale, that specter of female sexuality. Since the early days of Delilah and Circe, humanity contended with the threat of woman's desire by domesticating it, placing it under the authority of a man: "Your desire will be for your husband, and he will rule over you" (Gen. 3:16). Female sexuality was subjected to a male guardian – first a father, then a husband – who was meant to curb and control it. "She is always under her father's authority until she enters her husband's authority in marriage" (M Ketubot 4:5).[19]

---

motif in the portrayal of, respectively, shrews (the Wife of Bath insisting on her right to wine, for example, or Bertha Mason's permanent state of drunkenness) and femmes fatales (the Great Whore of Babylon intoxicating men with "the wine of her fornication," or Carmen and her keen love of drink).

17. To be fair, rabbinic literature expresses similar apprehension regarding men and drink (see, for example, Tanḥuma Noaḥ 13 and Yalkut Shimoni 61), but these concerns are of general loss of control – not, specifically, of sexual abandon. The rabbinic attitude toward the question of women and wine, says Shulamit Valler, is informed by the paternalistic view of women as "sexual, childish, irresponsible creatures, who must be policed and protected from their surroundings and from themselves." Valler, *Women and Womanhood,* 82.
18. This gradual descent – from degradation to sexual aggression to outright bestiality – is remarkably similar to the diatribe against the lecherous women of Rome by the satirist Juvenal: "Now their lust can't wait; they drop their pretenses; the temple rings with the cry 'Bring on the men.' Soon they need replacements; when they run out, they jump the servants; if there aren't any servants, they'll drag in any old beggar. If they can't find any men, they raid the stables and rape the donkeys." Juvenal, *Satire VI,* 326–34.
19. According to Jacob Neusner, the Mishna "provide[s] for a world in which it is normal for woman to be subject to man… and a system which regularizes the transfer of women from the hand of the father to that of the husband. The regulation of the transfer of women is the Mishna's way of affecting the sanctification of what, for

It followed that any woman not in the possession of a man was almost by definition dangerous. Without a male guardian to keep it in check, female desire was believed to run wild and wanton. Hence the talmudic imperative to limit the wine intake of *a woman whose husband is not with her*; compound such a woman's volatile sexuality with the aphrodisiac of alcohol and, it was feared, you'll have her chasing donkeys in the marketplace.[20]

"Our rabbis have taught: A maiden who gives herself up to prayer [and] a gadabout widow… behold, these bring destruction upon the world" (Sotah 22a). Herein is the great threat of the unattached woman: A *maiden* who has never married, and shows no interest in matrimony, and a *gadabout widow* who is no longer married, and is a little too free, and a little too roaming – *behold, these bring destruction upon the world*, no less! These women are a menace to society, a danger to themselves and to everyone around them.[21]

---

the moment, disturbs and disorders the orderly world." Jacob Neusner, *Method and Meaning in Ancient Judaism*, 96–97. We find a similar system in ancient Athens, where citizen women were passed from the guardianship of a father (or male next-of-kin) to the guardianship of a husband; in the event of divorce or the husband's death, the woman, if she had no children, would return to the jurisdiction of the original guardian or his heirs. See Sarah B. Pomeroy, *Goddesses, Whores, Wives, & Slaves: Women in Classical Antiquity*, 62–65.

20. It is not for nothing that the femmes fatales described in the previous section are practically all unmarried (the only exceptions – the Crafty Harlot of Proverbs, Lady Bertilak, and a number of the noir women – might as well be unmarried, as their husbands clearly fail to prevent their lecherous behavior). Nor is it coincidental that a number of them (the Crafty Harlot, the Daughters of Zion, the donkey-chasing woman here) are found in the market, a place entirely unseemly for a woman of good repute. On the immodesty of women in the marketplace, see pp. 160–62.

21. Admittedly, the danger of being overcome by desire is not specific to women; as the prevalence of rabbinic seduction stories shows, men too are highly susceptible to it. "There is no protection against sexual immorality" (Ketubot 13b, Ḥullin 11b), say the rabbis; sexual desire is a uniquely powerful force, and no one – man or woman – can guard themselves enough against it. However, it is only men who have the strength and self-control to even try: "'Happy is the man that fears the Lord' (Ps. 112:1). Happy is the man, but not happy is the woman?… Rabbi Yehoshua ben Levi says: Happy is one who triumphs over his sexual urge like a man" (Avoda Zara 19a). Women don't have a fighting chance in the war against their desire, which is why it must be controlled for them by a man.

Writing a millennium and a half after the Talmud, feminist thinker Simone de Beauvoir explains why even modern women require the protection of a male guardian: "Woman is her husband's prey, his possession.... Virgins unsubdued by man, old women who have escaped his power, are more easily than others regarded as sorceresses; for the lot of woman being bondage to another, if she escapes the yoke of man she is ready to accept that of the Devil."[22] Invoking the same talmudic categories of maiden ("virgins unsubdued by man") and widow ("old women who have escaped his power"), Beauvoir argues that female sexuality, when not under the restraining influence of a man, becomes dark and diabolical. The fear of the single woman, then, is not specifically rabbinic or even ancient; throughout history and across cultures, every unattached woman was essentially a femme fatale.

With that, let us continue in the sugya to the story of one very gadabout widow, Ḥoma.

> Ḥoma, Abaye's wife, came before Rava.
> She said, "Grant me an allowance of board," and he granted her.
> "Grant me an allowance of wine," she said.
> Said he, "I know that Naḥmani did not drink wine."
> "By the life of the master," she replied, "he would give me to drink in horns as large as this."
> As she was showing it to him, her arm was uncovered and a light shone upon the court.
> Rava rose, went home, and solicited Rav Ḥisda's daughter.
> "Who was in the court just now?" she said.
> "Ḥoma, the wife of Abaye," he replied.
> Thereupon Rav Ḥisda's daughter went after her, striking her with the lock of a chest until she chased her out of all Meḥoza.
> "You have," she said, "already killed three men and now you come to kill another!" (Ketubot 65a)

22. Simone de Beauvoir, *The Second Sex*, 184–87.

Our story is set in Meḥoza, one of the larger centers of Babylonian Jewry, during the 4th century.[23] Ḥoma, wife of the recently deceased Abaye, arrives at court to determine the size of her widow's allowance. The previously discussed financial obligations of a husband toward his wife do not end with the former's death; although the wife does not halakhically inherit her husband, she is given a stipend out of his estate so that she can maintain the same lifestyle to which she was accustomed during his life.[24] Presiding over Ḥoma's case is Rava, head of the Meḥoza yeshiva and her late husband's ḥavruta (or study partner). Ḥoma petitions the court for an allowance for food, and Rava duly grants it.

Ḥoma then requests an allowance for wine, and this time Rava is not as obliging. *"I know that Naḥmani did not drink wine,"* he says, calling Abaye by his real name.[25] A woman, we saw in the preceding halakhic discussion, may only receive a wine allowance if she was accustomed to drinking with her husband, and Rava, knowing his ḥavruta and his sober ways, does not believe this to have been the case. Moreover, as Abaye's study partner and friend, Rava refuses to let his widow descend into promiscuity now that Abaye is gone (recall how dangerous wine is thought to be to a woman, particularly, as Rava himself states, when her husband is no longer around). Installing himself as her male guardian in place of the deceased Abaye, Rava is determined to preserve Ḥoma's chastity.

Completely undeterred, Ḥoma swears that she and her husband did in fact drink, and that he would pour her wine *in horns as large as this*. And as she gestures, her sleeve falls away (think of Gilda, slowly stripping off a long black glove) and light from her exquisitely exposed arm shines onto the courtroom.[26]

---

23. Abaye's death, with which the story begins, is dated to the year 338.

24. "A widow is to be maintained out of the estate of [her husband's] orphans" (M Ketubot 11:1; see also 4:12). For more on a woman's inheritance, see p. 180 n. 48.

25. Abaye, who was orphaned at birth (Kiddushin 31b), was named Naḥmani after his grandfather, but his uncle and adoptive father Rabba bar Naḥmani dubbed him Abaye to avoid calling him by his own father's name.

26. See n. 3. The indecency of a woman baring her arm is mentioned later in the tractate, where it is listed, together with roaming the marketplace, as a valid cause for divorce (Ketubot 72b).

Rava rose, instantly aroused.[27] However, rather than fall into the clutches of the manipulative Ḥoma, he manages a narrow escape, and rushes home to consummate his passion with his lawfully wedded wife, Rav Ḥisda's daughter. Except that the latter, clearly unused to her husband coming home in the middle of the day to solicit her, is immediately suspicious. *"Who was in the court just now?"* she demands, and Rava, unable to lie, replies, *"Ḥoma, the wife of Abaye."*

Enraged, Rav Ḥisda's daughter picks up a *lock of a chest* (a bar which was threaded through the hoops of a chest to fasten it shut) and beats Ḥoma until she runs her out of town, crying, "You've already seduced and destroyed three men, do not come after mine!"

And here, in the story's dramatic dénouement, we discover a critical fact about our heroine. Ḥoma is not just a gadabout widow; she is a black widow, halakhically known as an *isha katlanit* – a woman who has lost a number of husbands and is suspected of somehow being the cause of their deaths.[28] The halakhic prohibition against recklessly endangering one's life[29] precludes marriage to such a woman, as the Talmud explains elsewhere:

> It was taught: If a woman was married to one husband who died, and to a second one who also died, she must not be married to a third; so said Rebbe. Rabbi Shimon ben Gamliel said: She may be married to a third, but she may not be married to a fourth.... Avimi of Hagronia said in the name of Rav Huna: The source is the cause. But Rav Ashi stated: The woman's ill luck is the cause. (Yevamot 64b)

27. "The primary rabbinic understanding of female nakedness is that it arouses sexual passion in men.... At stake is not only the fear that the man will become so aroused as to actually commit a forbidden sex act but also that he will lose self-control, which is itself highly valued by the rabbis." Michael Satlow, "Jewish Construction of Nakedness in Late Antiquity," 441–42.

28. The fear of the black widow inadvertently killing off her husbands was common to many cultures in Antiquity; the biblical Tamar (whose story is explored in Chapter 4), Sarah in the apocryphal Book of Tobit, the New Testament woman who is widowed by seven brothers (Mark 12:20–22), and the folktale of the Serpent Maiden whose bridegrooms repeatedly die on the wedding night are all examples of this pervasive ancient belief.

29. See Deut. 4:15, Berakhot 32b.

The rabbis debate whether it is intercourse with the *isha katlanit* ("source" being a euphemism for the female sexual organ) or her bad luck that causes the serial deaths of her husbands. They also discuss how many husbands a woman must lose before it becomes forbidden to marry her – two or three – a question which has direct implications for Abaye's ability to marry Ḥoma:

> This applies only when the fact had been established by the occurrence of three cases.... Abaye relied on this statement and married Ḥoma the daughter of Isi... although Reḥava of Pumbedita had married her and died, and Rav Yitzḥak son of Rabba bar bar Ḥana had married her and also died. And after Abaye married her, he himself died also. Said Rava: Would anyone else have exposed himself to such danger? (Ibid.)

Following the opinion that a woman only becomes an *isha katlanit* after the death of three husbands, Abaye marries the twice-widowed Ḥoma, and subsequently dies as well. Rava asks why anyone would put himself in harm's way as Abaye had done, evidently unhappy with his friend's decision to marry a potential black widow. No wonder Rava ran out of that courtroom in such a panic. Three men, including his own ḥavruta, have fallen prey to this woman's deadly charms; if he doesn't escape her, he might be next.

At the outset of our story, then, Ḥoma is, by all counts, an *isha katlanit*. The term itself is telling: *isha* – woman, *katlanit* – fatal. An *isha katlanit* is, literally, a femme fatale, a general literary archetype turned very real halakhic concept. And Ḥoma, when we encounter her, is about as fatale as a femme can get.

At face value, the story of Ḥoma is a classic femme fatale narrative: a dangerously beautiful black widow; a seduction by striptease; an otherwise pious man overcome by desire; and a betrayed woman, fighting to save her man from a treacherous femme fatale who's already killed three husbands – and is now coming for him.

But is this the story the Talmud is telling?

Baring Arms: Ḥoma Revisioned

As with Yalta, our revisioning of Ḥoma begins with another literary revisioning: a seduction narrative told from the perspective, not of the seduced man, but of the seducing woman. Nathaniel Hawthorne's *The Scarlet Letter* is the story of Hester Prynne, a young woman from Puritan New England who, in the absence of her husband, has an affair with another man and gives birth to his child. At the opening of the novel, Hester undergoes a difficult and humiliating trial, and is sentenced to wear a scarlet letter on her chest until the end of her days:

> The door of the jail being flung open from within, there appeared... a young woman... tall, with a figure of perfect elegance... her beauty shone out, and made a halo of the misfortune and ignominy in which she was enveloped.... The unhappy culprit sustained herself as best a woman might, under the heavy weight of a thousand unrelenting eyes, all fastened upon her, and concentrated at her bosom. It was almost intolerable to be borne.... She would become the general symbol at which the preacher and moralist might point, and in which they might vivify and embody their images of woman's frailty and sinful passion.... Who would have persuaded the struggling woman... that the outward guise of purity was but a lie, and that, if truth were everywhere to be shown, a scarlet letter would blaze forth on many a bosom besides Hester Prynne's?[30]

The malevolent character of the femme fatale is transformed, in Hawthorne's retelling, from villain to victim. Behind the mark of shame she is forced to wear, Hester Prynne is simply an unattached woman, ostracized by her community, censured by all, defended by none.

Imagining themselves to be far more pure than she, Hester's Puritan neighbors project onto her their own secret desires, with all of their attendant guilt and dread. And so, implies Hawthorne, is the

30. Nathaniel Hawthorne, *The Scarlet Letter*, chs. 2–5.

femme fatale created, the sum total of society's sexual projections. It's not the femme fatale's promiscuity people are afraid of but their own, not her seductiveness but their own susceptibility to seduction. Such repressed fears are externalized and personified in the archetype of the femme fatale, who accordingly grows into a terrifying figure, as powerful as human lust and as fatal as the fall it brings:

> Shaped from the projections of male fears and fantasies... [femmes fatales] confirm... the danger inherent within adult female sexuality.... Nightmarish women largely attempt to seduce men away from the field and from virtue, using sex as their primary weapon.... These women draw their strength from this realm of male imaginings and anxieties.[31]

The unattached woman is, in this respect, especially threatening. Desirable because available, and dangerous because desirable, she is more readily a site for projection. The rabbis admit as much when they say, "A woman who has a husband, whether she adorns herself or not, nobody stares at her.... A woman who has no husband, whether she adorns herself or not, everybody stares at her" (T Kiddushin 1:11). The single woman, an object of universal gaze, becomes a femme fatale regardless of what she says or does; her mere presence is a provocation.[32]

Close Reading

Having uncovered the psychological roots of the archetype, let us zoom in and reread Ḥoma's story, this time (like Hawthorne) from the point of view of the seductress:

31. Sheila T. Cavanagh, *Wanton Eyes and Chaste Desires: Female Sexuality in the Faerie Queene*, 44–45.
32. According to Judith Hauptman, the Talmud acknowledges that "men are easily aroused sexually by being in the presence of women, looking at them, dressed or undressed, or even just thinking about them" and that "a woman was considered fair game if she did not have a man to protect her. Her behavior, modest or immodest, did not much matter." Hauptman, *Rereading the Rabbis*, 31–51.

Act 1

Ḥoma, Abaye's wife, came before Rava.
She said, "Grant me an allowance of board," and he granted her.
"Grant me an allowance of wine," she said.
Said he, "I know that Naḥmani did not drink wine."
"By the life of the Master," she replied, "he would give me to drink in horns as large as this."
As she was showing it to him, her arm was uncovered and a light shone upon the court.

Act 2

Rava rose, went home, and solicited Rav Ḥisda's daughter.
"Who was in the court just now?" she said.
"Ḥoma, the wife of Abaye," he replied.

Act 3

Thereupon Rav Ḥisda's daughter went after her, striking her with the lock of a chest until she chased her out of all Meḥoza.
"You have," she said, "already killed three men and now you come to kill another!"

Act 1 – Court in Session	*Courtroom*	*Ḥoma, Rava*
Act 2 – Court Adjourned	*Bedroom*	*Rava, Rav Ḥisda's Daughter*
Act 3 – Passing Judgment	*Streets of Meḥoza*	*Rav Ḥisda's Daughter, Ḥoma*

Act 1 – Court in Session

Consider the scene: The lights come on on the Meḥoza courthouse. At the bench is Rava – presiding judge, head of the local yeshiva, representative of law and authority and power. Standing before him is Ḥoma – a woman, a single woman, and a fatal woman; you don't get any more marginalized, any more othered, than that. Here is an extreme imbalance of power. Like Hester Prynne, Ḥoma walks into the courtroom with the odds stacked firmly against her.

And like Hester Prynne, she walks into the courtroom surrounded by an air of prejudice, of people talking behind her back, whispering about that deadly femme fatale who's killed her three husbands. She also knows that this is her last day in court. The loss of a third husband renders her an *isha katlanit* according to all halakhic opinions; no one will ever marry her now. Whatever settlement she gets in today's hearing will be the sum she has to live off for the rest of her life.

So in addition to an allowance for food, Ḥoma requests an allowance for wine. Rava refuses, claiming knowledge of Abaye – *"I know Naḥmani"* – and his non-drinking habits. If Ḥoma and Abaye did not drink while the latter was alive, she should certainly not be given wine now that he's dead. Ḥoma, no less adamant, declares that they did drink, and in large quantities too. The scene devolves into a strange sort of love triangle, a tacit contest over who knew Abaye better – his wife or his ḥavruta? Who was more intimately familiar with him?

Broad Context: Abaye and Rava

One of the most prolific pairs of the rabbinic period, Abaye and Rava are the authors of hundreds of arguments scattered throughout the Talmud. So ubiquitous is their presence that the talmudic dialectic, the back-and-forth of halakhic dispute, is named for them: *havayot deAbaye veRava* – the debates of Abaye and Rava.[33]

In calling his ḥavruta by his real, rather than official, name, Rava asserts the familiarity and friendship that are the lot of rabbinic study partners.[34] The Talmud states that two people who learn together will necessarily "come to love each other" (Kiddushin 30b); the intimate act

33. Sukka 28a, Bava Batra 134a. For a list of the disputes between Abaye and Rava, see Richard Kalmin, *Sages, Stories, Authors, and Editors in Rabbinic Babylonia*, 285–92. Kalmin himself argues that, historically, these two rabbis would have had little direct contact. This, however, does not stop the talmudic storytellers from imagining a close, sometimes turbulent relationship for the pair, from their childhood tutelage under Rabba (Berakhot 48a) through their competition for the leadership of the Pumbedita yeshiva (Horayot 14a) to the rivalry between their respective disciples (Bava Batra 22a).
34. Significantly, in his dialogue with his wife in Act 2, Rava will revert to calling Abaye by his official name (other instances where Rava calls Abaye "Naḥmani" are in Shabbat 33a, 74a, Nedarim 54b, and Avoda Zara 58a).

of Torah study creates a deep and lasting bond.[35] After years of learning together, poring over the ins and outs of Jewish law, Rava knows Abaye, knows him as closely as only a ḥavruta can. Elsewhere, Rava is quoted as saying, "I know of Naḥmani that he practices hunger" (Shabbat 33a). Rava knows Abaye to have been an ascetic, a serious and somber scholar. He certainly did not drink wine.

Yet Ḥoma insists that he did, raising her hand to indicate the size of the drinking horns they would use. The drama reaches its climax, as grieving widow and grieving friend clash over ownership of Abaye's memory. Ḥoma gestures, her radiant arm is uncovered, sending a ray of light through the courtroom and a wave of desire through its judge.

This is not, I propose, a mere act of striptease, the base arousal of a man by the sight of a beautiful woman. What Rava sees when Ḥoma's sleeve falls away is not just a bit of skin, but an entirely different marital life. His own marriage (we can assume from his wife's response to his advances in the next act) is proper, prudish, perhaps even passionless. And here is Ḥoma, offering him a glimpse into something else – an intimate, intoxicated, erotic marriage. It is a moment of illumination, as Rava is suddenly struck by the thought that Abaye, the man he'd been studying with for so many years, might have been a great, solemn sage by day, and a passionate lover by night. And this is what excites him. This is what he wants. It isn't Ḥoma at all; it's the alternative kind of marriage she suggests.

Act 2 – Court Adjourned

So Rava runs home and sweeps his wife into his arms, and tries to do what he tries to do (what he probably imagines Abaye would have done with Ḥoma) – but Rav Ḥisda's daughter stops him cold. *"Who was in the court just now?"* she curtly asks. She is having none of it. None of this promiscuous behavior. Not in her home. She is, after all, a respectable woman.

35. "The talmudic academy consists of an all-male grouping structured around ... male intimacy." Daniel Boyarin, *Unheroic Conduct: The Rise of Heterosexuality and the Invention of the Jewish Man*, 131–32.

Broad Context: Rav Ḥisda's Daughter

The betrayed woman of our narrative, Rav Ḥisda's daughter is set up as a foil to Ḥoma; where the latter is fiery and sensual, Rav Ḥisda's daughter comes across as almost frigid. Which is hardly surprising, considering the sort of upbringing she received:

(i)

> Rav Ḥisda said to his daughters: Act modestly before your husbands. Do not eat bread before your husbands, do not eat greens at night, do not eat dates at night nor drink beer at night, and do not ease yourselves where your husbands do. And when someone calls at the door, do not say "Who is he?" but "Who is she?" Rav Ḥisda held a jewel in one hand and a clod of earth in the other; the jewel he showed them but the clod he did not show them, until they were upset, and then he showed it to them. (Shabbat 140b)

Rav Ḥisda rears his daughters up on the kind of finishing-school etiquette designed to keep women modest and ladylike in the eyes of their husbands. This includes what not to eat (so that they don't appear gluttonous or have bad breath or, God forbid, bowel movement), where not to defecate, and how not to talk to other men. He also demonstrates the importance of keeping themselves well concealed (the jewel he reveals to them is far less precious in their eyes than the clod of earth he keeps hidden).[36] Little wonder that Abaye and Ḥoma's intimacy came as such a surprise to Rava; his own wife probably never let him see her as she truly was.

In addition to the repressive nature of her education, the Talmud provides us with important details of Rav Ḥisda's daughter's personal history:

(ii)

> The daughter of Rav Ḥisda was sitting on her father's lap, and in front of him were sitting Rava and Rami bar Ḥama. He said

36. In another talmudic passage, Rav Ḥisda teaches that "it is forbidden for a person to have intercourse by day," which may explain his daughter's instinctive recoiling from Rava's daytime advances (Niddah 17a; see also Nedarim 20b, discussed on pp. 177–79).

> to her, "Which of them would you like?" She replied, "Both." Whereupon Rava said, "Let me be the second." (Bava Batra 12b)

(iii)

> When Ravin came he stated in the name of Rabbi Yoḥanan: A woman who waited ten years after separation from her husband, and then remarried, would bear children no more. Said Rav Naḥman: This was stated only with regard to one who had no intention of remarrying; if, however, she did intend to marry again, she may conceive. Rava said to Rav Ḥisda's daughter: The rabbis are talking about you. She answered him: I had my mind on you. (Yevamot 34b)

Sitting as a young girl on her father's knee, Rav Ḥisda's daughter professes a childish wish to marry both of her father's disciples. Knowing that this could only happen if one of them were to marry her and die, Rava immediately claims the right to be the second husband. And so it was: Rav Ḥisda's daughter marries Rami bar Ḥama, who dies, leaving her a widow for over a decade until she could marry Rava. Sometime after that marriage, Rav Ḥisda's daughter becomes pregnant, raising the suspicion that she might not have been celibate during her long widowhood (according to the opinion cited above, a sexually inactive widow of ten years would lose her ability to bear children – unless she intends to remarry, in which case she would remain fertile[37]). Rav Ḥisda's daughter responds to the charge by saying that she had indeed intended to marry again. In fact, she had had her eye on Rava all along.

Rav Ḥisda's daughter, turns out, has been widowed once before. Hence her terror of Ḥoma's seducing and destroying Rava. The loss of a second husband would make her, at least according to one opinion, an *isha katlanit*, no different to Ḥoma herself.

37. The ancients had a strong belief in the "correlation of a woman's private imagination or psychology with biological conception." Mairéad McAuley, *Reproducing Rome: Motherhood in Virgil, Ovid, Seneca, and Statius*, 56–57.

And Rav Ḥisda's daughter is nothing like Ḥoma, as far as she's concerned. Throughout her long widowhood, she had waited patiently to marry Rava. She never became a gadabout widow, never cultivated the dangerous independence Ḥoma had. The clearest indication of this is in her name: as opposed to Ḥoma, one of the few named women of the Talmud, Rav Ḥisda's daughter is nameless. She is, significantly, Rav Ḥisda's daughter – forever subsumed under a man.

Act 3 – Passing Judgment

If in Act 2 we were transported from the public sphere of the courtroom to the private sphere of the bedroom, in Act 3 we are once again back in public, with Rav Ḥisda's daughter charging out of the bedroom and onto the crowded street. The narrative shifts from one love triangle (Ḥoma—Abaye—Rava) to another (Ḥoma—Rava—Rav Ḥisda's daughter), as femme fatale and betrayed woman go head-to-head.[38] Taking up arms against the seductress who might kill her husband and turn her into an *isha katlanit*, Rav Ḥisda's daughter beats Ḥoma through the streets *until she chase[s] her out of all Meḥoza.*

The image of a married woman chasing a single woman with a bar – a bar which, as mentioned, was used as a type of lock – is highly symbolic. Locks, in the ancient world, were a popular metaphor for female chastity.[39] It is as if Rav Ḥisda's daughter is saying to Ḥoma: You're single, you're promiscuous, you're a danger to our men, you're a threat to society, and there is no room for you here. And thus is the widow Ḥoma driven out of town.

But if the Other can be eliminated, otherness itself cannot.[40] The people of Meḥoza might have banished Ḥoma from their midst, and yet the

---

38. The scene might be considered an early version of a catfight, a literary trope in which "two women, one usually a traditional wife (blond), the other a grasping, craven careerist (brunette), slug it out… usually they fight over men." Susan Douglas, *Where the Girls Are: Growing Up Female in the Mass Media*, 221.
39. The bride of Song of Songs is described as "a locked garden… a sealed fountain" (4:12; see also Ketubot 10a, Numbers Rabba 3:6, Song of Songs Rabba 4:12).
40. The point is made, post-Holocaust, by Jewish philosopher Emmanuel Levinas: "I can wish to kill only an existent absolutely independent, which exceeds my powers

rabbis – in telling her story – bring her back. They bring her back, specifically, to grapple with the ethical problem of her otherness. Where, then, are the rabbis in all of this? Let's zoom out and examine their framing of the narrative.

Immediate Context: Women and Wine

We've already looked at the passage that comes directly before our story. Still, given our revisioning of the text, its context bears rereading:

> No allowance for wine is made for a woman.... An objection was raised: If a woman is accustomed to drink, she is given an allowance of wine. Where she is accustomed to drink the case is different.... Abaye said:... If she was accustomed to drink two cups in the presence of her husband, she is given one cup in his absence; if she was accustomed to drink only one cup in the presence of her husband, she is given none at all in his absence.... It was taught: One cup is becoming to a woman; two are degrading; if she has three, she solicits publicly; and if she has four, she solicits even a donkey in the marketplace and cares not. Rava said: This was taught only with regard to a woman whose husband is not with her; but if her husband is with her, the objection does not arise.

An unattached woman, according to the sugya, must not be given too much wine, lest she lose control and solicit sex. Yet in our story, the unattached woman does neither of these things; it is the married man who solicits sex, and it is both he and his wife who lose control (Rava is overcome by desire, Rav Ḥisda's daughter – by rage).[41] In fact, the only character who remains calm and collected throughout the narrative is Ḥoma, that wild and wanton single woman. The juxtaposition

infinitely.... The Other... opposes to me... the infinity of his transcendence. This infinity [is] stronger than murder." Emmanuel Levinas, *Totality and Infinity: An Essay on Exteriority*, 198–99.

41. Tellingly, Rava's attempt to solicit his wife is described by the same root verb – T-V-A – used in the sugya in reference to the unattached woman's sexual solicitations. On the deeper meaning of this particular verb, see p. 108.

of text and context casts the latter in an ironic light, calling many of its premises into question.

The passage following our story is no less instructive:

> The wife of Rav Yosef son of Rava came before Rav Neḥemia son of Rav Yosef and said to him, "Grant me an allowance of board," and he granted her. "Grant me an allowance of wine," she said, and he granted her, saying, "I know that the people of Meḥoza drink wine." The wife of Rav Yosef son of Rav Menashya of D'vil came before Rav Yosef and said to him, "Grant me an allowance of board," and he granted her. "Grant me an allowance of wine," she said, and he granted her. (Ketubot 65a)

Two tales of women (one of them, incidentally, Rava's daughter-in-law) who petition the court for a wine allowance and are granted it, no questions asked. The ruling is justified, in the first of the two cases, by the fact that *the people of Meḥoza* (where, recall, our story takes place) *drink wine*. The excessive drinking habits of the wealthy Meḥozans are well documented in the Talmud.[42] Abaye, too, is portrayed as no stranger to the bottle, far from the teetotaler Rava imagines him to be.[43]

We are thus given grounds to believe that Ḥoma is actually telling the truth. That she is accustomed to drinking. That Abaye would pour her wine. And that she did know her husband better than his ḥavruta. The subsequent tales, establishing a widow's wine allowance as the legal norm, present Rava's rejection of Ḥoma's request as an aberration. This was a decision unduly influenced by the Rava's anger toward the *isha katlanit* who had killed his friend, and his determination to save all other men from what he sees as her fatal sexuality. As with Yalta, the framing of Ḥoma's story implies that the talmudic editors are completely on her side.

42. "The people of Meḥoza… drunkenness is common among them" (Taanit 26a; see also Gittin 69a).

43. "Abaye, when he would drink one cup, his mother would immediately place two cups in his two hands" (Pesaḥim 110a; see also Berakhot 42b and Rashi to Berakhot 56a). Not insignificantly, it is Abaye who, in the preceding sugya, sanctions the allotment of wine to women if they are used to drinking.

Yet the strongest evidence for where the rabbis stand with regard to Ḥoma is, once again, in the text's final line. *"You have," she said, "already killed three men and now you come to kill another."* Withholding the fact of Ḥoma's multiple widowhood until the very end, the rabbis ensure that the reader will not be prejudiced against Ḥoma in the way Rava, his wife, and the people of Meḥoza are.[44] Unaware of Ḥoma's status as an *isha katlanit* when she first walks into the courtroom, the reader is made to feel sorry for this newly bereaved widow, empathizing with her as no one in her own world does.

Not infrequently, we find in the Talmud a halakhic discussion articulating a certain position, followed by an aggadic narrative that completely turns that position on its head – questioning, critiquing, even directly contradicting it. The legend of Ḥoma is a case in point: Earlier in the sugya, the rabbis limit the wine allowance of a single woman, for fear of her promiscuity; elsewhere, they prohibit marriage to an *isha katlanit*, because of the risk it entails. And yet, by telling us the story of Ḥoma, the rabbis demonstrate that they are aware of the shortcomings of these legal positions, their unfairness toward unattached women and wretched three-time widows. In their broader concern for social order (compromised by the threat of an intoxicated single woman) and individual safety (endangered by the *isha katlanit* and the disease she is believed to sexually transmit), the rabbis do not change the halakha. But they do take pity on the women hurt by it and, in countering it with aggada, exhort us readers to do the same.[45]

44. Inbar Raveh argues that rabbinic storytelling often manipulates the reader's response through its strategic deployment of information: "The narrator sometimes withholds certain information in order to use it most effectively, adding it to the narrative's moral and emotional scales at just the right moment, as far as his interests are concerned." Raveh, *Fragments of Being*, 44.
45. For the role of aggada in redressing the individual harm caused by the broader social concerns of halakha, see pp. xxii–xxiii.

The Moral of the Story: The Danger of Projection

With its primary reading stripped away, the deeper truth of the story of Ḥoma is now laid bare. An unattached woman, whose sexuality we expected to run wild at any moment, is revealed to be a dignified widow who maintains her composure while everyone around her is losing control. A dangerous femme fatale who has seduced and destroyed three husbands is actually an ill-fated *isha katlanit* who's lost every man she ever loved. And a brazen striptease designed to manipulate the judge into giving her an allowance she doesn't deserve is really an attempt to secure a legitimate settlement as she's forced to live out the rest of her days on her own.

Yet neither her grief over the loss of her husband, nor the validity of her financial claim, are of any help to Ḥoma. By the end of the story, she is driven out of town, her allowance refused, her future prospects grim. The people of Meḥoza cannot contain her. A site of projection for their own repressed fears – of desire, of disorder, of death – Ḥoma's presence in the town becomes intolerable. She must be expelled.

Such is the destructive mechanism of projection. The Talmud, in a moment of keen psychological insight, observes: "Anyone who rejects another as flawed… has the same flaw" (Kiddushin 70a). Rejection is born of projection. We project onto the Other our deepest flaws, our most shameful secrets, and then we ostracize them, unable to bear in them that which we cannot acknowledge within ourselves. This is what the Meḥozans did to Ḥoma; it's what the people of Boston did to Hester Prynne; it's what we do to one another, more often than we know. But if the story of Ḥoma is meant to teach us anything, it's that we must be especially careful, especially compassionate, toward the Others in our midst. For those who appear dangerous are usually just different. And those who appear different are probably more like ourselves than we suspect.

Marta
The Prima Donna

The Archetype: There Is Nothing More Intolerable Than a Wealthy Woman

> The *Oxford English Dictionary* gives "the first or principal female singer in an opera" as its major definition of the prima donna, and records examples of the usage in English from the end of the 18th century. Although … by the 20th century, the term had stuck as a label of abuse…. To be a prima donna was not so much to be a great interpreter of operatic music as to be an outrageous *grande dame*, exacting, obstinate, torrential, grousing, and exasperating, and often lazy, greedy, stupid, conceited, emotionally unstable, mentally unbalanced, in short impossible in every respect.[1]

Taking her name from the leading ladies of the Italian opera and commedia dell'arte, the prima donna is as grandiose off stage as she is on. Her every wish must be indulged, her every demand immediately seen to. Vain, spoiled, and spectacularly self-absorbed, she lords over her

1. Vlado Kotnik, "The Idea of Prima Donna: The History of a Very Special Opera's Institution," 238.

inferiors – and all, to her, are her inferiors – as fastidious about her own needs as she is oblivious to theirs.

"Hear this word, you cows of Bashan on the hill of Samaria, who oppress the poor, who crush the needy, who say to their husbands, 'Bring, let us drink!'" (Amos 4:1). In his rebuke of the corrupt Israelite elite during the First Temple period, Amos reserves a special place for the prima donnas of Samaria. These rich, high-born women exploit the lower classes (and, to a lesser extent, their husbands) for their own extravagant existence, delighting in fine wine while those around them languish in want. Such selfish behavior, warns Amos, will be meetly punished, as the once pampered cows of Bashan will be captured, noosed, and led, cattle-like, into exile.

Somewhat less callous, though no less narcissistic, are the prima donnas of Jerusalem during the Second Temple period. The Talmud tells us of two widows, the daughter-in-law and daughter of the eminent philanthropist Nakdimon ben Gurion, who was so wealthy that "when he walked from his house to the beit midrash, his attendants would spread fine woolen garments beneath his feet" (Ketubot 66b–67a). Both widows petition the court for an allowance after their husbands' deaths.[2] In both cases, the allowance is for a luxury item – wine and perfume; in both cases, the allotted sum is a handsome one, as befits the widows' station in life; yet in both cases, the widows, discontented and ungrateful, throw it back in the judges' faces:

> There was the case of the daughter-in-law of Nakdimon ben Gurion, to whom the rabbis granted an allowance of two seahs of wine for her puddings, from one Shabbat eve to the next. She said to them, "May you grant so little to your own daughters".... There was the case of the daughter of Nakdimon ben Gurion, to whom the rabbis granted an allowance of four hundred gold coins for perfume for that day. She said to them, "May you grant so little to your own daughters," and they responded, "Amen." (Ketubot 65a–66b)

2. For the halakhic requirement to keep a widow in the same comforts she enjoyed during her husband's life, see p. 36 (these two tales, in fact, appear directly before and shortly after the story of Ḥoma).

So solipsistic are the widows of the Ben Gurion family, so utterly unaware of the socioeconomic reality of those around them, they don't realize the allowances they reject as meager are in fact exceedingly generous; as the concluding "Amen" implies, the judges would love nothing more than to bequeath such large sums to their own daughters. These heiresses, the Talmud goes on to recount, fare no better than the prima donnas of Samaria. After the destruction of Jerusalem, the daughter of Nakdimon ben Gurion is seen, naked and impoverished, "gathering barley grains from among the dung of Arab cattle" (Ketubot 66b).

Next we move from Jerusalem to Rome, whose rich women are the subject of the searingly critical *Satire VI* by 2nd-century poet Juvenal. Sometimes subtitled *Against Women,* the satire attacks the Roman matrons for their excessive spending, their sense of entitlement, and their mistreatment of their dependents:

Toilet of a Roman Lady, Juan Jimenez Martin

> The lady rules the roost, asking her husband for shepherds and Canusian sheep, and elms for her Falernian vines… all his slave-boys, in town and country; everything that her neighbor possesses, and that she does not possess, must be bought…. Her household is governed as cruelly as a Sicilian Court… the unhappy maid that does her hair will have her own hair torn, and the clothes stripped off her shoulders…. There is nothing that a woman will not permit herself to do, nothing that she deems shameful, when she encircles her neck with green emeralds, and fastens huge pearls to her elongated ears: there is nothing more intolerable than a wealthy woman.[3]

The European folktale "The Fisherman and His Wife" shows just how intolerable a wealthy woman can be, as the wife grows more and

3. Juvenal, *Satire VI,* 150–460.

more unpleasant the richer she becomes. Eternally dissatisfied with her lot, she sends her reluctant husband back to the magic flounder with increasingly unreasonable demands – a cottage, a palace, a kingdom, an empire – until the flounder, tired of her insatiable greed, returns her to the hovel whence she came.

The insatiable greed of Marie Antoinette, arguably the greatest prima donna of Western culture, is often cited as the cause for the French Revolution. Her lavish and luxurious lifestyle (the walls of her private residence were rumored to have been encrusted in gold and diamonds), together with her uncompromising refusal to consider a financial reform of any kind, were accused of single-handedly bankrupting the country's economy, reducing her subjects to abject poverty. Her infamous declaration "Let them eat cake," in response to a report that the people were starving for bread, has become a catchphrase for insensitivity and detachment.[4]

Portrait of Marie Antoinette,
Martin van Meytens

Half a century later, Nikolai Gogol's *The Government Inspector* gives us the ridiculous character of Anna Andreyevna – provincial, pompous, and profoundly shallow. Obsessed with her reputation and appearance (she changes outfits no fewer than four times throughout the play), this small-town mayor's wife fancies herself a member of the upper class, impatiently ordering her servants about:

> Anna: He has come? The Inspector? He has a mustache? What kind of a mustache?
> Mayor [from without]: Wait, dear. Later.

4. The phrase itself was coined by Jean-Jacques Rousseau in his *Confessions* (Book VI), some nine years before Marie Antoinette ascended the throne, and (like several other allegations) was misattributed to her, reinforcing her image of a frivolous prima donna. Here again, in the flattening out of a complex historical person to fit a one-dimensional cultural persona, do we find the archetype at work (see p. 4 n. 5.).

Anna: Wait? I don't want to wait. The idea, wait!… [She leans out of the window.] Here, Avdotya!… Off with you, off with you at once, do you hear? Run and ask everybody where they are. Be sure and find out who the newcomer is and what he is like, do you hear?… Quick, quick, quick![5]

The Present, Charles Robert Leslie

Another provincial wife with pretenses to the life of the beau monde is Emma Bovary, Gustav Flaubert's tragic heroine. Shutting out her own dreary reality, Emma lives in a fantasy world created by sentimental novels and daydreams, as a result of which she embarks on two adulterous affairs and endless spending sprees – neither of which she can afford. When her mounting debt is in danger of being exposed, she commits suicide, preferring to die an agonizing death rather than compromise her perfect dream of riches and romance.

For such is the way with the prima donna – reality always catches up with her in the end. Try as she might to seclude herself in her pampered and privileged bubble, at some point the bubble must burst. The prima donna narrative generally takes the form of a riches-to-rags morality tale, culminating in the heroine's fall from grace.

Though we find the prima donna in the writings of the Jews and the Romans, the Germans, the French, and the Russians, no culture provides us with quite as many specimens of the archetype as 19th-century England. The imperious British *grande dame* has everyone hovering nervously around her, for it is she who holds the purse-strings, and it is she who decides who may marry whom. The delicate and sickly Miss Crawley, surrounded by obsequious relatives hoping to inherit her when she finally dies, is introduced as "a large round bundle of shawls… who was conveyed upstairs forthwith, and put into a bed" – literally wrapped up in her own little world.[6] Lady Bracknell, an upper-class snob

5. Nikolai Gogol, *The Government Inspector*, 1:6.
6. William Makepeace Thackeray, *Vanity Fair*, ch. 14.

of the highest order, refuses to allow anyone to marry into her family before ascertaining the state of their finances and fashionability of their dinner parties. And, perhaps most iconic, Lady Catherine de Bourgh, powerful matriarch and local aristocrat, whom no one, save Elizabeth Bennet, dares cross:

> Her air was not conciliating, nor was her manner of receiving them such as to make her visitors forget their inferior rank.... There was little to be done but to hear Lady Catherine talk, which she did without any intermission till coffee came in, delivering her opinion on every subject in so decisive a manner, as proved that she was not used to have her judgment controverted.... Whenever any of the cottagers were disposed to be quarrelsome, discontented, or too poor, she sallied forth into the village to settle their differences, silence their complaints, and scold them into harmony and plenty.[7]

Pride & Prejudice, Universal Pictures

The golden age of Hollywood gives us Norma Desmond, the aging drama queen who is certain she is still "the greatest star of them all." Secluded in her Sunset Boulevard mansion, she is protected against the harsh reality of her dead career by her submissive butler (and former husband) Max, who forges her fan mail and props up her delusions of grandeur. In the film's penultimate scene, a deranged Norma, oblivious to the police and newsreels crowded round her, stares intently at her own reflection in a hand-held mirror, preparing for the close-up she believes will propel her back to stardom.[8]

7. Jane Austen, *Pride and Prejudice*, chs. 29–30.
8. The image-obsessed prima donna is frequently depicted as looking at herself in the mirror, that age-old symbol of narcissism; the convention dates back to the original *prima donna inamorata* of the Italian stage, who constantly gazes into a hand mirror, since "any imperfection can spell disaster." John Rudlin, *Commedia Dell'arte: An Actor's Handbook*, 108.

And who can forget Miss Piggy, that self-involved, snout-nosed diva?

The Muppets, The Walt Disney Company

The prima donna is thus a wealthy woman, a member (or would-be member) of the privileged class; fussy and fastidious, delicate and indulgent; surrounded by dependents who tend to her every need, terrified of incurring her displeasure; and often the subject of a morality tale, wherein she is punished for her selfish misdeeds.

With that, let us proceed to our prima donna – Marta bat Boethius.

Primary Reading: The Richest Woman in Jerusalem

Marta is the Aramaic version of Miriam, one of the two most popular female names in the late Second Temple period.[9] And it is in the late Second Temple period that we encounter Marta. Her legend is part of a lengthy story cycle in Tractate Gittin (lit., divorce bills), detailing the tragic events that led to the Destruction of the Temple (70 CE). The days are the days of the Roman siege of Jerusalem. The city has descended into famine. Jerusalemites are reduced to all manner of foraging, even cannibalism. People are dying in the streets. Enter Marta:

> Marta bat Boethius was one of the richest women in Jerusalem. She sent her servant out saying, "Go and bring me some fine flour." By the time he went, it was sold out.
> He came and told her, "There is no fine flour, but there is white flour." She said to him, "Go and bring me some." By the time he went, it was sold out.

9. Tal Ilan, "Notes on the Distribution of Women's Names in Palestine in the Second Temple and Mishnaic Period," 191–92. For the other most popular name, Shalom, see Chapter 6.

> He came and told her, "There is no white flour but there is dark flour." She said to him, "Go and bring me some." By the time he went, it was sold out.
> He returned and said to her, "There is no dark flour, but there is barley flour." She said, "Go and bring me some." By the time he went, this was also sold out.
> She was barefoot, but she said, "I will go out and see if I can find anything to eat."
> Some dung stuck to her foot and she died.
> Rabban Yoḥanan ben Zakkai applied to her the verse "The tender and delicate woman among you who would never venture to set her foot upon the ground" (Deut. 28:56)….
> When she was dying, she brought all her gold and silver and threw them out in the marketplace, saying, "What good are these to me?" And this is as it is written, "They shall cast their silver in the streets" (Ezek. 7:19). (Gittin 56a)

With the Romans surrounding the city and famine raging through the streets, the fabulously wealthy Marta sends her servant to the market for some fine flour, an expensive luxury food.[10] Like Marie Antoinette recommending cake to a starving populace, Marta is completely oblivious to the world beyond her palace walls.

By the time he went, it was sold out. The siege has resulted in an extreme food shortage, as products are rapidly disappearing from the market. With no fine flour to be had, the servant finds himself in a quandary; he cannot buy the flour that's been ordered, and knowing his overbearing mistress and her uncompromising ways, he dare not buy any other kind. So he returns home and asks for permission: *"There is no fine flour, but there is white flour."* Marta, in all likelihood discontented, demands that he buy her that instead, but until he gets back to the market it, too, has sold out.

10. "Marta's request for 'finest flour' stands out as a culturally significant claim of elite status, reflecting a common Mediterranean preference for white bread as a mark of high status." Julia Watts Belser, *Rabbinic Tales of Destruction: Gender, Sex, and Disability in the Ruins of Jerusalem*, 189. According to Daniel Sperber, the price of wheat (which Marta initially requests) was double that of barley (which she's ultimately forced to ask for). Daniel Sperber, *Roman Palestine 200–400: Money and Prices*, 112.

Thus begins a farcical sequence of events, in which Marta (like the fisherman's wife) repeatedly sends her servant back to the market for a particular type of flour; the flour gone, the servant reports back to Marta, and by the time he gets her approval for an inferior type, that type is sold out as well. The fourfold repetition (fine flour—white flour—dark flour—barley flour), remarkable in light of the Talmud's narrative economy, highlights the absurd nature of the scene: a spoiled prima donna, too fastidious to let her servant simply buy whatever he can find, and a helpless servant, too fearful of his mistress to stray from her orders one whit.

Finally, Marta grows impatient with her servant's incompetence and decides to go out and find some food herself. *She was barefoot;* shut up in her palatial home, with servants to come and go for her, Marta is clearly unaccustomed to leaving the house, and does not think to put her shoes on. She is, as Rabbi Yoḥanan describes her, *the tender and delicate woman who would not set her foot upon the ground.* Moreover, as we saw with Nakdimon ben Gurion, the wealthy of Jerusalem would often have carpets rolled out for them wherever they went. Marta, entirely out of touch with the reality around her, probably expects the carpets to be there now, at the height of the Roman siege. She has no sense of the depths of devastation waiting for her outside her door.

And the encounter with the outside world proves fatal. Rather than carpets and an entourage of servants, Marta is greeted by the cold, hard ground, with all the rot and filth of an enfamined city. Her laying of her foot directly in the dirt is symbolic of her first unmediated contact with reality. The shock, the terror and disgust are too much for her delicate soul to bear. She dies.

When she was dying.... The story ends with a dramatic flashback to the moment of Marta's death. With her dying breath, Marta takes her now worthless gold and silver – the gold and silver that couldn't save her from her fate – and casts them out in the market, crying, *"What good are these to me?"*

So goes the story of Marta. Ostensibly, it is a perfect prima donna narrative: a morality tale of an intolerably wealthy woman, whose selfish, solipsistic, and tyrannical nature leads to her inevitable downfall.

But, once again, is this the story the Talmud is telling?

Poor Little Rich Woman: Marta Revisioned

To revision the story of Marta, we must first trace the origin of her archetype. The prima donna, according to feminist theorists, is born of the tenuous relationship between women and money. Since for the best part of history, women were not economic agents in their own right, they could only ever spend money, not actually earn it. Hence the image of the indulgent prima donna, frittering away the wealth acquired for her by others:

> In Western society up to the present, women have been dependent on men for financial support, so that a wife who needed money – for running the household or for any other purpose – had to get it from her husband. Men earned the income, and, to some extent at least, women spent it. Women were often forced to nag or cajole for money and might easily become unduly mercenary in their attitude toward their husband or lover. It is a short step to the greedy, exploitative wife of literature.[11]

This character of the greedy wife, throwing around her husband's hard-earned cash, dates back, as we've seen, to Antiquity. "Your extravagant woman," writes Juvenal in his *Satire VI*, "is never sensible of her dwindling means; and just as though money were forever sprouting up afresh from her exhausted coffers, and she had always a full heap to draw from, she never gives a thought to what her pleasures cost her."[12] Similarly, Rava interprets Amos' aforementioned criticism of the "cows of Bashan" in reference to his own wealthy townswomen: "'You cows of Bashan'... Said Rava: These are like women of Meḥoza, who eat and do nothing" (Shabbat 32b–33a).[13] Taking the critique one step further, Rashi comments: "And in this manner they rob their husbands." Thus women,

11. Katharine M. Rogers, *The Troublesome Helpmate: A History of Misogyny in Literature,* 265.
12. Juvenal, *Satire VI,* 376–79.
13. Rava's disapproval may be linked to the rabbinic mandate that all women – no matter how rich – ought to do some form of (domestic) work, since "idleness leads to promiscuity" (M Ketubot 5:5).

traditionally barred from making money, were nevertheless blamed for not knowing its worth. If the prima donna is economically oblivious and financially reckless, it is probably because she was never allowed to take part in the economic system in the first place.

Broad Context: Marta

With this revised understanding of the archetype, let's zoom out and review some of the other mentions of Marta in rabbinic literature, and see if she really is the prima donna she appears to be.

(i)

> "You shall not take a widow's garment in pledge" (Deut. 24:17) – Whether poor or rich, and even if she were as rich as Marta bat Boethius. (Sifrei Deuteronomy 281)

This early source presents Marta as a paradigm of wealth, a woman whose name has become a byword for a rich widow. She is also, significantly, heir to the Boethius clan, a family of high priests descending from Shimon ben Boethius (appointed high priest in 23 BCE by his son-in-law King Herod). The Boethiuses were notorious for their tyrannical and nepotistic nature: "Aba Shaul ben Batnit said... 'Woe is me due to the house of Boethius, woe is me due to their clubs.'... Since they were high priests, and their sons were Temple treasurers, and their sons-in-law were Temple overseers, and their servants strike the people with clubs" (T Menaḥot 13:21). Marta, in this context, is portrayed as rich and high-born, daughter of an aristocratic and authoritarian family – so far quite consistent with the prima donna.

(ii)

> There was the case of Marta bat Boethius, to whom the rabbis granted an allowance of two seahs of wine every day.... Nevertheless, she cursed them and said, "May you grant so little to your own daughters." Rabbi Aḥa said, "And we responded, 'Amen.'" Said Rabbi Elazar bar Zadok... "I saw her gathering barley from among the hooves of horses in Akko, and I applied to her the verse 'The tender and delicate woman among you who would

> never venture to set her foot upon the ground' (Deut. 28:56)." (Y Ketubot 5:11)

This account, in Yerushalmi Ketubot, is a parallel of the twin tales of the Ben Gurion widows in Bavli Ketubot.[14] Like those two wealthy women, Marta is granted an exorbitant allowance (two seahs of wine, recall, were considered generous when allotted weekly to Nakdimon ben Gurion's daughter-in-law, whereas Marta is granted them daily); like them, she regards the allowance as paltry, economically ignorant as she is, and curses the judges in return; and like them (or at least, like Nakdimon ben Gurion's daughter), she ends up, post-Destruction, poverty-stricken and starving, foraging for food among the animals.[15] The Marta of this narrative is entitled, solipsistic, and ultimately falls from grace – still entirely compatible with the archetype.

(iii)

> A high priest may not marry a widow... [but] if he betrothed a widow, and was subsequently appointed high priest, he may consummate the marriage. There was an incident with Yehoshua ben Gamla who betrothed Marta bat Boethius, and the king appointed him high priest, and he consummated the marriage. (M Yevamot 6:4)

14. These are just two of several versions of the tale, scattered throughout rabbinic literature, of a former noblewoman plunged into misfortune in the wake of the Destruction of Jerusalem – the noblewoman being a metaphor for the city itself. For a comparative analysis of the tale's variants, see Ofra Meir, *The Poetics of Rabbinic Stories*, 57–80.
15. This Yerushalmi account of Marta is obviously inconsistent with our main text in Bavli Gittin, which has her die before the actual Destruction (for the ahistorical, and therefore sometimes contradictory, nature of rabbinic legend, see p. xx). The discrepancy notwithstanding, both traditions feature Marta's descent from riches to rags, both quote the same Deuteronomy verse about the delicate woman who had never set "her foot upon the ground," and both, accordingly, reference feet (Marta's foot stepping in dung in the Bavli; the horses' hooves in which Marta searches for grain in the Yerushalmi).

Among the various stringencies placed upon the high priest is the prohibition against marrying a widow.[16] If, however, a priest is already engaged to a widow and only then appointed high priest, he may proceed with the marriage. As evidence, the Mishna cites the case of Yehoshua ben Gamla, who was engaged to Marta bat Boethius when he ascended to the high priesthood – and went on to marry her anyway.

Yet the promotion of Marta's groom-to-be to the highest religious office in the land was not, the Talmud goes on to explain, a happy coincidence:

(iv)

> The king appointed him, but he was not worthy of being appointed. Rav Yosef said: I see a conspiracy here. Rav Assi related that Marta bat Boethius brought a potful of dinars to King Yannai before he appointed Yehoshua ben Gamla high priest. (Yevamot 61a)

The only reason Yehoshua ben Gamla became high priest is that Marta bribed the king to get him the job.[17] At this point, things start to look bad for Marta. If her noble birth and spoiled upbringing were not her fault, her corruption most certainly is. Not content with being born into a high priestly family, Marta insists on marrying into one as well, and like a true prima donna, spends an excessive amount of money to buy that which ought not be sold.[18]

---

16. In this, the high priesthood is not unlike royalty, whose members were traditionally required to marry only virgin brides. Anke Bernau, *Virgins: A Cultural History*, 132.
17. Though he never mentions bribery, Josephus describes how the king had taken the high priesthood away from another and handed it to Yehoshua ben Gamla, as a result of which "a sedition arose between the high priests, with regard to one another; for they got together bodies of the boldest sort of the people, and frequently came, from reproaches, to throwing of stones at each other.... And from that time it principally came to pass that our city was greatly disordered, and that all things grew worse and worse among us." Josephus, *Antiquities of the Jews*, 20.9.4. He later recounts that Yehoshua ben Gamla found his death in the violent infighting that took place in the years leading up to the Destruction. Josephus, *Wars of the Jews*, 4.5.2.
18. To be fair, Marta was hardly alone in her illicit purchase of the high priesthood, an institution which by then had become thoroughly corrupted, and was often sold to the highest bidder: "In the final years of the Second Temple, the high priesthood was

(v)

> There was the case of Martha bat Boethius[19] who was betrothed to Yehoshua ben Gamla, whom the king appointed high priest, and they were married. Once, she said: "I shall go and see him reading [the Torah] on the Day of Atonement in the Temple." They laid out carpets for her from the entrance of her house to the gateway of the Temple so that her feet not be exposed [to the dirt]. Nevertheless, her feet were exposed. (Lamentations Rabba 1:47)

No wonder Marta went tripping out the door with no shoes on. As one of Jerusalem's wealthiest, she was used to having carpets spread out for her, protecting her (like Miss Crawley's shawls) from any unwanted contact with reality. *Nevertheless, her feet were exposed.* For such is the way with the prima donna – reality always catches up with her in the end.[20]

Emerging from these sources is a portrait of a lady who is rich and upper class, powerful and privileged, entitled and wrapped up in her own little world – until reality, inevitably, comes crashing in. A prima donna if ever there was one.

---

procured for pay and regulated by the authorities (the Herodian dynasty and Roman procurators), according to the latter's judgment and interests." Jonah Fraenkel, *Studies in the Spiritual World of Aggadic Narrative*, 122.

19. Although the printed edition reads "Miriam bat Beothius," Naomi Cohen shows that the Leningrad manuscript version of "Marta" is the more accurate. Naomi G. Cohen, "The Theological Stratum of the Martha b. Boethus Tradition," 199.

20. The story continues, very much like the Yerushalmi account, with Marta's widowhood, her handsome wine allotment, and her tragic end. This text is situated in a larger story cycle in Lamentations Rabba describing the calamities which befell members of the Jerusalem elite after the Destruction. "The majority of stories in the cycle follow the literary genre of the fall – from the highest of the high to the lowest of the low.... The stories are all divided in two, where the first half describes the high social standing, wealth, and honor of the protagonists, and the second half – their dreadful state after the Destruction." This genre, too, is consistent with the prima donna archetype. Yassif, *The Hebrew Folktale*, 239.

Immediate Context: The Rich Men of Jerusalem

Still, let's not give up on poor Marta just yet. If the broad context cannot save her, perhaps the immediate context can. Let's return to her legend in Tractate Gittin and explore the passages that come directly before and after it.

> The emperor sent Vespasian the Caesar against them. He came and besieged Jerusalem for three years. There were three men of great wealth there: Nakdimon ben Gurion, Ben Kalba Savua, and Ben Tzitzit HaKesat.... Ben Tzitzit HaKesat was so called because his fringes [*tzitzito*] used to trail on blankets [*kesatot*].... One of these said to the people of Jerusalem, "I will keep you in wheat and barley." A second said, "I will keep you in wine, salt, and oil." The third said, "I will keep you in wood".... These men were in a position to keep the city for twenty-one years.... The zealots then rose up and burned the stores of wheat and barley and a famine ensued. (Gittin 56a)

Prefacing our story is an account of the unfortunate, and wholly avoidable, circumstances that led to Jerusalem's descent into famine. Despite the siege, the city had enough reserves to feed its population for twenty-one years; were it not for the militant zealots who tried to force the people into war with Rome by burning down the storehouses, Jerusalem might have survived. These reserves were courtesy of three rich men – Nakdimon ben Gurion, Ben Kalba Savua, and Ben Tzitzit HaKesat – who take it upon themselves to supply the people with basic necessities for the duration of the siege. Herein is a very unfavorable comparison with Marta: These three men are just as rich, and just as pampered, as Marta (both Nakdimon ben Gurion and Ben Tzitzit HaKesat are said to have carpeting laid out for them, just like her). And yet, rather than seclude themselves with their riches as Marta does, they come to the aid of the city, sharing their wealth with those in need.

On the other end of the story (in fact, directly before its epilogue, between Marta's death and her throwing out of her money) we have another version of what kills Marta:

> Some say that Marta ate a fig left by Rabbi Zadok, and became ill and died. For Rabbi Zadok observed fasts for forty years so that Jerusalem would not be destroyed. When he ate anything it could be seen from the outside [of his body]. When he wanted to restore himself, they would bring him figs, and he would suck the juice and throw the rest away. (Gittin 56a)

According to this second version of events, Marta's death was not by dung, but by dried fig. The saintly Rabbi Zadok, who practiced ritual fasting for forty years in an attempt to save Jerusalem, had become so emaciated he could eat nothing solid, and would merely suck the juice of figs. Marta finds the rind of one of these figs and, in her hunger-crazed state, eats it, only to die of disgust. This is another unflattering contrast: Rabbi Zadok is keenly aware of the imminent disaster, and undergoes severe privation to try and prevent it – while Marta, oblivious, indulges in fine cuisine.

At this stage, I think, we must admit defeat. Neither her story, nor its context, nor her other texts can save Marta from the charges leveled against her. As opposed to our previous two heroines, Marta cannot be revisioned; what seems to be a tale of a selfish, spoiled prima donna is indeed a tale of a selfish, spoiled prima donna.

This is an important lesson to be learned. We should not (as I have previously argued) reject the Talmud for failing to conform to our sensibilities – but we should not subject it to them either. If we are to read the Talmud on its terms, rather than our own, we must be prepared to listen even when it doesn't say exactly what we want to hear. The text will not always read the way we'd like it to read. Not every story can be revisioned, and not every character can be redeemed.

Save a Little: Marta Revisioned, Take II

By rights, the chapter ought to end here. Marta, we must accept, is a prima donna, and no amount of rereading will change that. But if we can't redeem her character entirely, perhaps we can try and save it a little. Marta's narrative, as mentioned, is part of a much larger story cycle in

Tractate Gittin. This three-page, eight-act drama describes the series of disastrous events that resulted in the Destruction of the Second Temple, the sack of Jerusalem, and the fall of Judea. The significance of this story cannot be overstated: The Destruction is, in many ways, the foundational event of rabbinic culture.[21] It is at this cataclysmic moment that the center of Jewish life shifts from the Temple to the beit midrash, from priest to sage, and from sacrifice to study. The world of the rabbis was born out of the ashes of Jerusalem.

It is thus not surprising that the Destruction story cycle – beginning with the famous incident of Kamtza and Bar Kamtza and ending with the only slightly less famous request of Rabbi Yoḥanan ben Zakkai to rebuild Judaism from the beit midrash of Yavneh – has become one of the most popular stories of the Talmud. It is the constant study of Jewish historians, who mine it in search of historical information;[22] a standard prooftext for Jewish pundits, who regularly draw comparisons between the infighting that preceded the Destruction and the political climate today; and a reigning favorite among Jewish educators of all stripes, who love to quote its message about the baseless hatred that destroyed Jerusalem. Within the countless studies, thinkpieces, and classes on the Destruction story cycle, the legend of Marta, a mere cameo in the lengthy cycle, is more often than not ignored – although this cameo stands at the very heart of the cycle and, I submit, serves as its critical turning point. To fully understand the story of Marta, then, we must go all the way back to the beginning.[23]

21. "The Destruction was undeniably a watershed moment in the development of the rabbinic class and its rise to dominance. From this point on, the rabbis' religious-intellectual method… began to spread throughout society, until it gained its authoritative status and became the lot of the entire Jewish community." Anat Yisraeli-Taran, *Legends of the Destruction*, 9.

22. Despite the patently ahistorical nature of the Destruction story cycle, it does contain certain details that are not inconsistent with the accounts of Josephus and other ancient historians. See Yitzhak Baer, "Jerusalem in the Times of the Great Revolt," 169–84.

23. The following reading is indebted, in ways too numerous to individually mention, to the extraordinary analysis of the cycle in Rubenstein, *Talmudic Stories*, 139–75.

The Destruction Story Cycle: A Drama in Eight Acts

Prologue

> Rabbi Yoḥanan said: What is meant by the verse "Happy is the man who fears always, but he who hardens his heart shall fall into evil" (Prov. 28:14)? Jerusalem was destroyed because of Kamtza and Bar Kamtza. (Gittin 55b)

The story cycle opens with a prooftext from Proverbs, which sets the scene for the entire narrative. *"Happy is the man who fears always, but he who hardens his heart shall fall into evil."* One must be constantly cautious, scrupulous, prudent – but not so much so that one becomes paralyzed, *hardened*, which shall surely lead to no good. This is the theoretical framework within which the tragedy of the Destruction must be read.

The prologue then flashes forward to reveal the story cycle's conclusion: *Jerusalem was destroyed.* In beginning the cycle by giving away its end, the talmudic editors emphasize the narrative's educational, rather than historical, nature. They are less interested in what happened than in why it happened, less concerned with chronicling historical events than with articulating the lessons that may be drawn from them.[24] For the rabbis, *Jerusalem was destroyed* not because of a doomed war waged by the small Jewish polity against the mighty Roman Empire, but *because of Kamtza and Bar Kamtza.*

Act 1 – The Banquet

> A certain man had a friend Kamtza and an enemy Bar Kamtza. He once held a banquet and said to his servant, "Go and bring me Kamtza." He went and brought him Bar Kamtza. The host came

24. "Whereas classical historians, beginning with Thucydides, searched for a natural causality that determined the flow of history, the rabbis applied a totally different system of reasoning. World powers rose and fell regardless of the natural or social conditions governing their behavior, but solely on the basis of moral criteria ... moral virtue or culpability." Isaiah Gafni, "Rabbinic Historiography and Representations of the Past," 297.

> and found him sitting at the banquet. Said he, "Since you are my enemy, what are you doing here? Get up and leave." Said Bar Kamtza, "Since I am here, let me stay, and I will pay you for what I eat and drink." Said he, "No." Said Bar Kamtza, "I will pay you half the cost of the banquet." Said he, "No." Said Bar Kamtza, "I will pay for the whole banquet." Said he, "No." He took Bar Kamtza by his hand, forced him up, and threw him out. (Gittin 55b–56a)

The point of departure of our story cycle is a simple case of mistaken identity. A servant is charged with inviting his master's friend Kamtza to a banquet and, confused by the similarity in names, invites his enemy Bar Kamtza instead. When the host finds Bar Kamtza at his table, he indignantly demands that the latter leave. No use are Bar Kamtza's pleas to let him stay, to accept payment for the meal, to spare him the embarrassment; the host takes him up bodily and throws him out.

Hence the cycle's popular interpretation that Jerusalem was destroyed because of baseless hatred. If you were to stop reading here (as many, mistakenly, do[25]), you may well come away with the understanding that it was the animosity between the host and Bar Kamtza that brought about the city's downfall. And indeed, elsewhere the Talmud does state that it was baseless hatred that caused the Destruction (Yoma 9b). But this is not the story here. Within the context of our cycle, the real story begins now.

Act 2 – Bar Kamtza's Revenge

> Said Bar Kamtza, "Since the rabbis were sitting there and did not protest, this shows that they agreed with him. I will go and inform against them at the palace." He went and said to the emperor, "The Jews are rebelling against you." Said the emperor, "How can I tell?" Said Bar Kamtza, "Send them a sacrifice and see whether they will offer it." So he sent with him a fine calf. While Bar Kamtza was on the way he made a blemish on its upper lip,

25. Such fragmentary reading is a common error with rabbinic stories (for another example of a story which is seldom read in its entirety, see Chapter 6).

> and some say on the white of its eye, in a place where we count it as a blemish but they do not. The rabbis were inclined to offer it for the sake of keeping the peace with the government. Rabbi Zekharia ben Avkulas said to them, "People will say that blemished animals may be offered on the altar." They then proposed to kill Bar Kamtza so that he should not go and inform against them. Rabbi Zekharia ben Avkulas said to them, "People will say that one who makes a blemish on sacrificial animals is to be killed." Rabbi Yoḥanan said, "The humility of Rabbi Zekharia ben Avkulas destroyed our Temple, burned our Sanctuary, and exiled us from our land." (Gittin 56a)

Act 2 opens with a revelation. *Since the rabbis were sitting there and did not protest*. This is the first we hear of the rabbis, who had apparently been sitting at the banquet all along.[26] In neglecting to mention them earlier, the text enacts their effective (if not literal) absence; the rabbis are not noted as present since they might as well have been absent.[27] In face of the cruel public humiliation of Bar Kamtza, they remain silent. Afraid of upsetting the host, by all appearances a rich and powerful man, they are – just as in the Proverbial prooftext – paralyzed into inaction. "All that is necessary for the triumph of evil," says John Stuart Mill, in what might almost be a paraphrase of the verse from Proverbs, "is that good men do nothing."[28] This is the first instance of good men doing nothing, the first of many, an ongoing failure of leadership that will ultimately lead to the Destruction.

And so Bar Kamtza decides to have his revenge. He goes to the Roman emperor and informs him that his Jewish subjects are rebelling. When the latter sends back a sacrifice to test their loyalty, Bar Kamtza

26. While the Destruction is considered the founding event of rabbinic culture, there were a number of rabbis who "were necessarily active before the Destruction." Seth Schwartz, "The Political Geography of Rabbinic Texts," 76. It is likely, though, that the talmudic editors enhance the size and significance of this otherwise small group.
27. On the deliberate deploying of information in rabbinic storytelling, see p. 49 n. 44.
28. The exact quote is "Bad men need nothing more to compass their ends, than that good men should look on and do nothing." John Stuart Mill, *Inaugural Address at St. Andrews*, 36.

injures it in such a way that renders it blemished for the Jews but not for the Romans.[29] The rabbis are inclined to offer it nonetheless, so as not to incur the wrath of the emperor. This, halakhically, is the correct course of action; the meta-halakhic principle of *shalom malkhut* (keeping the peace with the government[30]) overrides the prohibition against sacrificing a blemished animal, particularly when the blemish is so borderline and the government so brutal and bloody.

But Rabbi Zekharia ben Avkulas sends his rabbinic colleagues back into paralysis when he warns, *"People will say that blemished animals may be offered on the altar."* This is a second instance of leadership failure. If in Act 1 the rabbis were afraid of what the host might do, now they are afraid of what the people, the unnamed masses, might say. Once again, they do nothing.

They then proposed to kill Bar Kamtza. A much better solution! Rather than sacrifice an animal with a very minor blemish, let Bar Kamtza be killed. This is an extreme course of action perhaps, but one that is equally halakhically valid. Endangering the life of fellow Jews by informing on them to a hostile government is, according to Jewish law, a capital offense, and Bar Kamtza was rightly deserving of death.[31]

Rabbi Zekharia ben Avkulas, however, persists in his naysaying. *"People will say that one who makes a blemish on sacrificial animals is to be killed."* People might get the wrong idea, draw the wrong halakhic conclusions. The law itself might be compromised. Faced with this threat, the rabbis, yet again, are stymied. Their overabundance of caution prevents them from doing what they know has to be done.

Rabbi Yoḥanan said, "The humility of Rabbi Zekharia ben Avkulas destroyed our Temple, burned our Sanctuary, and exiled us from our land." And here, in a moment of trenchant rabbinic self-critique, are we given the true reason for the Destruction: not the host's hatred, but the rabbis' humility.[32] The choice of word is remarkable; throughout rabbinic

29. Even within Jewish law, there is a dispute as to whether the injuries in question – on the upper lip or eye – are considered blemishes (see Ḥullin 128b, Zevaḥim 35b).

30. See Gittin 80a, Bava Batra 10b.

31. Bava Kama 117a.

32. Rabbi Zekharia is, in this regard, representative of the entire rabbinic class. Significantly, in the story's parallel in Lamentations Rabba, it is he – rather than the group of

literature, "humility" is unequivocally valorized.[33] This is one of just two cases where the word is used in a negative sense. The second case, also concerning Rabbi Zekharia, tells of his inability to take a side in a Hillel—Shammai dispute over the clearing of waste from the Shabbat table, resulting in his throwing the waste "under the couch." Although in that instance, the damage is nothing worse than a mess on the dining room floor, there too we are told, "The humility of Rabbi Zekharia ben Avkulas burned the Sanctuary" (T Shabbat 16:7).[34]

For this, precisely, is when humility goes wrong. When it undermines our confidence. When it paralyzes. When the fear of making a mistake prevents us from doing anything – which is often the greatest mistake of all. So humble are the rabbis, so lacking in conviction and a sense of their own authority, they dare not take a stand where one is urgently needed. Humility goes wrong when it makes good men do nothing.

The Sugya: Rabbinic Amendments

Jerusalem did not have to fall. There were two halakhic solutions the rabbis could have adopted to avert the impending disaster. Yes, they were not perfect, yes, their consequences were uncertain, but either one of them would have saved the city. Yet the rabbis chose neither, refusing to consider a compromise of any kind. The Talmud's condemnation of this halakhic purism as the cause of the Destruction – *the humility of Rabbi Zekharia ben Avkulas destroyed our Temple* – becomes even more pronounced in light of the sugya in which the Destruction story cycle is situated.

---

anonymous rabbis – who remains silent at the banquet (4:3). "The narrator redoubles his irony and condemnation of the rabbis through the character of Rabbi Zekharia ben Avkulas." Mandel, "Tales of the Destruction," 153.

33. Different rabbinic sources describe humility as the greatest of virtues (Avoda Zara 20b), an attribute of God (Berakhot 16b, Megilla 31a) and of the righteous (Bava Metzia 85a, Sanhedrin 11a), whose reward is prophecy (Nedarim 38a) and the entry into Heaven (Sanhedrin 88b).

34. Scholars have suggested that the name Avkulas is a pun on the Greek *eukolos*, which may be interpreted to mean humility. See Daniel R. Schwartz, "More on 'Zechariah ben Avkules: Humility or Zealotry?,'" 313–16.

The halakhic context for the story cycle is a list, in Mishna Gittin 4–5, of *takkanot* – amendments made by the rabbis to various laws. The root T-K-N (lit., to amend) recurs throughout these chapters, as several of the amendments are instituted for the sake of the meta-halakhic principle of *tikkun olam* (amending the world; M Gittin 4:2–7, 4:9, 5:3), as well as *takkanat hashavim* (an amendment for the sake of penitents; M Gittin 5:5) and *tikkun hamizbe'aḥ* (an amendment for the sake of the altar; ibid.).[35]

Within this list of *takkanot*, the Mishna preceding our story cycle deals with an amendment to the law of *sikarikon* – Romans (and Roman collaborators) who seized Jewish land in the aftermath of the Destruction. According to the law of *sikarikon*, if a Jew wanted to buy land thus seized, he had to first compensate the original Jewish owner for its full value:

> From the time that people were being killed in the war, the law of *sikarikon* applied.... If [one purchased land] from the owner and then purchased it from the *sikarikon*, his purchase stands.... This was the earlier Mishna. A later court said: One who purchased from the *sikarikon* must give one-fourth to the owner. (M Gittin 5:6)

The effect of the law in its initial formulation was a doubling of the cost of land (which would have to be purchased twice, first from the original owner and then from the *sikarikon* who stole it), so that all such sales became untenable. The rabbis therefore amended the law, reducing the compensation to just a quarter of the land's value – a change which was admittedly unfair to the original owner, but without it the land could never be redeemed back into Jewish hands.

The stark contrast between the Mishna's context and the story cycle text heightens the force of the latter's critique: As opposed to the rabbis at the time of the Destruction, the rabbis of the Mishna – who

35. A subsequent set of amendments is made in the name of the principle of *darkhei shalom* (keeping the peace; M Gittin 5:8–9), which itself recalls the principle of *shalom malkhut* invoked in Act 2.

lived in the century after the Destruction, and learned from the mistakes of their forebears – took stock of the situation they found themselves in, and realized they could not afford to be purists about it. They understood that the law, however perfect in theory, must sometimes be amended in face of an imperfect reality. They were not afraid to assert their religious authority, in spite of what people might say, and make the compromises they deemed necessary. If only the rabbis of the Destruction had done the same, our story might have had a very different ending.

Act 3 – Nero's Defection

> The emperor sent Nero the Caesar against them. When he came, he shot an arrow to the east, and it fell in Jerusalem. He shot one to the west, and it again fell in Jerusalem. He shot to all four directions, and each time it fell in Jerusalem. He said to a child, "Repeat the verse you have learned to me." He said to him, "And I will lay My vengeance upon Edom by the hand of My people Israel" (Ezek. 25:14). Nero said, "The Holy One, blessed be He, desires to lay waste His house and to lay the blame on me." So he fled and converted, and Rabbi Meir descended from him. (Gittin 56a)

The emperor, whose loyalty test the Jews had failed when they refused to sacrifice his calf, declares war, sending Nero to capture Jerusalem.[36] Herein lies the story's tragic irony: The rabbis' paralysis, caused by the fear of being misinterpreted by their fellow Jews, leads to a far more fatal misinterpretation by the Romans. Their uncompromising insistence on protecting the purity of the altar results in the altar being burned to the ground.

Before launching his campaign, Nero is careful to ascertain his chances of success. He employs two soothsaying techniques: shooting arrows in all directions of the wind, from which he learns that God intends for Jerusalem to be destroyed, and asking a child to recite the

36. This is consistent with Josephus' account, by which "the true beginning of our war with the Romans" was the Jews' "reject[ion of] the sacrifice of Caesar" (*Wars of the Jews*, 2.17.2).

verse he's just been taught, from which he learns that God will punish whoever actually destroys it.[37] Like the rabbis, Nero is faced with a difficult choice, one in which there are no ideal options – either desertion and death at the hand of the emperor, or destruction and punishment at the hand of God. Unlike the rabbis, though, he makes a decision, preferring an imperfect course of action to no action at all. Embodying the Proverbial prooftext, Nero is cautious but not overly cautious, fearful without letting the fear paralyze him. The text's juxtaposition of his bold choice in Act 3 with the rabbis' humility in Act 2 once again underscores the criticism directed at the rabbis, who fail where the non-Jew succeeds.[38] The result of Nero's decision to escape and convert is Rabbi Meir, a leader of immeasurable contribution to Jewish life and literature;[39] the result of the rabbis' indecision is the end of Jewish life as they knew it.

Act 4 – The Siege

> The emperor sent Vespasian the Caesar against them. He came and besieged Jerusalem for three years. There were three men of great wealth there: Nakdimon ben Gurion, Ben Kalba Savua, and Ben Tzitzit HaKesat.... One of these said to the people of Jerusalem, "I will keep you in wheat and barley." A second said, "I will keep you in wine, salt, and oil." The third said, "I will keep you in wood".... These men were in a position to keep the city for twenty-one years. There were certain zealots among the people of Jerusalem. The rabbis said to them, "Let us go out and make peace with the Romans." But the zealots did not let them. The zealots said to the rabbis, "Let us go out and engage in battle against the Romans." The rabbis said to them, "You will not succeed." The zealots then rose up and burned the stores of wheat and barley and a famine ensued. (Gittin 56a)

37. Asking a child to repeat the last verse he had learned that day was a standard practice of divination in the rabbinic world (see Ḥagiga 15a, Ḥullin 95b, Esther Rabba 7:13).
38. For the aggadic use of non-Jewish characters to chastise Jews, see p. xxiii.
39. For more on Rabbi Meir, see Chapter 5.

After Nero's defection, his replacement, Vespasian, comes and lays siege to Jerusalem. Three local philanthropists step up to feed the populace. The rabbis, once again, do nothing.

There were certain zealots among the people of Jerusalem. Three years of rabbinic paralysis have created a leadership void, into which step the zealots, a gang of warmongering thugs bent on fighting Rome. The zealots are the antithesis, the dark double, of the rabbis (even their names – *biryonei* and *rabbanei* – mirror each other), as the two groups typify the negative extremes of the Proverbs prooftext: If the rabbis have too many scruples, the zealots haven't scruples enough. They rise to power in the besieged city, not so powerful as to lead the people into war, but powerful enough to prevent the rabbis from suing for peace, when the latter finally decide to do so. To overcome the rabbis, and force the people to join their fight, the zealots burn down the food stores, plunging the city into hunger.

Yet nowhere are we told, "The unscrupulousness of the zealots destroyed our Temple." No; the rabbis realize this is on them, that the zealots were an outgrowth of their own leadership failure. Good men have done nothing, and so evil has triumphed.

Act 5 – Marta

At this point, we return to the tragedy of Marta. Having grounded it in the context of the Destruction story cycle, we may now read her narrative, if not redemptively, then in a somewhat different light:

Scene 1

> Marta bat Boethius was one of the richest women in Jerusalem. She sent her servant out saying, "Go and bring me some fine flour." By the time he went, it was sold out.
> He came and told her, "There is no fine flour, but there is white flour." She said to him, "Go and bring me some." By the time he went, it was sold out.
> He came and told her, "There is no white flour but there is dark flour." She said to him, "Go and bring me some." By the time he went, it was sold out.

He returned and said to her, "There is no dark flour, but there is barley flour." She said, "Go and bring me some." By the time he went, this was also sold out.

Scene 2

She was barefoot, but she said, "I will go out and see if I can find anything to eat."

Some dung stuck to her foot and she died.

Rabban Yoḥanan ben Zakkai applied to her the verse "The tender and delicate woman among you who would never venture to set her foot upon the ground"....

Scene 3

When she was dying, she brought all her gold and silver and threw them out in the marketplace, saying, "What good are these to me?" And this is as it is written, "They shall cast their silver in the streets." (Gittin 56a)

Scene 1 – It Was Sold Out	*Home (Market)*	*Marta, Servant*
Scene 2 – I Will Go Out	*Home → Market*	*Marta, Rabbi Yoḥanan ben Zakkai*
Scene 3 – Threw Them Out	*Market (Home)*[40]	*Marta*

Scene 1 – It Was Sold Out

By the time he went, it was sold out. Marta did not have to die. There were three other types of flour the servant could have bought to stave off starvation. Yes, they were not perfect, yes, he couldn't be sure of his fussy mistress's approval, but any one of them would have saved her life. In returning to ask for Marta's permission each time, the servant displays the same kind of purism, the same fear of getting it wrong, the same

40. Although all three scenes are split between the private sphere of the home and the public sphere of the market, the locus for Scene 1 is the home, whence the servant is sent and to which he returns, while the locus for Scene 3 is the market, where Marta draws her final breath.

humility as the rabbis. The implications of this parallelism are radical: If the servant, in his fear of deviating from his mistress's orders, ends up causing her death, then the rabbis, in their fear of deviating from their Master's orders, end up destroying Him.[41]

Scene 2 – I Will Go Out

She said, "I will go out and see if I can find anything to eat." This is the turning point of Marta's narrative, and, I would argue, of the story cycle at large. The fastidious Marta decides to come down off her high horse and go to the market herself. She doesn't care that it's beneath her. She doesn't care that what she finds there will not be perfect. She doesn't even care about what others might say. She decides to go outside.

In this sense, her choice of words is instructive: *"I will go out and see"* (*eipok ve'eḥezei*) echoes the talmudic principle of "Go out and see (*puk ḥazei*) [what the people do]." In times of halakhic uncertainty, the Talmud empowers rabbis to make decisions based on reality on the ground, however imperfect that reality might be.[42]

By going out and seeing, Marta creates a major shift in the narrative: She is the first (Jewish) character who does not shy away from a difficult choice; who confronts her hopeless situation, and takes matters into her own hands; the first character who is not afraid to act.

Scene 3 – Threw Them Out

She brought all her gold and silver and threw them out in the marketplace. Marta's final act, casting her gold and silver in the market, signifies her newfound awareness of reality. She realizes that her money – the money which was the source of her corruption, which separated her from her fellow man, allowing her to live in comfort while those around her starved – that money is now worthless. She throws it out, giving full effect to the words of the prophecy, "*They shall cast their silver in the streets*, and their gold shall be removed; their silver and their gold shall not be

41. In rabbinic literature, the Destruction of the Temple is often likened to the downfall of the Divine Presence. See Ephraim E. Urbach, *The Sages: Their Concepts and Beliefs*, 42–43.

42. See, for example, Berakhot 45a, Eiruvin 14b, Bava Kama 84b.

able to deliver them in the day of the wrath of the Lord. They shall not satisfy their souls, neither fill their bowels, because it is the stumbling block of their iniquity" (Ezek. 7:19).[43]

This is a moment of *tikkun* for Marta. It doesn't save her, but it does conclude her story on a note of repentance. She is no longer the oblivious, entitled, uncompromising woman she used to be. Marta may have lived a prima donna, but she dies a penitent one. And in her death, she irrevocably alters the course of events that follow.

Act 6 – Escape from Jerusalem

> Aba Sikra, the head of the zealots of Jerusalem, was the son of the sister of Rabban Yoḥanan ben Zakkai. He sent to him saying, "Come to visit me in secret." When he came, Rabbi Yoḥanan said to him, "How long are you going to carry on in this way and kill all the people with starvation?" He replied, "What can I do? If I say a word to them, they will kill me." He said, "See if there is a way for me to go out. Perhaps I will be able to save a little." Aba Sikra said to him, "Pretend to be ill, and let everyone come to inquire about you. Bring something foul-smelling and put it by you, so that they will say you are dead. Let then your disciples get under your bed, but no others, so that they will not notice that you are still light, since they know that a living being is lighter than the dead." He did so, and Rabbi Eliezer went under the bier from one side and Rabbi Yehoshua from the other. When they reached the gate, the zealots wanted to put a lance through the bier. Aba Sikra said to them, "People will say that they have stabbed their master." They wanted to give it a push. He said to them, "People will say that they have pushed their master." They opened the gate and he got out. (Gittin 56a)

---

43. Marta's money (as opposed to the actual goods of the three rich men) is easily depreciated because its value is entirely symbolic, "detached from production and its real conditions: a pure, empty form … operating on nothing but its own revolving motion"; it is, in this respect, not unlike Marta's former detached self. Jean Baudrillard, *The Transparency of Evil: Essays on Extreme Phenomena*, 35.

Directly after Marta's death, we have the first instance of rabbinic initiative in the story. Rabbi Yoḥanan ben Zakkai approaches Aba Sikra, leader of the zealots and his own nephew, to devise a strategy for him to break out of the city.[44] Specifically, he asks his nephew for a *takkanta* – a way to amend the otherwise hopeless situation. Rabbi Yoḥanan knows about Marta's death; his description of her (in Scene 2) as *the tender and delicate woman* from Deuteronomy implies that he witnessed it firsthand.[45] His presence at the tragic scene in Act 5, followed by his immediate turn from spectator to principal actor in Acts 6–8, is not just a temporal sequence of events; it is the inspiration of Marta that jolts Rabbi Yoḥanan out of his rabbinic paralysis. Her heroic ability to take stock of her reality and do something about it emboldens him to try to do the same. This causal connection is reflected in the verbal parallel between the acts: If Marta attempted to *go out and see* (*eipok ve'eḥezei*) whether she could save herself, Rabbi Yoḥanan, following her example, tries to *see* (*ḥazei*) whether he can *go out* (*de'eipok*) and *save a little.*

So Aba Sikra comes up with a plan: With the Romans guarding the city gates from without, and the zealots guarding them from within (to make sure no one escapes who can stay and fight), Rabbi Yoḥanan must feign his own death and be smuggled out of Jerusalem as a corpse. The plan is successfully executed, with Rabbi Yoḥanan escaping actual death when Aba Sikra convinces the zealot sentinels not to drive a lance through the coffin (the zealots may be antithetical

44. Aba is a common rabbinic honorific (see p. 169 n. 19), and Sikra is understood to be a play on sicarii, an extremist faction of the zealots; the word derives from the Latin *sicarius*, a general term for a violent criminal (which some scholars link to the previously discussed *sikarikon*). Martin Hengel, *The Zealots: Investigations into the Jewish Freedom Movement in the Period from Herod 1 until 70 AD*, 46–53.

45. Were this verse simply a later editorial insertion, it would have been quoted by the story's narrator (like the Ezekiel verse in Scene 3). That the text places it in the mouth of Rabbi Yoḥanan, who goes on to become the protagonist of the story's three final acts, suggests that he was actually there when Marta met with her unfortunate end. Note that Rabbi Yoḥanan ben Zakkai is not the Rabbi Yoḥanan who introduces the story cycle's prooftext and its condemnation of Rabbi Zekharia; the latter is Rabbi Yoḥanan bar Nafḥa, a leading 3rd-century rabbi who is often the narrator of stories of the Destruction (see, for example, Y Taanit 4:5, Taanit 29a, and Bava Metzia 30b).

to the rabbis in every other way, but they seem to share their fear of what *people will say*). There is a poignant symbolism in Rabbi Yoḥanan's being carried out of the city in a coffin. Jewish life must die in Jerusalem so that it can be resurrected – like Rabbi Yoḥanan, and by him – in the beit midrash of Yavneh.

Act 7 – Confronting Vespasian

> When he reached the Romans, Rabbi Yoḥanan said, "Peace to you, O king, peace to you, O king." Vespasian said to him, "You are deserving of death on two counts: One, I am not a king and you call me king. And again, if I am a king, why did you not come to me until now?" He replied, "As for your saying, 'I am not a king,' in truth you are a king. For if you were not a king, Jerusalem would not be delivered into your hand.... And as for your asking, 'If I am a king, why did you not come to me until now?,' the zealots among us did not let me." Vespasian said to him, "If there is a jar of honey round which a serpent is wound, would they not break the jar to get rid of the serpent?" Rabbi Yoḥanan was silent. Rav Yosef, and some say Rabbi Akiva, applied to him the verse "God... turns wise men backward and makes their knowledge foolish" (Is. 44:25). He ought to have said, "We take a pair of tongs and remove the serpent and kill it, and leave the jar intact." (Gittin 56a–b)

Once out of Jerusalem, Rabbi Yoḥanan makes his way to the Roman camp and presents himself to Vespasian, prophesying that the commander in chief will one day become emperor. When Vespasian reproaches him for not coming sooner, Rabbi Yoḥanan is forced to admit that the zealots have taken over the city and have prevented all peacemaking efforts. Vespasian responds with a parable, likening Jerusalem to *a jar of honey round which a serpent is wound*. Just as the jar becomes worthless and ought to be smashed when surrounded by a deadly snake, so Jerusalem loses its value and ought to be destroyed when overrun by lawless, violent men.

Act 8 – Give Me Yavneh

> Just then, a messenger arrived from Rome, and said to Vespasian, "Rise, for the emperor has died, and the noblemen of Rome have decided to make you their leader".... Vespasian said to Rabbi Yoḥanan, "I am going, and will send someone to take my place. But ask something of me and I will give it." He said to him, "Give me Yavneh and its sages, and the dynasty of Rabban Gamliel, and physicians to heal Rabbi Zadok." Rav Yosef, and some say Rabbi Akiva, applied to him the verse "God... turns wise men backward and makes their knowledge foolish." He ought to have said to him, "Let the Jews off this time." But he thought that Vespasian would not give so much, and so he would not even save a little. (Gittin 56b)

The conversation is interrupted by a messenger from Rome, who breaks the news that the emperor is dead and that, just as Rabbi Yoḥanan had predicted, Vespasian has been chosen to succeed him. The pleased Vespasian condescends to grant Rabbi Yoḥanan one request before returning to Rome, and Rabbi Yoḥanan, in a decision that spells the end of Jerusalem and the dawn of the rabbinic era, asks for *Yavneh and its sages*.

Rabbi Yoḥanan makes a bold and controversial choice, and is denounced as *foolish* for it. According to Rav Yosef (or Rabbi Akiva), he had gone from extreme purism to extreme pragmatism. His request for Yavneh was a little too expedient. He should have tried to save Jerusalem.

But according to Rabbi Yoḥanan, who is given the final word in the story, *Vespasian would not give so much.*[46] Rabbi Yoḥanan has seen the disastrous effects of the refusal to compromise, of preferring the perfect and the unattainable to the imperfect and the plausible, and he is determined not to make the same mistake. He also recognizes the truth of Vespasian's parable, that in the current reality Jerusalem is no longer the

46. On the significance of the last word, see pp. 17–18. Rabbi Yoḥanan's assumption is given credence in the story's parallel in Lamentations Rabba, where he actually does ask for Jerusalem to be spared and Vespasian responds, "Did the Romans make me king that I should abandon the city? Make another request" (1:31).

city it once was. And he decides that saving something, however little, however imperfect, is better than saving nothing at all.

And so, returning to the beginning of the story, *Jerusalem was destroyed*. Judaism is left to begin again at Yavneh, where, under the leadership of Rabbi Yoḥanan ben Zakkai, it is radically transformed into the rabbinic Judaism we know today.[47] The various changes Rabbi Yoḥanan institutes to adapt Jewish life to a post-Temple world are referred to, significantly, as *takkanot*.[48] Like the rabbis in the mishnaic context of our story, Rabbi Yoḥanan is not afraid to assert his religious authority, and make the compromises required by the new, imperfect reality. It may have come years too late, and at a terrible price, but Rabbi Yoḥanan finally achieves his *takkanta*.

Having read the Destruction story cycle from beginning to end, we can now see just how pivotal Marta's role is in the larger narrative:

	Act 5: Marta	**The Destruction Story Cycle**
Part	**Act 5, Scene 1: It Was Sold Out**	**Acts 1–4: The Banquet, Bar Kamtza's Revenge, Nero's Defection, The Siege**
Setting	Home	Jerusalem (inside the city)
Attitude	Purism	Purism

47. "Rabbi Yoḥanan's legacy is not just as a builder of the nation and its institutions after their demise, but also as one of the greatest builders of Judaism throughout the generations, adjusting its character to fit the new reality after the Destruction." Shmuel Safrai, "New Inquiries into the Status and Activities of Rabban Yohanan ben Zakkai After the Destruction," 218.

48. M Sukka 3:12, M Rosh Hashana 4:1–4, M Menaḥot 10:5.

Plot	The servant, fearful of adopting any course of action the least bit imperfect or uncertain, fails to save Marta	The rabbis, fearful of adopting any course of action the least bit imperfect or uncertain, fail to save Jerusalem
Part	**Act 5, Scene 2: I Will Go Out**	**Act 6: Escape from Jerusalem**
Setting	Home → Market	Jerusalem (inside the city) → Outside the city
Attitude	Purism → Pragmatism	Purism → Pragmatism
Plot	Marta takes matters into her own hands and attempts to go out and see (*eipok ve'eḥezei*) if she can save herself	Rabbi Yoḥanan takes matters into his own hands and attempts to see if he can go out (*ḥazei … de'eipok*) and save a little
Part	**Act 5, Scene 3: Threw Them Out**	**Acts 7–8: Confronting Vespasian, Give Me Yavneh**
Setting	Market	Outside the city
Attitude	Pragmatism	Pragmatism
Plot	Marta's newfound courage and awareness of reality allow her to let go of what no longer has value, a renunciation which does not save her, but is her *tikkun*	Rabbi Yoḥanan's newfound courage and awareness of reality allow him to let go of what no longer has value, a renunciation which does not save Jerusalem, but is his *takkanta*

The three scenes of Marta's story (Act 5) perfectly correspond to the overarching narrative's three parts (Acts 1–4, 6, 7–8): Marta's resolve to *go out* from home to market foreshadows Rabbi Yoḥanan's fateful decision to leave Jerusalem; the initiative she shows in attempting to save herself inspires Rabbi Yoḥanan to try and *save a little*; and her move from purism to pragmatism encapsulates the same turn in the rabbinic mindset, from Rabbi Zekharia's humility to Rabbi Yoḥanan's courage. As such, Marta's story is a perfect microcosm of the Destruction story cycle, and Marta – though still a prima donna – is its true heroine.

The Moral of the Story: The Danger of Purism

The Destruction is not just the founding event of rabbinic culture; it is also its foundational trauma. Rabbi Yoḥanan and his rabbinic heirs lived under the shadow of the Destruction, a tragedy which, in their self-critical account, was the direct result of the failure of the rabbis before them. If the rabbis of the Mishna and Talmud seem especially daring in their halakhic decision-making, in the adaptations they make and amendments they institute, it is because they were trying to get as far away as possible from Rabbi Zekharia ben Avkulas and his purist peers.[49]

This is the lesson of the Destruction story cycle in general, and of the legend of Marta in particular: We must act, even if it means we make a mistake. We must choose, even if we choose incorrectly. We must get past our own humility. The world is not a perfect place; uncertainty is the fundamental human condition. We can sit around, paralyzed, waiting for certainty, waiting for conditions to be just right – and then we will never do anything at all. Or, like Marta, we can take matters into our own hands, go out into the world, and try, each in our own way, to save a little.

49. "By introducing these amendments the sages assert authority and exert power. They display the self-confidence to modify the law, to recognize that certain situations demand legal intervention and remedy. The Mishna testifies to rabbinic initiative, confidence, and action." Rubenstein, *Talmudic Stories*, 163.

Ḥeruta
The Madonna/Whore

The Archetype: Mistresses for Pleasure, Wives to Bear Us Children

> Since the beginning... we find two opposite feminine archetypes: the positive, loyal, moral woman, who is beloved, wise, and charged with the preservation of the family unit and cultural continuity; and opposed to her, the sensual, attractive woman... who is independent, lascivious, enticing, self-indulgent, and loyal primarily to herself.[1]

Of all the archetypes imposed upon women, perhaps the most primal is not one archetype, but two – the division of women into basic binary opposites: the good woman and the bad woman, the pure and the promiscuous, the saintly and the seductive, the maternal and the immoral. This division, otherwise known as the madonna/whore paradigm, cuts through history and across cultures, halving all of womankind in two. Whatever the literature, whatever the mythology, whatever the folklore, a woman can be either madonna or whore; there is no middle ground.

1. Nitza Abarbanell, *Eve and Lilith*, 15–24.

In Jewish culture, the paradigm is best represented in the characters of Eve and Lilith. The one is the "mother of all life" and a loyal helpmate to Adam (Gen. 3:20); the other, a defiant demoness who abandons him to haunt the earth, cause death to infants, and seduce men in their sleep.[2]

Eve and Lilith (Anonymous; John William Waterhouse)

In Mesopotamian mythology, it is Ninsun and Ishtar – the wise and loving mother of the hero Gilgamesh who aids him in his quests, and the dangerous temptress who seeks to destroy him.

Greek literature gives us Penelope and Circe – the faithful wife who waits for years for Odysseus to return, rejecting all other men in his absence, and by contrast, the treacherous witch who entices Odysseus to love-making "with evil purpose in her heart."[3]

Christianity, of course, has its two Marys – the Virgin Mary, archetypal madonna, and Mary Magdalene, the prostitute.

So pervasive, in fact, was this dichotomy in the ancient world, it exceeded the fictional realms of mythology and literature and became an actual split in the household. It was not uncommon for the men of Antiquity to have two women, one for procreation and the other for sexual gratification. "Mistresses," the Athenian Apollodorus famously proclaimed, "we keep for pleasure… and wives to bear us legitimate children and be our housekeepers."[4]

2. Shabbat 151b; *The Alphabet of Ben Sira*, 5.
3. Homer, *The Odyssey*, 10:317.
4. Demosthenes, "Apollodorus Against Neaera," 122. According to historian Kevin Reilly, the ancient world "considered [prostitution] a noble solution to the problem of providing men with seductive and interesting women while ensuring that their own wives (and thus their own family lines) would remain pure. In short, they created a society of two types of women: the sexless wives and virginal daughters of the men of substance, and the women (drawn mostly from the lower class) who were trained

The great medieval poem *The Divine Comedy* features its madonna and whore, respectively, as part of Dante's journey through Heaven and Hell. Beatrice, "a fair, saintly lady," gently guides Dante through Paradise, "as the mother… to her boy";[5] while Semiramis, guilty of incest with her own son, is punished in the violent storms of the underworld.

Beatrice and Semiramis (Gustave Doré)

Don Quixote, arguably the first modern novel, illustrates the paradigm in the characters of Dulcinea and Aldonza. The latter is a rough-and-ready farm girl, vulgar, loud, and of easy virtue. It's only in Don Quixote's deranged mind, the same mind that turns windmills into giants and old horses into steeds, that this wanton country wench becomes "Dulcinea del Toboso… queen and lady… in beauty no one equals her and in good name few approach her."[6]

Drawing on European folktales, the 19th-century ballet *Swan Lake* is the love story of Odette, a beautiful princess magically transformed into a swan, and Prince Siegfried, who falls for Odette but is lured away by her dark double, Odile. These two roles (often danced by the same ballerina) are

Odette and Odile (*Swan Lake*, Ballet Company National Opera of Ukraine)

to satisfy men's pleasure." Kevin Reilly, *The West and the World: A History of Civilization from the Ancient World to 1700*, 161.

5. Dante Alighieri, *The Divine Comedy*, 1:2, 3:22.
6. Miguel de Cervantes, *Don Quixote*, 1:13–25.

deliberately contrasted on stage: Odette, dressed in white, her head bowed and her body limp in the prince's arms, is compliant, devoted, and chaste; whereas Odile, in black, confidently dances round the prince, her pirouettes provocative and proud.

The eponymous hero of *Daniel Deronda* is similarly torn between two madonna- and whore-like women. The attractive and selfish Gwendolen Harleth (whose name makes no secret of her nature) is the object of much male attention, but is disinclined toward marriage, a state "in which a woman could not do what she liked, had more children than were desirable… and became irrevocably immersed in humdrum." Conversely, Mirah Lapidoth, the penniless Jewish refugee Deronda ultimately marries, is innocent and meek, "capable of submitting to anything in the form of duty."[7]

Moving from Victorian London to the Antebellum South, we find Melanie Hamilton and Scarlett O'Hara, another quintessential madonna/whore pair. Scarlett is as flagrant as Melanie is demure, as devious as Melanie naïve. After Ashley Wilkes chooses Melanie over Scarlett, and Scarlett marries Melanie's brother in revenge, the two women struggle to survive the Civil War together, Melanie genuinely affectionate toward Scarlett and Scarlett secretly scornful of Melanie:

Melanie and Scarlett
(*Gone with the Wind*, Metro-Goldwyn-Mayer)

> Scarlett saw Melanie… and, with a surge of dislike, she realized that the fly in the ointment of Atlanta would be this slight little person in black mourning dress, her riotous dark curls subdued to matronly smoothness and a loving smile of welcome and happiness on her heart-shaped face…. [Melanie] always saw the best

7. George Eliot, *Daniel Deronda*, chs. 4, 45.

> in everyone and remarked kindly upon it.... Scarlett exercised the same charms as Melanie but with a studied artistry and consummate skill. The difference between the two girls lay in the fact that Melanie spoke kind and flattering words from a desire to make people happy... and Scarlett never did it except to further her own aims.[8]

The 1958 Hitchcock thriller *Vertigo* tells of Scottie, a retired detective who fails in his mission to protect the life of Madeleine Elster. Wracked with guilt and obsessed with the memory of his dead beloved, Scottie imagines he sees Madeleine everywhere, until one day he runs into Judy Barton, her mysterious lookalike. Their uncanny similarity notwithstanding (both women are played by actress Kim Novak), Madeleine was blond, wealthy, and dignified, while Judy is dark-haired, low-class, and loose. Nevertheless, Scottie tries to turn Judy into Madeleine, forcing her to dye her hair and don a prim grey suit – a perverse attempt that ends, predictably, in tragedy. The feminine dichotomy is absolute; a madonna can never be a whore, as a whore can never become a madonna.

But of all the 20th-century madonna/whore duos – Elizabeth and Margaret, Betty and Veronica, Krystle and Alexis – perhaps the most iconic are Jackie Kennedy and Marilyn Monroe. The first lady and the film star, wife and (alleged) mistress, epitome of elegance and symbol of sexuality. Over two millennia after Apollodorus made his hard-and-fast distinction between wives and mistresses, very little, it seems, has changed. Women are still either one or the other.

Jackie and Marilyn (Jaques Lowe; Alamy)

8. Margaret Mitchell, *Gone with the Wind*, ch. 8.

Against the universality of the madonna/whore paradigm, from ancient Mesopotamia to modern America, rabbinic culture stands out as somewhat more complex. Practically speaking, the keeping of two women for the fulfillment of one's sexual and procreative needs is strongly condemned (if not entirely forbidden[9]) as the height of immorality and injustice. Indeed, when the rabbis seek to identify the sin of the generation of the Flood – the very sin that destroyed the world – it is this practice that they point to:

> This is what the men of the generation of the Flood would do: Each took two wives, one for procreation and the other for pleasure. The former would stay like a widow throughout her life, while the latter was given a cup of sterility to drink so that she would not bear, and would sit before him made up as a harlot. (Genesis Rabba 23:2)[10]

Rabbinic legend, like midrash, does not take kindly to this instrumental use of women. When Rebbe's son, for instance, returns home after twelve years of study to discover his wife can no longer bear children, Rebbe refuses to let him take a second wife, for fear that "it would be said: One is his wife and the other his mistress." He prays for his daughter-in-law to regain her fertility instead (Ketubot 62b).

---

9. While there is scant evidence of actual polygamy in the rabbinic period, "it remains very significant that it was halakhically acceptable." Rachel Biale, *Women and Jewish Law: The Essential Texts, Their History, and Their Relevance for Today*, 49–50. A halakhic prohibition against polygamy was introduced only in the Middle Ages.
10. The midrash goes on to establish Adah and Zilla, the two wives of Lamech (who lived one generation before the Flood), as a typical madonna/whore pair: "Adah – because she became pregnant [*adah*]... Zilla – because she sat in his shade [*zillo*]" (Genesis Rabba 23:2; for an inverse midrash on the names, which has Adah as the whore and Zilla as the madonna, see Y Yevamot 6:5). Another (albeit modern) interpretation detects a madonna/whore dynamic in Jacob's marriage to Leah and Rachel; according to the 17th-century commentator *Kli Yakar* (Gen. 30:25), Jacob was reluctant to return to Canaan as long as Rachel remained childless, embarrassed that his father might think that he had married two wives – one, plain and fecund, for childbirth, and the other, beautiful and barren, for sexual gratification.

But if the rabbis reject the feminine dichotomy in practice, they certainly seem to accept it in theory. Throughout rabbinic literature, both in its halakhic and aggadic parts, references to the madonna/whore paradigm abound.

Halakhically, we find the paradigm at work in numerous rabbinic debates. One notable example is the discussion of the biblical law against a priest "marry[ing] a harlot" (Lev. 21:7). The Talmud presents three opinions as to who the harlot in question might be:

> The harlot mentioned in the Torah… Rabbi Yehuda says: A harlot is a congenitally infertile woman. The rabbis say: A harlot is… one who engaged in licentious sexual intercourse. Rabbi Elazar says: An unmarried man who had intercourse with an unmarried woman not for the purpose of marriage renders her a harlot. (Yevamot 61b)

According to the rabbis' opinion, the harlot is *one who engaged in licentious sexual intercourse,* i.e., an actual prostitute. Rabbi Yehuda says she is a woman who has never developed sexually and is therefore incapable of conceiving. Herein is an explicit contrast of the two feminine categories; if a woman cannot be a madonna, she is necessarily a whore.[11] Rabbi Elazar takes the contrast one step further, arguing that she is any woman who has sexual relations *not for the purpose of marriage*; the harlot, for him, is not just non-mother, but non-wife.[12]

Aggada, for its part, features several passages which establish a firm distinction between the modesty and demureness of a good woman and the brazenness and abandon of her fallen sister:

> "All the honor of the king's daughter is within" (Ps. 45:14) – If she acts to keep herself modest and is worthy… she will raise up priests who wear high priestly garments…. But if she walks about

11. This is not to say that Jewish law requires that all sexual relations between husband and wife lead to conception; see n. 27 below.
12. Similar definitions of harlotry as non-procreative or non-marital intercourse are found in M Ketubot 5:1, Sifra Kedoshim 7:2, Sifra Emor 1:7.

> a lot and goes out into the marketplace, she will come to corruption, to harlotry. (Tanḥuma Buber Vayishlaḥ 12)

> Rabbi Yosei the Galilean says: Seven things were said about the adulteress. Haughty eyes... a lying tongue... blood-shedding hands... a wicked heart... evil-bound feet... a false witness... and a hate-monger.... It is about her that Solomon said, "And I find more bitter than death the woman" (Eccl. 7:26).... [Conversely,] it is the manner of the daughters of Israel that they are neither loud in their voice, nor haughty in their gait, nor wanton with merrymaking. (Tanḥuma Buber Naso 3–4)

Hence, for all of their formal criticism of the feminine dichotomy, the rabbis aren't able to rid themselves of the notion that there are, in truth, two different types of women – the good, virtuous, maternal woman and the bad, sinful, sexual one.[13] It is this tacit acceptance of the madonna/whore paradigm that makes our next story all the more remarkable.

Primary Readings: The Old Woman, The Devil, and the Trickster

> It was Rav Ḥiyya bar Ashi's custom, whenever he prostrated himself in prayer, to say, "May the Merciful One save me from the evil inclination."
> One day his wife heard him. She said, "For many years he has separated himself from me. Why does he say this?"
> One day he was studying in his garden.
> His wife made herself up and passed before him repeatedly.

13. "The rabbinic world was characterized by dichotomies and separations, and so, too, was their perceived world of women.... Distinctions divide modest homebodies from immodest gadabouts, and the pious wives of rabbis and rabbinic students from the wives of people derelict in their observance of ritual obligations. The fertile wife fulfilled social expectations while... the seductive beauty... could lead Jewish men away from faithful worship of God and observance of divine commandments." Baskin, *Midrashic Women*, 162–63.

He said to her, "Who are you?"
She said, "I am Ḥeruta, and I just returned today."
He demanded her services.
She said to him, "Bring me the pomegranate from the top of that tree."
He jumped up, went, and brought it to her.
When he came home, his wife was firing the oven.
He went and sat in it.
She said to him, "What is this?"
He said, "Such and such happened."
She said, "It was me."
He paid no attention to her until she gave him the signs.
He said to her, "Nevertheless, my intention was to violate a prohibition."
That righteous man fasted all of his days until he died of that death. (Kiddushin 81b)

Set in the 3rd century in the small Babylonian Jewish community of Korkoneya,[14] our story begins, like many a rabbinic legend, with a routine about to be broken.[15] Intimated in Rav Ḥiyya's prayer – *"May the Merciful One* (i.e., God[16]) *save me from the evil inclination* (i.e., the sexual urge[17])*"* – and in his wife's subsequent response to it, this routine is one

14. See Avoda Zara 16b.
15. "Rabbinic stories open with an exposition of a routine... [followed by] its disruption." Raveh, *Fragments of Being*, 181–82.
16. Berakhot 60b, Shabbat 88a, Bava Kama 83b.
17. Although in early rabbinic literature "evil inclination" (*yetzer hara*) refers to all manner of sinful urges, in the Talmud it comes to be identified primarily with sexual desire (see, among others, Berakhot 20a, Shabbat 62b, Sukka 52a, Sotah 8a, Kiddushin 21b). This is not to say that the rabbis view desire as unequivocally evil. Far from it; they readily recognize its positive, even creative, potential: "'Behold, it was good' (Gen. 1:31) refers to the good inclination; 'and behold, it was very good' (ibid.) refers to the evil inclination. But is the evil inclination good? Inconceivable. Rather, without the evil inclination no man would build a house, take a wife, or beget children" (Genesis Rabba 9:7; see also Yoma 69b, Sanhedrin 64a). At the same time, the rabbis regard the evil inclination as an inherently dangerous force (p. 34 n. 21), one which can only be controlled through supreme willpower and divine aid. "Eight out of nine

of marital abstinence. *For many years* Rav Ḥiyya *has separated himself* from his wife. Such abstinence is unparalleled in rabbinic literature, and our story, accordingly, has been the subject of a great deal of scholarly discussion.[18] Broadly speaking, scholarship surrounding the story may be classified into three distinct primary readings.

I. A Reawakening of Desire

The first, traditional reading is attributed to Rashi, who glosses the wife's words *"he has separated himself from me"* as "because of old age." This is usually taken to mean that Rav Ḥiyya and his wife were an elderly couple, past their sexual prime, and that the story, essentially, is about a reawakening of desire. With a dash of makeup and some seductive role-play, the wife jolts Rav Ḥiyya out of years of sexual inactivity, and rekindles his lost passion for her. A romantic reading, to be sure, but one that is completely at odds with the narrative details: Rav Ḥiyya, from the very outset, fights to resist his sexual urge, which is clearly far from dormant; he climbs a tree, so he is by no means geriatric; and he ultimately starves himself to death, which is hardly a romantic happy end. Rashi's comment thus cannot be read as a full explanation of the story; it might reflect the reason the wife gave for her husband's abstinence, but it can't possibly be the true reason.

II. A Rabbinic Seduction Story

A second, modern reading examines the text within its immediate context. Located toward the end of Tractate Kiddushin (lit., marriages), our

narratives that mention the evil *yetzer* in the Bavli discuss sexual issues.... The *yetzer* appears as sexual desire, with which men, usually sages, are in constant struggle, and that demands external assistance or supervision in order to win." Ishay Rosen-Zvi, *Demonic Desires: Yetzer Hara and the Problem of Evil in Late Antiquity*, 111.

18. While there are several legends of rabbis separated from their wives by long sojourns in the yeshiva (most notably, the legends of Ketubot 62b–63a), this is the only instance of lengthy abstinence between a husband and wife living under the same roof. "In this respect, the story is singular in all of talmudic literature." Rosen-Zvi, "The Evil Inclination," 80.

story concludes a sequence of narratives about rabbis who are brought to their knees by the Devil or evil inclination (which in rabbinic literature are often one and the same[19]). Before it, we have the legend of Rav Amram's lustful climb to an attic full of women,[20] followed by these twin tales:

> Rabbi Meir used to scoff at transgressors. One day the Devil appeared to him as a woman on the opposite bank of the river. As there was no ferry, he seized the rope bridge and proceeded across. When he had reached halfway along the rope, the Devil let him go, saying: "Had they not proclaimed in Heaven, 'Take heed of Rabbi Meir and his Torah,' I would have valued your life at two pennies."
>
> Rabbi Akiva used to scoff at transgressors. One day the Devil appeared to him as a woman on the top of a palm tree. Grasping the tree, he went climbing up. When he reached halfway up the tree, the Devil let him go, saying: "Had they not proclaimed in Heaven, 'Take heed of Rabbi Akiva and his Torah,' I would have valued your life at two pennies." (Kiddushin 81a)

The preceding story cycle establishes an unmistakable pattern: (a) a seduction (b) by the Devil in disguise (c) of an exceptionally pious man (d) who must overcome a considerable physical obstacle to fulfill his desire. Within this context, our story reads as simply another seduction narrative, the ensnaring and undoing of a great rabbi by the Devil or evil inclination – who, in our case, assumes the guise of the rabbi's own wife. In the words of Shulamit Valler,

> The devious evil inclination... takes the shape of Rav Ḥiyya bar Ashi's wife... manipulating [him] into a situation from which there is no way out, other than death.... Of no use are Rav Ḥiyya's daily prayers for help, his abstinence from his wife, his

19. "Reish Lakish says: The Devil [and] the evil inclination... are one" (Bava Batra 16a).
20. See pp. 26–27.

> rich spiritual life.... [The story] demonstrates that man cannot free himself from the firm grip of the evil inclination.[21]

Rav Ḥiyya's abstinence, according to this reading, is all a piece with his valiant war against the evil inclination. Separating himself from his wife, Rav Ḥiyya tries desperately to overcome his sexual urge, only to succumb to it in the end – as all the rabbis had before him.

Such an interpretation is supported by a parallel narrative in the late midrash, in which a heretic who denies the power of the evil inclination is seduced, like Rav Ḥiyya, by a "made-up" woman in a "garden"; when he falls ill with remorse, the woman reveals herself to him as a demoness sent by God to expose his fallibility (Tanḥuma Buber Miketz 15).

Yet the many similarities between text and context are outweighed by the far more significant differences between them: Unlike the preceding accounts, our story is longer and more detailed (and therefore, presumably, a great deal more complex[22]); unlike Rabbi Meir and Rabbi Akiva, Rav Ḥiyya doesn't "scoff" at the sexual urge, but struggles mightily against it; unlike the bids to seduce the former, which are abandoned at the last moment, Rav Ḥiyya's seduction is carried through (and with tragic results); and unlike the Devil, whose role is merely to occasion the seduction, Rav Ḥiyya's wife is not a secondary character, but the story's protagonist – a rich, multidimensional heroine through whose point of view the story, uniquely, is told.[23]

Hence, in spite of various attempts at comparison, the legend of Ḥeruta is too different to the narratives that come before it, and cannot be read as just another rabbinic seduction story.

21. Shulamit Valler, *Women in Jewish Society in the Talmudic Period*, 49–50.
22. For the importance of each and every detail in rabbinic storytelling, see p. xxvii.
23. On the convention of telling seduction tales through the perspective of the seduced man, rather than seducing woman, see p. 27.

III. An Anti-Abstinence Polemic

A third reading – this one, too, modern – analyzes the story in light of an important feature of its historical context: the conflict with early Christianity and the consequent anti-Christian polemic that underlies many of the Talmud's passages.[24] Several scholars regard the story as a rabbinic cautionary tale against the ideal of abstinence, an ideal which many Jews at the time had adopted from their Christian neighbors. In a widely cited essay, Shlomo Naeh argues that

> the Syriac Christian idea of a war for freedom from the sexual impulse... captivated... members of the Babylonian Jewish community.... The point of the story is its negative portrayal of the ascetic ideal, or at least its presentation as irremediably at odds with the common Jewish ideal of family life.[25]

Rav Ḥiyya's abstinence, according to this interpretation, is not commended by the rabbis – it is criticized. If you try, like Rav Ḥiyya, to abstain from sexual relations with your lawfully wedded wife, you will end up, like Rav Ḥiyya, sinning with a prostitute.

This reading is supported by a number of parallel narratives in biblical and rabbinic literature, in which a man depriving a woman of sexual relations is tricked by her into having intercourse: from the biblical incident of Judah and Tamar (Gen. 38), an obvious intertext for our story;[26] through the midrash on the conception of King David,

---

24. "The confrontation with Christianity lies at the very heart of midrashic and talmudic Judaism, which deal intensively with a renewed self-definition of who is a Jew and what is Judaism.... It was essential to define this in relation to those who wished to see themselves as Jews but were rejected by the sages of the Mishna and the Talmud because of their belief in the messiahhood of Jesus.... The process of appropriation and the struggle over that which is appropriated characterized the world of anti-Christian polemic during the rabbinic period." Israel Jacob Yuval, *Two Nations in Your Womb: Perceptions of Jews and Christians in Late Antiquity and the Middle Ages*, 23.

25. Shlomo Naeh, "Freedom and Celibacy: A Talmudic Variation on Tales of Temptation and Fall in Genesis and Its Syrian Background," 88–89.

26. See below, pp. 111–12.

achieved when David's mother takes the place of Jesse's new wife in the marriage bed (Yalkut HaMakhiri Psalms 118:28); to this rather typical bed-trick tale:

> A woman was propositioned by a man. She said to him, "Where will you go?" What did she do? She went and told his wife. The wife went to that place and he slept with her. Then he regretted it and sought his death. Said his wife to him, "From your bread you have eaten and from your cup you have drunk, but... you are rude of manner." (Numbers Rabba 9:3)

Here, then, is a compelling reading, informed by multiple levels of context, and accepted by a majority of critics. Still, there are a number of key questions such an interpretation leaves unanswered: What about the conjugal obligation which a husband, according to Jewish law, has toward his wife?[27] Can it be that a man like Rav Ḥiyya – not a simple Jew susceptible to Christian influence, but a highly learned rabbi[28] – elected simply to ignore it? Moreover, why does the wife not address this blatant violation of her marriage contract, and sue for divorce, as is her legal right? And, perhaps most importantly, how could a man who has spent years fighting his sexual urge fall so immediately at the sight of a prostitute, without so much as a hint of resistance?

---

27. One of the three obligations that make up the Jewish marriage contract (see p. 32), the conjugal obligation requires that a husband have intercourse with his wife at regular intervals. According to the Mishna, if the husband abstains from his conjugal duty for more than a couple of weeks, he is considered in violation of the marriage contract, and his wife is released from the marriage with full payment of the contract (M Ketubot 5:6). The Talmud, for its part, states that abstinence is not just a violation of the marriage contract, but an actual transgression: "Rabbi Yehoshua ben Levi said: Anyone who knows that his wife is God-fearing and does not have intercourse with her is called a sinner" (Yevamot 62b). Of issue is not just procreation, but "the happiness of conjugal rights" (Pesaḥim 72b) – the joy of marital intimacy between husband and wife.
28. See, for example, Berakhot 11b, Eiruvin 51b, Zevaḥim 94a.

The Madonna Who Became a Whore: Ḥeruta Revisioned

Contrary to the prevailing readings, I'd like to propose that the key to understanding Rav Ḥiyya's abstinence is not physiological, ethical, or theological – but psychological. Noting the recurrence of madonnas and whores in world mythology and folklore, Sigmund Freud posits that these archetypes are an expression of a deep psychological force.[29] He thus translates the madonna/whore paradigm into the madonna/whore complex – a disorder which affects men who fail to establish a healthy attitude toward sex, and who consequently "regard the sexual act basic-ally as something degrading, which defiles and pollutes not only the body." Such an attitude, when taken to extreme, is apt to develop into a complex whereby

> the whole sphere of love... remains divided in the two directions personified in art as sacred and profane (or animal) love. Where they love they do not desire and where they desire they cannot love....
>
> If someone makes an impression that might lead to a high psychical estimation of her, this impression does not find an issue in any sensual excitation but in affection which has no erotic effect.... [This] psychical impotence... manifests itself in a refusal by the executive organs of sexuality to carry out the sexual act, although before and after they may show themselves to be intact and capable of performing the act.[30]

The madonna/whore complex is a psychological split between women who are objects of love and women who are objects of desire; "where they love they do not desire and where they desire they cannot love." If a man suffering from this complex comes to love a certain woman, he will not be able to regard her erotically, he will not be able to desire

29. On archetypes as originating within the human psyche, see pp. xxviii–xxix.
30. Sigmund Freud, "On the Universal Tendency of Debasement in the Sphere of Love," 11:179–86.

her, and ultimately, he will not be able to perform with her sexually. It is, says Freud, a form of psychological impotence.

What do men do who suffer from this complex? According to Freud, such men will frequently find an outlet in a type of lower-class, loose woman they see as a "debased sexual object":

> [Man] is assured of complete sexual pleasure only when he can devote himself unreservedly to obtaining satisfaction, which with his well-brought-up wife, for instance, he does not dare to do. This is the source of his need for a debased sexual object, a woman who is ethically inferior, to whom he need attribute no aesthetic scruples, who does not know him in his other social relations and cannot judge him in them. It is to such a woman that he prefers to devote his sexual potency, even when the whole of his affection belongs to a woman of a higher kind.[31]

This, for Freud, is the true origin of the feminine dichotomy, the division of women into loved and undesired madonnas, and desired but unloved whores.[32] Drawing on his psychological theory, I submit that it is not, as most critics claim, an aversion to sexual relations in general that plagues Rav Ḥiyya; it is an aversion, specifically, to sexual relations with his wife – the madonna.

Close Reading

Act 1

> It was Rav Ḥiyya bar Ashi's custom, whenever he prostrated himself in prayer, to say, "May the Merciful One save me from the evil inclination."
>
> One day his wife heard him. She said, "For many years he has separated himself from me. Why does he say this?"

---

31. Ibid., 185.
32. Although the madonna/whore complex, with its resulting impotence, afflicts only some, Freud claims that the separation of love from desire is fairly universal.

Act 2

One day he was studying in his garden.
His wife made herself up and passed before him repeatedly.
He said to her, "Who are you?"
She said, "I am Ḥeruta, and I just returned today."
He demanded her services.
She said to him, "Bring me the pomegranate from the top of that tree."
He jumped up, went, and brought it to her.

Act 3

When he came home, his wife was firing the oven.
He went and sat in it.
She said to him, "What is this?"
He said, "Such and such happened."
She said, "It was me."
He paid no attention to her until she gave him the signs.
He said to her, "Nevertheless, my intention was to violate a prohibition."
That righteous man fasted all of his days until he died of that death.

Act 1 – Revelation	*Home*	*Rav Ḥiyya, Wife*
Act 2 – Seduction	*Garden*	*Rav Ḥiyya, Ḥeruta*
Act 3 – Confrontation	*Home*	*Rav Ḥiyya, Wife*

Act 1 – Revelation

The point of departure for our story, as mentioned, is a routine of marital abstinence, a husband and wife who have gone for years without a moment's intimacy. If Rav Ḥiyya does indeed suffer from the madonna/whore complex, as this reading suggests, he would regard his wife – an object of what Freud calls "sacred love" – as far beyond the realm of the sensual, divested of all erotic desire. His sexual drive may remain potent, and dangerously so, yet his wife can no longer arouse it. Rav Ḥiyya, by this reading, does not refuse to fulfill his conjugal duty; he simply cannot.

And so we find Rav Ḥiyya, his face to the ground, praying to be protected from the sexual urge raging within him: *"May the Merciful One save me from the evil inclination."*[33] The lust from which Rav Ḥiyya begs to be saved is not, as it is usually read, for his own wife. Quite the contrary; his wife, saintly and pure and safely asexual, poses no danger whatsoever. It is for the women beneath her, the low, promiscuous women who threaten to burst the dam of his surging desire. Which, we shall see, is precisely what happens.[34]

And the wife? What did she make of her husband's prolonged celibacy? Judging by her surprised reaction to Rav Ḥiyya's unwitting revelation – *"Why does he say this?"* – the wife had evidently believed her husband to be beyond the hold of carnal passion, a holy man who had fought his evil inclination – and won. As such, she may have agreed to waive her conjugal right (which is her halakhic prerogative[35]), submitting to what she presumed to be her husband's wishes.

Herein lies the full tragedy of the Bar Ashis' marital life. A husband and wife, both contending with unfulfilled sexual needs, both believing themselves to be alone in their struggle. For what makes their situation all the more pitiable is their apparent inability to talk about it. Throughout the entire first act (which, although short, does describe a period of *many years*), Rav Ḥiyya and his wife engage in no dialogue at all. Rav Ḥiyya prefers to confess his yearnings in prayer, afraid perhaps that such an admission made to his chaste, madonna-like wife would sink him in her estimation. And the wife, for her part, does not dare tell her

33. According to Ari Elon, in rabbinic times prayer in prostration "was not an integral part of the fixed daily prayer... [but] an intimate supplication, occurring in the prostrator's innermost chamber... revealing the depths of his soul." Elon, "The Symbolization of the Plot Components," 35–109.

34. Such an interpretation more readily accounts for the urgency of Rav Ḥiyya's prayer, as extramarital relations are far more serious an offense than the breach of one's self-imposed abstinence from one's own wife.

35. Although a husband must perform his marital obligation at regular intervals, the Talmud does make the caveat that, if the wife grants her permission, the obligation may be deferred (Ketubot 61b).

holy man of a husband of her desire, for fear of incurring his contempt. Hence it is not just sexual relations that Rav Ḥiyya and his wife abstain from; it is all relations.

Until this routine is *one day* broken. Overhearing Rav Ḥiyya's anguished prayer, the wife realizes how wide the gulf between them has become, how her husband is no more a holy man than she is a madonna, how her own secret longings are mirrored by his. She does not, however, confront him on the subject, probably because she intuits that Rav Ḥiyya is so consumed by his complex that talking, at this point, would be completely futile.[36] Her husband will not touch her as long as she remains a madonna in his eyes. To bring down the barrier between them, she must become a whore instead.

Act 2 – Seduction

Act 2 begins with another *one day*, a second, more radical break in the routine. *One day [Rav Ḥiyya] was studying in his garden.* The action is transported from the order and propriety of the home to the garden, in all of its wildness and disorder. Gardens, in the Talmud, are depicted as enclosed spaces, typically at some distance from the home,[37] and are hardly ever used as a place of study.[38] The lush surroundings (and ultimately, the feminine seduction and the plucking of the fruit) bear ominous connotations to the Garden of Eden and the Tree of Knowledge. Rav Ḥiyya's controlled, celibate world is about to descend into sin.

And, just as the scenery changes, so is our heroine transformed. From a demure and dutiful madonna, she becomes a flagrant, defiant whore. Like the wanton women of the generation of the Flood, the wife *ma[kes] herself up*, seeking, in her painted disguise, to lure her husband into releasing his pent-up sexual energy, and at the same time, to satisfy her own desire (the Aramaic root K-SH-T – lit., make up or adorn – often

36. To say nothing of the fact that if the wife were to bring it up with Rav Ḥiyya, there would be no story to tell.

37. Beer, *The Babylonian Amoraim*, 107.

38. "We do find a number of instances of rabbis in their gardens, but it is always in the context of agricultural work." Ido Hevroni, "An Arrow in Satan's Eye: Contexts and Meaning in a Polemical Talmudic Story," 190.

denotes female preparation for sexual relations[39]). This is not, as is sometimes argued, a fidelity test, determining whether Rav Ḥiyya will succumb to the charms of another woman.[40] This is a sincere attempt to regain lost intimacy with her husband.

And indeed, no sooner does Rav Ḥiyya see this "ethically inferior" woman (to use Freud's words) than he demands her identity, his failure to recognize his own wife attesting to the degree of alienation between them. The wife responds, assuming the name Ḥeruta, the infamous local courtesan.[41] This two-line dialogue, while serving no direct plot-related purpose (in fact, the dramatic sequence would have been far more taut without it), constitutes the story's critical turning point.[42] For one thing, it is the first instance of dialogue in the narrative. The yearnings so carefully concealed in Act 1 are now openly announced, as the wife, hiding behind the mask of a prostitute, brazenly asserts her sexuality, while Rav Ḥiyya, faced with a woman who (again to quote Freud) "does not know him in his other social relations and cannot judge him in them," freely solicits her services.

Furthermore, the wife's declaration *"I am Ḥeruta, and I just returned today"* signifies – far more than her promiscuous dress or provocative manner – her transformation from a nameless, selfless wife-of to an independent, full-fledged subject. The former madonna has now

39. The wanton women are described as "made up as a harlot" (Genesis Rabba 23:2; see above, p. 92). Similar uses of the root are found in M Sotah 1:7, Shabbat 25b, Taanit 23b, and Tanḥuma Buber Miketz 15 (above, p. 98). "[The] root *K-SH-T* is commonly used for the act of adorning oneself by various methods, including the application of cosmetics, but also hairstyling, dress, and jewelry… [associated with] intercourse." Gail Labovitz, "'Even Your Mother and Your Mother's Mother': Rabbinic Literature on Women's Usage of Cosmetics," 14–20.

40. That the wife is not at all interested in trying her husband's loyalty is confirmed by her unruffled response to his confession of infidelity in Act 3 (see below, p. 109).

41. The general understanding of Ḥeruta as the name of a well-known prostitute dates back to Rashi who, according to Jonah Fraenkel, based it on an ancient tradition. Jonah Fraenkel, *The Aggadic Narrative: Harmony of Form and Content*, 65.

42. One might argue that the conversation serves to establish Rav Ḥiyya's ignorance of the courtesan's true identity, but this point is made abundantly clear in the exchange in Act 3.

returned, changed,[43] come into her own, established an identity unhinged from that of her husband. Naming, in Antiquity, was believed to confer power over the named object;[44] thus the wife, in naming herself, exhibits the autonomy and self-determination acquired in her new role as whore.

Third, and most significant, is the name the wife chooses. Ḥeruta, a name which appears nowhere else in rabbinic literature, has scholars disagreeing as to its meaning. It's been variously interpreted as liberty (given its similarity to the Hebrew equivalent *ḥerut*), reveler, wedding party, withered branch, and released prisoner.[45] Yet the most rigorous analysis of the name is found in Naeh's aforementioned essay. Surveying the mentions of Ḥeruta in contemporaneous Syriac sources (texts from roughly the same period and geographical region as our story), Naeh concludes that

> the word is remarkable for its Janus-like duality of meaning. On the one hand, it reflects a life of self-control and suppression of impulse – the celibacy and dignity that are the obligation of the social class of "free persons".... On the other hand, it expresses the enticements of the sort of freedom that entails unrestrained behavior, debauchery, and licentiousness.[46]

In referring to herself by a word which puns on the double meaning of "liberty" (as "freedom to" and "freedom from"), the wife proclaims her ability to exercise both sexual freedom, as a wanton harlot, and freedom from sexuality, as a freeborn noblewoman. The very name Ḥeruta collapses the categories of madonna and whore; it is, in this sense, symbolic of the narrative as a whole.

---

43. The Aramaic word for return, *hadar*, is also used to mean change (see, for example, Berakhot 5b, Shabbat 111a, Megilla 26b).
44. Adam's naming of the animals in the Garden of Eden (to which our story, as mentioned, alludes) is an expression of his dominion over the animal kingdom (Gen. 1:28); similar connections between naming and power are found, among others, in Plato (*Cratylus*, 389a) and Philo (*On the Creation*, 148).
45. Tal Ilan, *Silencing the Queen: The Literary Histories of Shelamzion and Other Jewish Women*, 88–89.
46. Naeh, "Freedom and Celibacy," 83.

These subtleties, however, are completely lost upon Rav Ḥiyya. Unable to resist his evil inclination any longer, he lays aside the Torah he's just been studying, and *demand[s] her services* (the Aramaic verb *tvaa* – lit., solicited – commonly refers to sexual relations of a coarse or animalistic kind;[47] such sexual conduct is typical of men suffering from the madonna/whore complex who, according to Freud, "do not usually show much refinement in their modes of behavior in love"[48]).

But our heroine is no longer a compliant wife. Before yielding to Rav Ḥiyya's demand, she requires that he bring her a pomegranate from the uppermost bough of the tree. This is more than just a standard fee for her services;[49] this is an integral part of her plan. If she is to cure her husband of his complex, she must be able to prove her identity to him after the deed is done. Rav Ḥiyya, his desire aflame, scrambles up the tree, plucks the fruit for her – and the narrator modestly draws the curtain on the scene.[50] The seduction, we can only infer, has succeeded.

Act 3 – Confrontation

With the opening of Act 3, the plot has shifted back indoors, into the order and civility of the home – and our heroine, accordingly, has slipped back into her role of devoted housewife. As the curtain once again rises, we find her *firing the oven*, making dinner, engaged in the most wifely of chores. She has gone from madonna to whore to madonna – from kindling her husband's lust to kindling the kitchen fire – with complete effortlessness. Pure and promiscuous, saintly and seductive, dutiful and defiant; all feminine binaries seem to dissolve in her person.

But if the wife can integrate dignity and desire, Rav Ḥiyya, sadly, cannot. The events of the past few hours, which have left her entirely

47. See, for example, Moed Katan 12a, Ḥagiga 15a, Ketubot 65a.

48. Freud, "On the Universal Tendency of Debasement," 184.

49. "A pomegranate is an accepted form of payment in situations of this type." Hevroni, "An Arrow in Satan's Eye," 202.

50. We might consider the possible phallic symbolism in Rav Ḥiyya's prostrate position in Act 1 and his ascent here (indeed, two of the accounts in the preceding story cycle feature seduced men who, in a surge of passion, climb to great heights to satisfy their lust).

unfazed, have traumatized him to the point of suicide. He comes home, sees his pure, innocent wife standing by the oven and, overcome with guilt and shame, throws himself into it.[51]

Perhaps from the sense of shock, perhaps from the newfound courage she acquired when she played the part of prostitute, the wife breaks her years of silence and turns to her husband in question: *"What is this?"* The barrier of communication is shattered; as opposed to the dual monologues of Act 1, and the masked dialogue of Act 2, Rav Ḥiyya and his wife, for the very first time, communicate directly. Unable to keep it from his wife, Rav Ḥiyya admits to his transgression – *"Such and such happened"* – probably afraid that now that she learns the truth about him, she will despise him forever.

And yet, rather than pain or anger or derision, his confession is met with one of her own: *"It was me."* The harlot in the garden, the debased sexual object, was her. Rav Ḥiyya, however, *pa[ys] no attention to her*. Clinging fiercely to his madonna-like conception of his wife, he refuses to believe her capable of such promiscuous conduct. But our heroine, knowing how far gone her husband is, was prepared for this disbelief. She presents him with the *signs* she was careful to obtain – most likely the pomegranate she had demanded as pay. If she could only get him to see her as she is – a good woman and a sexual woman, an object of love and desire – perhaps she could extricate him from the throes of the madonna/whore complex.

But to no avail. What should have come as inexplicable relief, the knowledge that his grave sin was not that grave after all, only devastates Rav Ḥiyya even more.[52] *"Nevertheless, my intention was to violate*

51. The image of a fiery oven has been long associated with the sexual urge ("They are all adulterers, as an oven heated by the baker"; Hosea 7:4) and is invoked elsewhere in the Talmud as a punishment for sexual transgression (Kiddushin 40a). "Because of the unique way in which it was fired up, the oven symbolized sin and its punishment." Yehoshua Brand, *Ceramics in Talmudic Literature*, 604.

52. Although having relations with one's wife while thinking she is someone else is roundly criticized (indeed, the very thought of another woman during intercourse is likened to extramarital sex; see Nedarim 20b, discussed on pp. 177–79), it is still nowhere near as grievous as adultery itself.

a prohibition," he says stonily, and turns away from his wife, perhaps in guilt, perhaps in contempt. Whether he cannot forgive himself for succumbing to his evil inclination, or cannot forgive her for failing to be the saint he had idolized, or both, is uncertain. What is clear, however, and tragically so, is that the wife's plan has miscarried. Rav Ḥiyya's complex is still firmly anchored in his mind, and within it she must remain – either a deified and untouched madonna, or a despised and untouched whore. Or a widow. For, unable to live with his burning sense of shame, the tormented Rav Ḥiyya fasts *until he die[s] of that death.*

In this context, it is interesting to note the parallelism between the story's second and third acts:

Act 2	**Act 3**
She makes herself up, passes before **him**	**He** throws himself into the oven before **her**
He questions **her** (*"Who are you?"*)	**She** questions **him** (*"What is this?"*)
She reveals her sexual self (*"I am Ḥeruta"*)	**He** reveals his sexual self *("Such and such happened"*)
He reciprocates, solicits her (*He demanded her services*)	**She** reciprocates, exposes herself (*"It was me"*)
She does not yield, demands wages	**He** does not yield, requires proof
He obtains the pomegranate	**She** produces the pomegranate
Encounter	Separation (death)

Here again, we may observe the stark difference between Rav Ḥiyya and his wife. After many years of silent struggle, as described in Act 1, Act 2 is the wife's (disguised) admission of sexuality, while Act 3 is Rav

Ḥiyya's. And yet, the very same sequence of events, when initiated by the wife, in whom madonna and whore are happily integrated, leads to an encounter, to a promise of renewed marital life; when they are initiated by Rav Ḥiyya, who cannot come to terms with his own sexuality, they lead to separation and, ultimately, death.

Broad Context: Judah and Tamar

Why, then, does the story end by calling Rav Ḥiyya *that righteous man*?

One answer is that the story's final line is a post-talmudic editorial insertion, added to blunt the edge of this otherwise scandalous narrative.[53] Another is the ironic sense in which *that righteous man* is sometimes used.[54] But I'd like to claim that the phrase is a direct allusion to our story's primary intertext – the biblical incident of Judah and Tamar:

> As soon as Tamar was told that her father-in-law was on his way to Timna to shear his sheep, she took off her widow's clothes, covered herself with a veil to disguise herself, and sat down at the entrance to Enaim, which is on the road to Timna. For she saw that Shela was grown up, and she hadn't been given to him in marriage. When Judah saw her, he thought she was a prostitute, for she had covered her face. Not realizing that she was his daughter-in-law, he went over to her by the roadside and said, "Come now, let me sleep with you." "And what will you give me to sleep with you?" she asked. "I'll send you a young goat from my flock," he said. "Will you give me something as a pledge until you send it?" she asked. He said, "What pledge should I give you?" "Your seal and its cord, and the staff in your hand," she answered. So he gave them to her and slept with her, and she became pregnant by him. After she left, she took off her veil and put on her widow's clothes again.... About three months later, Judah was told, "Your daughter-in-law Tamar is guilty of prostitution, and as a result she is now pregnant." Judah said, "Bring her

53. Significantly, the final line does not appear in the talmudic manuscripts, although it is included in all early printed editions. See Fraenkel, *The Aggadic Narrative*, 64.
54. See, for instance, Shabbat 55b, Megilla 16b, Nedarim 62a.

> out and let her be burned." As she was being brought out, she sent a message to her father-in-law. "I am pregnant by the man who owns these," she said. And she added, "See if you recognize whose seal and cord and staff these are." Judah recognized them and said, "She is more righteous than I, since I wouldn't give her to my son." (Gen. 38:13–26)

The similarities between the two narratives are clear: a woman suffering in silence through a long period of sexual privation,[55] a masquerade as prostitute, the man's failure to recognize his kinswoman, an outdoor seduction, a demand of pay (to be later used as proof), a punishment of death by fire, and, perhaps most importantly, a transition from madonna to whore with a simple change of dress.[56] Two remarkably similar stories, two diametrically opposite endings; for, while our story ends with death, the Genesis account ends with new life, as Tamar "give[s] birth [to] twin boys" (Gen. 38:27). The difference, I believe, lies in the men's response to discovering the true nature of their transgression: Judah is quick to admit to his misconduct and recognize that Tamar *"is more righteous than I"*; whereas Rav Ḥiyya holds fast to his image as *that righteous man*, digging himself ever deeper into self-flagellation and guilt, unable to see his wife to the end.

So far, our close reading has demonstrates how, through its tragic plotline (the disastrous consequences of the madonna/whore paradigm), its complex characterization (a heroine who easily transforms from madonna to whore), and its subtle symbolism (the heroine's choice of name, signifying both madonna and whore), the story systematically deconstructs the binary view of women. There is, however, a fourth and

55. Earlier in the chapter, we are told that Tamar had previously been widowed by Judah's first two sons and was waiting to marry his third (according to the ancient custom of levirate marriage, if a man died childless, his widow would be married to his brother to produce an heir). But Judah kept delaying the marriage, fearing that Tamar might be a black widow (see pp. 37–38).

56. Like Ḥeruta, Tamar's dual identity is also suggested by her name, interpreted to mean "she converted (*hemira*) herself into a whore" (Genesis Rabbati 38:6).

final aspect to consider: the way in which the narrative, in its very structure, dramatizes the disintegration of the feminine dichotomy.

The story, we have seen, comprises three acts, acts which form an elegant thesis—antithesis—synthesis triad: Act 1, the thesis, centered on the madonna in the home; Act 2, the antithesis, featuring the whore in the garden; and Act 3, the synthesis, effectively fusing the two. For, though we are back in the decorous home, and our heroine is once again a respectable housewife, there are nevertheless a number of whorish elements that punctuate the scene: the oven, at once maternal and menacing (a fitting symbol, as such, of woman's duality); the wife's assertiveness in demanding *"What is this?"*; her avowal *"It was me"* (*ana havai*), echoing her previous declaration *"I am Ḥeruta"* (*ana Ḥeruta*); the pomegranate, a double symbol of fertility and lust[57] – all these conflate the two preceding acts, blurring the boundaries between home and garden, order and chaos, propriety and passion. The narrative itself, like its heroine, enacts the collapse of the binary view of women; madonna and whore become one.

The Sugya: Deconstructing the Madonna/Whore Paradigm

It is not only the story that is governed by this threefold madonna (thesis)—whore (antithesis)—madonna/whore (synthesis) structure, it is also the wider halakhic discussion in which the story is situated. The sugya, in Kiddushin 80b–82a, deals with the laws of *yiḥud,* forbidden seclusion with members of the opposite sex. At the beginning of the discussion is a thesis, put forth by the Mishna: "A man may be alone with his mother and his daughter" (4:12). The text lists the women with whom one may seclude oneself – the safe, asexual women, the mothers divested of all carnal desire, the daughters who pose no erotic threat.

The Talmud then follows with an antithesis – the women one must beware – in a story cycle that reads like a catalog of adultery and sexual misconduct (80b–81b): a recently bereaved widow seduced by another at her husband's grave; a married woman engaging in an orgy with ten profligates; a suspected adulteress guarded by two sages lest she

57. Admiel Kosman, *Women's Tractate: Wisdom, Love, Faithfulness, Passion, Beauty, Sex, Holiness*, 87.

seduce her husband on the way to the *sotah* ritual; Rav Bibi trapped in Rav Yosef's attic to prevent his secluding himself with the latter's wife; Rav Amram, tempted by an attic full of captive women, climbing halfway up a ladder; Rabbi Meir and Rabbi Akiva, tempted by the Devil disguised as a woman, vaulting halfway across a river and up a palm tree; and at the end of the list, a perfect microcosm, the legend of Ḥeruta, with its madonna—whore—madonna/whore structure. The feminine dichotomy disintegrates.

The discussion is then brought to a close with a synthesis, as the Talmud revisits the opening words of the Mishna ("A man may be alone with his mother"; 81b). Now, however, the rabbis don't sound as sure. Can one seclude oneself with one's mother? It is, apparently, a matter of debate: Rav Assi permits, Shmuel forbids. The daughters are cast in a similarly uncertain light, as Rabbi Meir, we are told, was careful not to be alone with his daughter; Rabbi Tarfon took pains not to seclude himself with his daughter-in-law; and Rav Aḥa bar Aba, who held his little granddaughter in his lap, was admonished by her father for "handl[ing] a woman" (81b). The safely asexual women of the Mishna no longer seem as safe, nor as asexual. By the time the sugya reaches its end, the deconstruction of the madonna/whore paradigm is complete.

The Moral of the Story: The Danger of Instrumentalization

The rabbis might not have been able to transcend their patriarchal culture entirely, but there are certain instances in the Talmud where they show themselves to have been way ahead of their time. The story of Ḥeruta is one such instance. In a world steeped in the feminine dichotomy, the story emerges as an exceptional critique of the madonna/whore paradigm. Women, it implies, are not simply reproductive or sexual creatures. No woman is wholly pure, as no woman is altogether promiscuous. Regarding them as such is not just profoundly unethical; it is also patently untrue.

As ever, this lesson applies to all Others. No one, the rabbis seem to say (centuries before Kant's famous categorical imperative), should be treated solely as a means to an end.[58] No person should be reduced to a role or function that they fill for you. Such instrumentalization is not just wrong – as no one is that one-dimensional, and no person was put on this earth just to serve you – it is also unethical, it is dangerous, it will end in death. We must see the Other as we ourselves wish to be seen – in all of their fullness, in all their beauty, as an end to themselves. Only then can there really be a relationship, only then can we really have an encounter.

58. Writing some 1,200 years after the Talmud, philosopher Immanuel Kant made this rule the cornerstone of Western ethics: "Act in such a way that you treat humanity, whether in your own person or in the person of any other, never merely as a means to an end, but always at the same time as an end" (*Groundwork of the Metaphysics of Morals*, 4:429).

Beruria
The Overreacherix

The Archetype: A Woman with the Soul of a Man

> The malevolent female is one who usurps her role from the masculine domain, and... is condemned for acting like a man... sexual immorality... and refusal to become [a] "proper" woman of society.[1]

It is a story as old as time, or at least Greek tragedy. Prometheus stole fire from the gods and was bound to a rock, an eagle pecking at his liver for all eternity. Sisyphus cheated death and was made to push a boulder up a hill until the end of days. Icarus attempted to fly on waxen wings, came too close to the sun, and fell crashing to his death. This classic archetype is known as the overreacher, and his formula is simple: Man likens himself to a god. Man is guilty of hubris, the Greek term for unbridled arrogance. Hubris leads to nemesis, a fall, wherein man is destroyed by the very human nature he sought to overcome.[2]

1. Sarah Appleton Aguiar, *The Bitch Is Back: Wicked Women in Literature*, 5–29.
2. Harry Levin, *The Overreacher: A Study of Christopher Marlowe*, 24–25.

Moving this formula down the traditional hierarchy – from the God—man relationship to the man—woman relationship[3] – I'd like to propose a feminine equivalent. The overreacherix, as I shall call her, is a woman who likens herself to a man, engaging in a typical masculine pursuit. This, too, is an act of hubris. And here, too, hubris leads to nemesis, as the overreacherix falls precisely because of the feminine nature she thought herself able to transcend.

In the Bible, perhaps the most obvious example of the archetype is Jezebel, the mighty and Machiavellian queen. Though only a queen consort, Jezebel acts more like a reigning monarch, exploiting the king's powers to crush anyone who gets in her way. She is contemptuous of the law, constantly meddles in affairs of state, and murders the prophets of Israel en masse. Yet this thoroughly masculine queen is ultimately accused of feminine "harlotries and sorceries" (II Kings 9:22). Jezebel may have lived her life as a man, but she dies very much a woman. In her final moments, she is reduced to "paint[ing] her eyes… and dress[ing] her hair" (II Kings 9:30), in a desperate ploy to seduce her accuser and would-be assassin, Jehu. Unmoved by her advances, Jehu orders two eunuchs (tellingly, feminized men) to hurl her from the palace window, and she falls crashing to her death.

Jezebel, Basilica del Carmine

In rabbinic literature, it is Devora and Hulda, the two biblical prophetesses, who are charged with overreaching. Though presented in the Bible in an entirely positive light, Devora and Hulda's insistence on prophesying while female does not sit well with Rav Naḥman, who condemns their behavior as arrogant:

> Rav Naḥman said: Haughtiness does not befit women. There were two haughty women, and their names are loathsome, one being

3. "The analogy between a man's relation to God and a woman's relation to her husband is found explicitly in all three of the monotheistic religions." Wegner, "The Image and Status of Women," 98 n. 31.

> called a hornet [Devora] and the other a weasel [Hulda]. Of the hornet it is written, "And she sent and called Barak" (Judges 4:6), instead of going to him. Of the weasel it is written, "Say to the man" (II Kings 22:15), instead of "Say to the king." (Megilla 14b)

At least in the former case, such hubris leads to nemesis, with Devora's haughtiness causing her to lose her powers of prophecy.[4]

But it is not only prophecy that is regarded as beyond a woman's sphere. Talmud study, the heart of Jewish life, its chief occupation and highest of values, is also seen as an improper female pursuit. "Anyone who teaches his daughter Torah," says Rabbi Eliezer ben Hyrcanus, in what has become the prooftext for the exclusion of women from the beit midrash, "teaches her licentiousness" (M Sotah 3:4).[5] Herein is the entire story of the overreacherix, in one neat rabbinic formulation: Any woman who learns Talmud, that most male of male activities, will inevitably come to lechery, brought down by her inexorable female desire.[6]

In classical mythology, the overreacherix takes the form of the Amazons, the legendary kingdom of warrior women. Highly skilled in the arts of combat, riding, and archery (for which they seared off their right breasts), the Amazons vanquished armies of men across the ancient world. One day, so the myth goes, the Amazon queen, Hippolyta, fell in love with the king of Athens, Theseus, and betrayed her comrades to

---

4. "Anyone who acts haughtily… if he is a prophet, his prophecy departs from him, as is learned from Devora" (Pesaḥim 66b).
5. This is not the place to discuss the centrality of this Mishna in the historical debate over women and Talmud study, nor the many interpretations it has received in halakhic responsa throughout the generations. A few comments, however, are in order: First, the Torah Rabbi Eliezer speaks of is not the Written, but the Oral, Torah, i.e., Talmud. Second, the word here translated as "licentiousness," *tiflut*, is used elsewhere to mean frivolity (Y Taanit 4:5, Horayot 12b), but in this context clearly refers to sexual license (the Mishna will go on to say that, according to Rabbi Yehoshua, "A woman prefers one kab of food and *tiflut* to nine kab of food and abstinence"). Third, and most significant, this is one of two opinions that appear in the Mishna, the other one being that "a man must teach his daughter Torah." For a careful teasing out of the voices for and against women's Talmud study in rabbinic literature, see Boyarin, *Carnal Israel*, 170–81.
6. On the danger of the female sexual urge, see p. 34 n. 21.

fight at his side. Thus were the otherwise "man-like Amazons"[7] destroyed by the weakness of a woman's heart; the Athenians won the war, Hippolyta was killed, and the Amazons suffered a devastating defeat.

Amazon Preparing for Battle, Pierre Eugene-Emile Hebert

A similar fate befell the historical, though no less legendary, Cleopatra, ruler of Egypt and self-proclaimed "queen of kings." A shrewd stateswoman, Cleopatra used her charms to forge alliances – and liaisons – with the two most powerful men of the Roman Empire, Julius Caesar and Mark Antony. She bore them both sons, and drew on their patronage to solidify her hold over Egypt and rid herself of rivals to the throne. This earned her a reputation of "*regina meretrix* (the harlot queen), inflated with vanity and disdainful arrogance,"[8] and ultimately led to her undoing; her relationship with Mark Antony sparked a civil war in Rome, culminating in her capture, death by suicide, and the fall of the three-hundred-year Ptolemaic dynasty.

If Cleopatra was dubbed *regina meretrix*, Valeria Messalina, her near-contemporary to the north, was known as *meretrix augusta* (the imperial harlot). Messalina, third wife of the Roman Emperor Claudius, was notorious for her cold and calculating nature, ruthlessly killing off all political enemies, including many members of her own family. She was also overtly promiscuous, engaging in multiple adulterous affairs and frequent visits to the brothels of Rome:

When Claudius Is Away Messalina Will Play, A. Pigma

> To cruelty in the prosecution of her purposes, she added the most abandoned incontinence. Not confining her licentiousness within the limits of the palace, where she committed the most

7. Homer, *The Iliad,* 3:249.
8. Pliny the Elder, *Natural History,* 9:58.

> shameful excesses, she prostituted her person in the common stews, and even in the public streets of the capital… [her] lewdness resounded throughout the empire.[9]

It was this insatiable lust – both for power and for sexual pleasure – that brought about Messalina's ruin. With her husband out of town, Messalina married her lover, Senator Gaius Silius, in an apparent bid to unseat Claudius. News of the extravagant wedding reached Claudius, and Messalina was executed, her name going down in history as a byword for cruelty and depravity.

Yet for all of the overreacherixes of Antiquity, it is in the Middle Ages that the archetype really comes to the fore. Medieval biblical commentaries, Jewish and Christian alike, emphasize the link between a woman's conducting herself like a man and her fall into promiscuity. Interpreting the verse "A woman must not wear a man's garment" (Deut. 22:5), Rashi says: "So that she resembles a man, in order to consort with men, which can only lead to unchastity"; Ibn Ezra, for his part, explains that "a woman is created only for childbirth, and if she were to join men in war she would come to harlotry"; and Thomas Aquinas, writing from an entirely different religious tradition, contends: "Of itself it is sinful for a woman to wear male clothing… since this can be a cause of lasciviousness."[10]

Confirming these warnings against the dangers of cross-dressing was the scandalous account of Pope Joan, an exceptionally learned young woman who disguised herself as a man, rose in the ranks of the Catholic Church, and was eventually elected to its highest office:

> John Anglicus, born at Mainz, was pope for two years, seven months and four days, and died in Rome, after which there was a vacancy in the Papacy of one month. It is claimed that this John was a woman, who as a girl had been led to Athens dressed in the clothes of a man by a certain lover of hers. There she became proficient in a diversity of branches of knowledge, until she had no

9. Suetonius, *Remarks on the Life and Times of the Emperor Claudius*, ch. 46.
10. Thomas Aquinas, *Summa Theologica*, 2:2:169.

> equal, and, afterward in Rome, she taught the liberal arts and had great masters among her students and audience. A high opinion of her life and learning arose in the city; and she was chosen for pope. While pope, however, she became pregnant by her companion. Through ignorance of the exact time when the birth was expected, she was delivered of a child while in procession from St. Peter's to the Lateran, in a lane once named Via Sacra (the sacred way) but now known as the "shunned street".... After her death, it is said she was buried in that same place.... Nor is she placed on the list of the holy pontiffs, both because of her female sex and on account of the foulness of the matter.[11]

According to one version of events, Pope Joan's death was caused, not by complications of childbirth, but by an angry mob who lynched her after discovering she was not a man.

Another medieval cross-dresser punished for her gender transgressions was Joan of Arc, arguably the most famous overreacherix of Western history. At just seventeen, Joan, with no military training but with an iron will and indomitable sense of purpose, led the French army to a series of victories over the English. She fought with the ferocity of a born soldier, and in standard army uniform. When finally captured, she was tried and convicted for "[wearing] clothing and armor such as is worn by men... a thing contrary to divine law and abominable before God," and was burned at the stake.[12]

Catherine the Great, empress of Russia, was one of the most powerful female monarchs of the modern era. Formidable and ambitious, Catherine seized the throne from her husband, Peter III, and went on to turn Russia into one of the largest and greatest countries in Europe. Over the course of her long reign, Catherine took a series of lovers (many of them significantly younger than herself), and was sometimes called "Messalina of the Neva." "She had two passions which never left her but with her last breath," wrote a court biographer, "the love of man,

11. Martin Polonus, *Chronicle of the Popes and Emperors*, ch. 12.
12. W.S. Scott, ed., *The Trial of Joan of Arc: Being the verbatim report of the proceedings from the Orleans Manuscript*, 52.

which degenerated into licentiousness, and the love of glory, which sank into vanity."[13] Rumors of Catherine's sexual escapades ran wild, culminating in the popular report of her death being the result of a failed attempt to have intercourse with her favorite stallion.

An Imperial Stride, William Holland

None of these historical overreacherixes, it must be said, were quite the harlots history has proclaimed them to be. Cleopatra presumably only ever had two sexual partners in her life; Messalina and Catherine, adulteresses though they were, probably did not engage in outright prostitution or bestiality; Joan of Arc was a devout Christian who only wore men's clothes to fight in battle and protect herself from assault in prison; Pope Joan, like the Amazons, was a myth and never actually existed.[14] All these legends were part of calculated smear campaigns by rival religious or political factions, for whom the aberration of a woman in power was an easy target.

What is historically true, however, is the 19th-century phenomenon of cross-dressing doctors. Since for the best part of modern history, a woman could not study or practice medicine, the 19th century saw several cases of highly gifted women who passed themselves off as men in order to pursue successful medical careers. Margaret Ann Bulkley became Dr. James Barry, a distinguished military surgeon who advanced to the rank of inspector general, improved medical conditions in hospitals across the British Empire, and performed the first recorded Caesarean section in Africa. Sarah Emma Edmonds turned herself into Franklin Flint Thompson, enlisted in the Union Army as a military nurse, and was praised for being fierce and resourceful on the battlefield. Enriqueta Favez took on the dress and military rank of her deceased husband, enrolled in the Sorbonne, and went on to become the first female surgeon in modern times, initially in the French army, and then in a thriving private practice in Cuba. Yet in spite of their considerable achievements,

13. Charles François Philibert Masson, *Secret Memoirs of the Court of St. Petersburg*, 1:88.

14. On the cultural significance of ahistorical representation, see p. 4 n. 5.

none of these doctors in disguise came to a good end. James Barry developed a brash and violent temper (set off by insinuations of "his" effeminacy), got into a series of conflicts and physical fights, and was on a number of occasions arrested and demoted for aggressive behavior; despite her dying wish to be buried in her clothes, her sex was discovered and leaked to the press by a charwoman who laid out her body, causing a scandal that rocked British society. Private Thompson contracted malaria, abandoned her army post for fear of being found out, and was subsequently charged with desertion. Dr. Enrique Favez was exposed by a servant, put on trial for the illegal practice of medicine and for deceiving another woman into marriage, and sentenced to four years in prison.

Another vocation historically denied to women was that of artistic creation. Trying to explain "why no woman wrote a word of extraordinary literature when every other man, it seemed, was capable of song or sonnet," Virginia Woolf imagines what life would have been like for Judith Shakespeare, fictional sister of the famous William. Although Judith, as described by Woolf, was every bit as talented as her brother, her attempt to enter his profession could only end in tragedy:

> Shakespeare himself went, very probably... to the grammar school, where he may have learned Latin – Ovid, Virgil, and Horace – and the elements of grammar and logic.... Very soon he got work in the theatre, became a successful actor, and lived at the hub of the universe, meeting everybody, knowing everybody, practicing his art on the boards, exercising his wits in the streets, and even getting access to the palace of the queen. Meanwhile his extraordinarily gifted sister, let us suppose, remained at home. She was as adventurous, as imaginative, as agog to see the world as he was. But she was not sent to school. She had no chance of learning grammar and logic, let alone of reading Horace and Virgil. She picked up a book now and then, one of her brother's perhaps, and read a few pages. But then her parents came in and told her to mend the stockings or mind the stew and not moon about with books and papers.... The force of her own gift alone drove her to it. She made up a small parcel of her belongings, let herself down by a rope one summer's night and took the road to

> London. She was not seventeen. The birds that sang in the hedge were not more musical than she was. She had the quickest fancy, a gift like her brother's, for the tune of words. Like him, she had a taste for the theatre. She stood at the stage door; she wanted to act, she said. Men laughed in her face. The manager – a fat, loose-lipped man – guffawed. He bellowed something about poodles dancing and women acting – no woman, he said, could possibly be an actress. He hinted – you can imagine what. She could get no training in her craft. Could she even seek her dinner in a tavern or roam the streets at midnight? Yet her genius was for fiction and lusted to feed abundantly upon the lives of men and women and the study of their ways. At last... Nick Greene the actor-manager took pity on her; she found herself with child by that gentleman and so – who shall measure the heat and violence of the poet's heart when caught and tangled in a woman's body? – killed herself one winter's night and lies buried at some cross-roads where the omnibuses now stop outside the Elephant and Castle. That, more or less, is how the story would run, I think, if a woman in Shakespeare's day had had Shakespeare's genius.[15]

And, of course, there's Yentl, the rabbi's daughter who had "the soul of a man." After years of secretly learning with her father, Yentl dresses in his rabbinic garb, cuts her hair, and enters a yeshiva to pursue her love of Talmud. "Only now did Yentl grasp the meaning of the Torah's prohibition against wearing clothes of the other sex.... I'm wicked, a transgressor... she told herself. Her only justification was that she had taken all these burdens upon herself because her soul thirsted to study Torah."[16] Disaster isn't far to follow; Yentl falls in love with her ḥavruta, is married off to a wealthy man's daughter,

Yentl, Metro-Goldwyn-Mayer

15. Virginia Woolf, *A Room of One's Own*, 69–75.
16. Isaac Bashevis Singer, "Yentl the Yeshiva Boy."

and when the lies close in on her, she escapes, leaving destruction and heartbreak in her wake.

Hence the overreacherix – whether queen or doctor, scholar or soldier, pope or prophetess – is a woman who transgresses gender boundaries, taking up a traditionally male role; talented and ambitious, she excels in her pursuit, rising above the men in her field; is accordingly arrogant and aggressive in her behavior; and is ultimately felled by her inescapable feminine (so as not to say, sexual[17]) nature. Overreaching leads to hubris leads to nemesis.

Which leads us to Beruria.

Primary Reading: The Curious Incident of Beruria's Transgression

Best known and most complex of the women of the Talmud, Beruria poses a unique challenge for readers.[18] She is the one woman in rabbinic literature described as an actual Torah scholar; the Talmud attaches her name to the verb *tanya* (lit., to learn or teach by recitation), ascribing to her the official activity of the beit midrash.[19] Beruria is thus placed squarely within the ranks of the rabbis, a rare woman in the world of Torah, sage among sages. As such, she has become the poster woman for a variety of modern causes: Jewish feminism, women's study of Talmud, female religious leadership. These causes – whether one is for or against them – have inevitably colored the way Beruria is read. Schools have been named for her, responsa written against her; she's been hailed as

---

17. Femininity, writes Simone de Beauvoir, has always been equated with sexuality: "[Woman] is called 'the sex,' by which is meant that she appears essentially to the male as a sexual being. For him she is sex – absolute sex, no less." Beauvoir, *The Second Sex*, 16.
18. The name Beruria has been interpreted as either a variation of the Latin name Valeria or a compound of the Hebrew root B-R-R with the common -ya suffix. David Goodblatt, "The Beruriah Traditions," 68 n. 1.
19. Pesaḥim 62b (discussed below, p. 136). While it is true that both Yalta (Chapter 1) and Ima Shalom (Chapter 6) are depicted as halakhically knowledgeable, neither has Beruria's scholarly credentials.

a heroine and denounced as a transgressor; held up as both model and cautionary tale. The stakes of interpretation are high, and many is the reader who's allowed their ideology to influence their understanding of the text. We are all of us, as mentioned, entitled to our biases – but we cannot let them get in the way of our reading.

Furthermore, Beruria is not just the most ideologically charged woman of the Talmud, she is also the most textually diffuse. From 3rd-century Israel to 7th-century Babylonia to 11th-century Europe, references to Beruria span nearly a thousand years of texts, and sometimes portray wildly different women, making her character particularly difficult to pin down.

But of all the narratives of Beruria, perhaps the most famous is the "Beruria Incident" – the scandalous account of Beruria's adulterous affair and subsequent suicide. The Incident, widely accepted as part of the rabbinic portrayal of Beruria, is not actually in the Talmud; it is in Rashi's 11th-century commentary, written some four hundred years after the Bavli. Yet this is the story for which Beruria is best known:

> Once Beruria mocked the words of the rabbis, "Women are flighty."
> Rabbi Meir said to her, "By your life! You will ultimately admit to their words."
> He instructed one of his disciples to tempt her to transgression.
> The disciple entreated her for many days until she gave in to him.
> When the matter became known to her, she strangled herself, and Rabbi Meir fled because of the disgrace. (Rashi, Avoda Zara 18b)

At first reading, the Beruria Incident is a classic overreacherix tale: Beruria, the female sage, the woman in the world of Torah, *mock[s] the words of the rabbis*. The saying "Women are flighty" appears a number of times in rabbinic literature, and is generally understood to mean that women are weak-minded (and therefore susceptible to seduction).[20] But Beruria, in her arrogance, believes she knows better than the rabbis,

20. Shabbat 33b, Kiddushin 80b, Tanḥuma Vayera 22. This notion is not unique to rabbinic culture, and is found throughout the ancient world; the Romans, for instance,

believes she herself can disprove their dictum; she, after all, is a scholar, and not the least bit weak-minded. Scolding her for her derision, and determined to prove her wrong, Beruria's husband Rabbi Meir sends a disciple *to tempt her to transgression*. Sure enough, Beruria is seduced, falls into disrepute, and *strangle[s] herself*, destroyed by the very feminine flightiness she thought she could transcend.[21] Overreaching. Hubris. Nemesis.

It is not only Beruria who is destroyed by this fall. The notorious Incident is an indictment not just of Beruria, but of all women Torah scholars. Rabbi Eliezer's warning is in effect confirmed: Beruria's father had taught her Torah, and so she came to licentiousness.

Accordingly, the Beruria Incident has become a favorite exemplum of halakhic decisors writing against the study of Talmud for women. From the Maharil (Rabbi Jacob Moellin) in the 14th century to the *Tzitz Eliezer* (Rabbi Eliezer Waldenberg) in the 20th, decisors quote the story of Beruria's infamous end to prove that women learning Talmud cannot but fall into promiscuity: "Beruria's end demonstrates her beginning... since at first they would teach [women Talmud], but from what had happened to Beruria they agreed that the law followed Rabbi Eliezer."[22] As such, Beruria is something of an Eve figure, for whose original sin all Jewish women are punished, forever banned from the world of Torah.

But is this really the story the Talmud is telling? Or rather, is this the story the Talmud is telling at all?

In Search of the Beruria Incident

Two questions, then, confront us as we try and unpack the character of Beruria: One, is she really the overreacherix the Beruria Incident makes her out to be, and two, how does Rashi come by his outrageous story?[23]

decreed that women should remain under the perpetual guardianship of men "on account of their instability of judgment." Gaius, *Institutes*, 1:144.

21. In this respect, the Beruria Incident is something of a gender reversal of the standard rabbinic seduction story we find throughout the Talmud (see pp. 26–27).

22. Rabbi Eliezer Waldenberg, *Tzitz Eliezer*, 9:3.

23. The story's shocking details – a great rabbi sending his disciple to seduce his own wife, the consequent adultery, the ultimate suicide – are so at odds with rabbinic

Rashi, famously, does not write stories. Rashi writes commentary, explaining linguistic and logical difficulties in the talmudic text. On the rare occasion when Rashi does quote a narrative in his comments, it is precisely that – a quote of an earlier tradition.[24] In this case, however, no such earlier tradition exists; not in rabbinic, geonic, or early medieval literature. The Beruria Incident is nowhere to be found.

Broad Context: Beruria

Our search for the Beruria Incident begins, as ever, with context. Since Beruria appears so many times throughout rabbinic literature, let's explore these appearances and see if they can shed light on her nature and the provenance of her Incident.

(i)

> A *claustra*: Rabbi Tarfon pronounces it impure, and the rabbis pronounce it pure. Beruria says: He may remove it from one door and hang it on another on Shabbat. These things were said to Rabbi Yehoshua. He said: Beruria has spoken well. (T Kelim Bava Metzia 1:6)

The first mention of Beruria is in the early rabbinic work of the Tosefta. The passage in question concerns a *claustra*, a door bolt which could be removed from the door and used as an independent utensil (for grinding spices and the like). Rabbi Tarfon and the rabbis debate whether such an object can contract impurity, and Beruria declares that it may be moved on Shabbat.[25] A seemingly unremarkable law, noteworthy

values, there have been several attempts to explain them away. One commentator claims that the disciple was surreptitiously replaced by Rabbi Meir moments before the deed was done (Rabbi Gedalia Ibn Yahya, *Shalshelet HaKabbala*, s.v. "Rashbag II"); another says the disciple was a eunuch, and therefore incapable of consummating the seduction (Rabbi Yosef Hayim of Baghdad, *Ben Yehoyada*, Avoda Zara 18b). These obviously apologetic readings have no basis in the text itself.

24. Avraham Grossman, *Rashi*, 140.

25. At the heart of the debate is the *claustra*'s object status: is it a utensil in its own right (in which case it can become impure) or is it part of the door (in which case it remains

only because of the gender of the transmitter; this is one of just two laws in all of early rabbinic literature that are transmitted by a woman, and the only one where the woman is named. This might explain why the Tosefta adds that *Rabbi Yehoshua said: Beruria has spoken well.* Such approbations by a senior rabbinic authority are relatively rare, and this one was probably needed to lend credence to the law, given the identity of its transmitter. For our purpose, however, it is fortuitous, as it allows us to date Beruria: Rabbi Yehoshua is Rabbi Yehoshua ben Ḥanania, a leading figure of the first generation of rabbis, one of the founders of the beit midrash of Yavneh.[26] This places Beruria at the very beginning of the rabbinic period, in the late 1st or early 2nd century.

The same *claustra* law appears, practically word for word, in the Mishna, with one conspicuous difference:

> A *claustra* is impure… Rabbi Yehoshua says: He may remove it from one door and hang it on another on Shabbat. (M Kelim 11:4)

The approbator in the Tosefta becomes, in the more authoritative text of the Mishna, the transmitter. Since the Tosefta contains a great deal of material not included in the Mishna, and since it is far more plausible that a woman would be edited out of – rather than into – a halakhic discussion, we can assume that Beruria was the original transmitter, and that the editors of the Mishna chose to erase her name. A woman Torah scholar was, for them, an aberration.[27] Beruria's Torah may have been preserved by the Mishna, but Beruria herself was not.

The Beruria of the Tosefta is thus fully consistent with the archetype of the overreacherix: a female sage, taking part in the exclusively

pure, and may be moved on Shabbat). For a similar discussion, see p. 186 n. 60.

26. When early rabbinic literature mentions simply "Rabbi Yehoshua" without an additional appellation ("ben Korḥa," "ben Levi," etc.), the reference is to Rabbi Yehoshua ben Ḥanania. Strack and Stemberger, *Introduction to the Talmud and Midrash*, 70. It was Rabbi Yehoshua who, together with Rabbi Eliezer ben Hyrcanus, smuggled Rabbi Yoḥanan ben Zakkai out of the besieged Jerusalem in a coffin (see p. 79; for the charged relationship between these two founding fathers of rabbinic culture, see Chapter 6).

27. Tellingly, there are no laws transmitted by a woman in the Mishna.

male role of transmitting laws (although it has been claimed that the *claustra* law is no evidence of a formal rabbinic education, but rather that Beruria, as a woman, simply knew her way around the kitchen[28]).

However, it is when we move from the Tosefta (3rd-century Israel) to the Talmud (7th-century Babylonia) that the character of Beruria becomes really interesting.

(ii)

> Rabbi Simlai came before Rabbi Yoḥanan. He said to him, "Let the master teach me the Book of Genealogies." He said to him, "Where are you from?" He answered, "From Lod." "And where is your residence?" "In Nehardea." He said to him, "We teach this book neither to Lodites nor to Nehardeans, and certainly not to you, who are from Lod and whose residence is in Nehardea." Rabbi Simlai pressed him, and he consented. Rabbi Simlai said to him, "Let the master teach me the book in three months." Rabbi Yoḥanan took a clod of earth, threw it at him, and said, "If Beruria, the wife of Rabbi Meir, the daughter of Rabbi Ḥanania ben Teradyon, learned (*detanya*) three hundred traditions in a day from three hundred rabbis, and even so did not fulfill her responsibility in three years – how can you say in three months?" (Pesaḥim 62b)

Beruria doesn't actually appear in this talmudic story, but the reference to her is significant. Rabbi Simlai, so the story goes, asks Rabbi Yoḥanan to teach him the Book of Genealogies, an arcane and complicated text taught only to very advanced students.[29] He is refused, because of, well, his genealogy. Rabbi Simlai is a Nehardean, and used to be a Lodite, and neither group was deemed capable of learning such a difficult text

28. "Details of rabbinic law relating to the kitchen and house would be known by a woman who grew up in a rabbinic household. Girls would learn these rules from their mother when they helped out with the housework.... Talmudic literature refers to several women who possess knowledge of this type." Goodblatt, "The Beruriah Traditions," 83. On the domesticity of women, see Chapter 6.

29. The Talmud goes on to explain that the book is about the genealogical lists discussed in the opening chapters of I Chronicles.

(according to the Yerushalmi version of the story, Nehardeans were considered uncouth, Lodites ignorant[30]). After prevailing on Rabbi Yoḥanan to teach him nonetheless, Rabbi Simlai, pressing his advantage, asks that they complete their study in just three months. Exasperated, Rabbi Yoḥanan throws a handful of dirt at him, remonstrating that *if Beruria,* who *learned three hundred traditions in a day from three hundred rabbis,* could not complete the book in three years, how dare he presume to do it in three months?

Herein are two important elements the Talmud adds to the portrayal of Beruria. The first are her family connections. Beruria is described as *the wife of Rabbi Meir, the daughter of Rabbi Ḥanania ben Teradyon.* These connections, although consistent throughout the Talmud, are entirely absent from Beruria's original appearance in the Tosefta. Where, then, do they come from?

As mentioned, there are only two laws in early rabbinic literature transmitted by a woman. Beruria's was one. This is the other:

> From what time does an oven become unclean?... Said Rabbi Ḥalafta of Kfar Ḥanania: I asked Shimon ben Ḥanania who asked Rabbi Ḥanania ben Teradyon's son and he said, From the time when it is removed from its place. And his daughter said, From the time when it is disassembled. When these things were said before Rabbi Yehuda ben Bava, he said: His daughter has spoken better than his son. (T Kelim Bava Kama 4:17)

This law is strikingly similar to Beruria's: Both concern the purity of objects (and are quoted in different divisions of Tosefta Kelim, lit., objects), both are transmitted by women, and both, consequently, are sanctioned by a rabbinic authority. Given the anomaly of a learned woman in the rabbinic world, the talmudic editors take it for granted that these two female transmitters are one and the same, and accordingly conflate them. Thus does Beruria become the daughter of Rabbi Ḥanania ben Teradyon.

30. Y Pesaḥim 5:3 (interestingly, this version makes no mention of Beruria).

That Beruria's family ties are a strict talmudic invention is evidenced by the fact that there is no reference to them in the Tosefta, which as a legal work, is far less prone to fiction,[31] and as a text originating in 3rd-century Israel, is closer to Beruria in time and place and therefore more historically reliable.[32] In addition, from what the Tosefta does tell us of Beruria, we know her to have been a contemporary of Rabbi Yehoshua ben Ḥanania, who lived one generation before Rabbi Ḥanania ben Teradyon (noted for being one of the martyrs of the Bar Kokhba Revolt, c. 135 CE[33]) and two generations before Rabbi Meir, making it highly unlikely that she was the former's daughter or the latter's wife. Finally, since the Talmud routinely links rabbis to one another through fictitious familial relationships, it is more than probable that it does so here, as well.[34]

So Beruria's characterization as *the wife of Rabbi Meir, the daughter of Rabbi Ḥanania ben Teradyon* is a talmudic fiction.[35] What of it? The stories of the Talmud, as I have said before, are literature, not history. If the Talmud consistently presents Beruria as Rabbi Meir's wife and Rabbi Ḥanania's daughter, what should it matter that these relationships (like so much else in talmudic storytelling) are a literary construct? Why should we care about the historicity of Beruria's

---

31. Tal Ilan, *Integrating Women into Second Temple History*, 178.
32. Neusner, *Development of a Legend*, 297.
33. See Avoda Zara 17b–18a (below, pp. 139–40).
34. In an influential essay on the subject, Shmuel Safrai shows how the Babylonian Talmud typically depicts important figures of rabbinic culture as related to one another, even though there is no indication of these relationships in earlier (and hence more credible) sources. Shmuel Safrai, "Tales of the Sages in the Palestinian Tradition and the Babylonian Talmud," 229–32. More often than not, such fictional ties are created through the character of a woman; Queen Shlomzion, for instance, connects her brother Rabbi Shimon ben Shataḥ with her husband King Yannai (Berakhot 48a), Kalba Savua's daughter connects him with her husband Rabbi Akiva (Ketubot 62b), and Beruria, similarly, links Rabbi Ḥanania ben Teradyon to Rabbi Meir.
35. The point is conclusively demonstrated in Goodblatt, "The Beruriah Traditions," 81–82; and Ilan, *Integrating Women*, 176–97. Ilan argues elsewhere that the Talmud's endowing of Beruria with male relations who were themselves great scholars serves to "tame" Beruria, making her "a dutiful sage's daughter… and the docile wife of another sage." Ilan, *Mine and Yours*, 110. I'm not sure, however, that "dutiful" and "docile" are apt descriptions of Beruria's talmudic portrayal, as we shall see.

family connections, any more than the real-life relationship of Abaye and Rava,[36] or whether Jerusalem was in fact destroyed because of Kamtza and Bar Kamtza?[37]

The Non-Beruria Narratives

The answer, of course, is that we shouldn't. But if the ahistorical nature of Beruria's family ties shouldn't stop us from trying to understand the Beruria of the Talmud, it should give us pause when considering other, non-talmudic narratives.

Specifically, there are two stories in rabbinic literature that feature Rabbi Ḥanania ben Teradyon's daughter, without referring to Beruria by name. Both stories deal with tragedies which befall the Ben Teradyon family: the martyrdom of the parents and forced prostitution of the daughter,[38] and the criminal life and assassination of the son.[39] Both appear in texts which, like the Tosefta, originate in Israel and precede

---

36. P. 42 n. 33.

37. P. 68.

38. "When they arrested Rabbi Ḥanania ben Teradyon … they said to him, 'You have been sentenced to be burned together with your Torah scroll.' He recited this verse: 'The Rock, His work is perfect, for all His ways are justice' (Deut. 32:4). They said to his wife, 'Your husband has been sentenced to be burned, and you have been sentenced to be killed.' She recited this verse: 'A God of faithfulness and without iniquity, just and right is He' (ibid.). They said to his daughter, 'Your father has been sentenced to be burned, your mother to be killed, and you have been sentenced to prostitution.' She recited this verse: 'Great in counsel and mighty in deed; whose eyes are open to all the ways of men, rewarding every man according to his ways and according to the fruit of his doings' (Jer. 32:19)" (Sifrei Deuteronomy 307).

 This account closely resembles the Talmud's description of Rabbi Ḥanania's martyrdom in Avoda Zara 17b–18a.

39. "It happened that the son of Rabbi Ḥanina ben Tardion [sic] fell into evil ways. Brigands seized him and slew him. His mutilated body was found after three days. They then brought him into the city and eulogized him out of respect for his father and mother. His father recited this verse over him: 'How have I hated instruction, and my heart despised reproof, neither have I hearkened to the voice of my teacher, nor inclined my ear to them that instructed me I was nigh in all evil' (Prov. 5:12–14).… His mother recited this verse over him: 'A foolish son is a vexation to his father, and bitterness to her that bore him' (Prov. 17:25). His sister recited this verse over him: 'Bread of falsehood is sweet to a man; but afterward his mouth shall be filled with gravel' (Prov. 20:17)" (Semaḥot 12:13).

the Talmud: Sifrei Deuteronomy and Tractate Semaḥot.[40] And since the identification of Beruria with Rabbi Ḥanania's daughter was only made in the Babylonian Talmud, centuries later, both cannot be read as Beruria narratives.[41]

Likewise, there is a story which speaks only of Rabbi Meir's wife, again without naming Beruria. This story, a rabbinic meditation on the verse "A good wife who can find?" (Prov. 31:10), tells of the time Rabbi Meir's two sons had died and his pious wife kept it from him until after Shabbat, when she broke the news gently and in full acceptance of God's judgment.[42] The story is frequently included in analyses of Beruria's character, even though it appears in Midrash Mishlei, a work of uncertain

40. The two works are traditionally dated to the late 3rd century; Strack and Stemberger, *Introduction to the Talmud and Midrash*, 229, 273.

41. What's more, according to Avoda Zara 18a, Rabbi Ḥanania ben Teradyon had two daughters (see below, pp. 139–40); even if we were to suppose that the Beruria—Rabbi Ḥanania's daughter association was made as early as the 3rd century, and in Israel, we would still have no proof that the daughter mentioned in these passages is actually Beruria and not her sister.

42. "It once happened that Rabbi Meir was sitting and lecturing in the beit midrash on Shabbat afternoon, and his two sons died. What did their mother do? She laid the two of them on the bed and spread a sheet over them. After the departure of the Shabbat, Rabbi Meir came home from the beit midrash. He said to her, 'Where are my two sons?' She said, 'They went to the beit midrash.' He said, 'I was watching the beit midrash, and I did not see them.' She gave him a cup for *Havdala* (the blessing for the end of Shabbat), and he recited the *Havdala*. He again said, 'Where are my two sons?' She said to him, 'They went to another place and will soon come.' She set food before him, and he ate and blessed. After he blessed, she said, 'Rabbi, I have a question to ask you.' He said to her, 'Ask your question.' She said to him, 'Rabbi, some time ago a man came and gave me something to keep for him. Now he comes and seeks to take it. Shall we return it to him or not?' He said to her, 'My daughter, whoever has an object in trust must return it to its owner.' She said to him, 'Rabbi, I would not have given it to him without your knowledge.' What did she do? She took him by the hand and led him up to the room. She led him to the bed and removed the sheet that was on them. When he saw the two of them lying dead on the bed, he began to cry and say, 'My sons, my sons'.... At that time she said to Rabbi Meir, 'Rabbi, did you not say to me that I must return the trust to its master?' He said, 'The Lord gave and the Lord has taken away; blessed be the name of the Lord' (Job 1:21). Rabbi Ḥanina said: In this way she comforted him, and his mind was set at ease. Regarding such an instance does it say, 'A good wife who can find?' (Prov. 31:10)" (Midrash Mishlei 31:10).

provenance,[43] and even though the woman it describes – dutiful, self-denying, submissive – is wholly inconsistent with the assertive, self-assured Beruria portrayed (as we shall see) in the Talmud.[44] Given the lack of name, the discrepancy in characterization, and the fact that Rabbi Meir, according to the Talmud, was at some point married to another woman (the daughter of one Zeruz[45]), there is no reason to assume that this narrative is about Beruria, either.

Beruria's relationships with Rabbi Ḥanania and Rabbi Meir are a literary fiction unique to the Talmud (not for nothing when other rabbinic texts tell of Rabbi Ḥanania's daughter or Rabbi Meir's wife, Beruria is never once named). This does not detract from Beruria's otherwise consistent representation in the Talmud, but it does prevent us from reading into the Beruria corpus non-talmudic narratives where only the relationships, rather than Beruria herself, are mentioned.

The second critical addition the Talmud makes to the portrayal of Beruria is her scholarship. As opposed to the single law in the Tosefta (which, as we said, leaves the question of her formal education open), the Talmud describes Beruria as a bona fide scholar (*Beruria detanya*), disciple of *three hundred rabbis,* a regular of the beit midrash. And not just regular; Beruria is exemplary. Renowned for having studied *three hundred traditions in a day,* it is Beruria, rather than any other rabbi, whom Rabbi Yoḥanan holds up as a model of excellence, an example for everything a Torah scholar can and ought to be.

The Beruria of the Talmud, then, goes from a one-time transmitter of a negligible law in the Tosefta to a fierce and formidable scholar,

43. While all theories agree that Midrash Mishlei postdates the Talmud, they differ as to whether it was composed in Israel, Babylonia, or Italy; none of these theories have been conclusively proven. Burton L. Visotzky, "Midrash Mishle: A Critical Edition," 5–12.

44. On the significance of consistency, rather than historical accuracy, for our ability to read rabbinic stories in light of one another, see p. xxvi n. 27.

45. Ḥullin 6b.

outperforming men in the study of Torah – a most distinctive overreacherix indeed.

(iii)

> There were certain thugs in Rabbi Meir's neighborhood who used to trouble him greatly. He prayed that they should die. Beruria his wife said to him, "What is the reason for your opinion? Is it because it is written, 'Let sins cease' (Ps. 104:35)? But is 'sinners' written? It is 'sins' that is written. Furthermore, cast your eyes to the end of the verse: 'And they are wicked no more.' Since sins will cease, they will be wicked no more. So pray that they repent and be wicked no more." He prayed for them, and they repented.
>
> A certain heretic said to Beruria, "It is written, 'Sing, barren woman, who did not bear' (Is. 54:1). Because she did not bear, she should sing?" She said to him, "Fool! Cast your eyes to the end of the verse, where it is written, 'For the children of the desolate woman will be more than the children of her that married, said the Lord.' What then does 'barren woman, who did not bear' mean? It means, Sing, Congregation of Israel, who is like a barren woman who did not bear sons of Hell like you." (Berakhot 10a)

A second talmudic reference features twin tales of Beruria debating men, demonstrating great skill in close and contextual reading of Scripture. In the first, an oft-quoted story about the power of repentance, Beruria's close reading of a verse in Psalms convinces Rabbi Meir that he ought to pray for the atonement, rather than death, of his sinful next-door neighbors. In the second, Beruria's contextual reading of a verse in Isaiah proves to a heretic that the verse he thought was ludicrous actually makes perfect sense.

Here again, we find nothing to contradict the characterization of Beruria as an overreacherix. She once more bests men in a typical male pursuit – this time, midrashic interpretation; note how she goes from a simple transmitter of law to a formal student of the beit midrash to an active interpreter in her own right, proficient in the most advanced kind of Torah scholarship.[46] There is also more than a hint of hubris in her behavior toward the heretic, whom she contemptuously calls a *fool* and a *son of Hell.*

(iv)

> Rabbi Yosei the Galilean was walking along the road. He met Beruria. He said to her, "By which road shall we go to Lod?" She said to him, "Galilean fool! Did not the rabbis say, 'Do not converse too much with a woman'? You should have said, 'By which to Lod?'"
>
> Beruria found a certain disciple who was reciting his lesson in a whisper. She kicked him and said to him, "Is it not written, 'Ordered in all and secure' (II Sam. 23:5)? If it is ordered in your 248 limbs, it will be secure, and if not, it will not be secure." (Eiruvin 53b–54a)

This next talmudic passage, second only to Rashi's Incident in the number of times it is cited in connection to Beruria, provides us with yet another pair of stories. The first has Beruria encounter Rabbi Yosei the Galilean on the highway. When the latter asks for directions, Beruria berates him for talking to her, in violation of the Mishna *"Do not converse too much with a woman"* (Avot 1:5[47]). The danger, says the Mishna, is that "as long as one converses too much with a woman... he neglects the study of the Torah"; since women are ignorant of Torah, talking to them is a waste of time that could otherwise be spent in study.[48] Beruria, who is hardly ignorant herself, expresses her scorn for this prohibition

46. "[Midrash] was learned in the higher schools.... We must distinguish between the lowest... primary schools for the study of the Oral Torah... [and] more qualified study... [where students] would practice the techniques of interpretation and dialectics." Birger Gerhardsson, *Memory and Manuscript: Oral Tradition and Written Transmission in Rabbinic Judaism and Early Christianity*, 90–91.

47. Other variations of this rabbinic dictum appear in Ḥagiga 5b and Avot DeRabbi Natan 7.

48. Like with Rabbi Eliezer's edict (above, p. 119), "Torah" here is a reference to the Talmud.

by pointing out, sarcastically, that Rabbi Yosei's question could have been made two whole words shorter.[49] The second account has Beruria back in the beit midrash, this time as a teacher, walking past a disciple who is studying too quietly for her liking. She *kick[s] him,* telling him off (again with the use of a verse) for not putting his all into his learning.

Beruria's overreacherix nature in this passage is especially pronounced. Once again, she vanquishes men through her superior knowledge of Torah. She is also aggressive, both verbally (*"Galilean fool"*) and physically (*kicked him*). And she is profoundly derisive, mocking Rabbi Yosei, and through him, the prohibition against talking to a woman, and through it, the general rabbinic view of women. "Don't you know," she says to Rabbi Yosei, "you're not supposed to talk to women? Don't you know we're lacking in Torah? Here, let me quote a Mishna on the ignorance of women, just to show how ignorant we women are."

(v)

> At once they sentenced Rabbi Ḥanania ben Teradyon to be burned, his wife to be killed, and his daughter to be consigned to a brothel.... Rabbi Yoḥanan related that once the daughter was walking before the nobles of Rome who remarked, "How beautiful are the steps of this maiden." Whereupon she took particular care of her steps.... They brought Rabbi Ḥanania, wrapped him in the Torah scroll, surrounded him with bundles of twigs, and set them on fire. They brought tufts of wool, soaked them in water, and laid them on his heart, so that he would not die quickly. His daughter said to him, "Father, how can I see you thus?" He said to her, "If I alone were being burned, it would be difficult for me. But now that I am burned along with the Torah scroll, He who will seek to avenge the humiliation of the Torah scroll will seek to avenge my humiliation"....
>
> Beruria the wife of Rabbi Meir was the daughter of Rabbi Ḥanania ben Teradyon. She said to Rabbi Meir, "It is a disgrace for me that

49. In the original Hebrew, Rabbi Yosei's question is four words long, whereas Beruria shortens it to two.

> my sister sits in a brothel." He took a potful of dinars and went [to Rome]. He said, "If no transgression has been committed with her, a miracle will occur. If she has committed a transgression, no miracle will occur for her." He went and presented himself to her as a cavalryman, and said to her, "Submit to me." She said, "I am menstruating." He said to her, "I will wait." She said to him, "There are many here more beautiful than I." He said, "Evidently she has not committed a transgression, and says this to anyone who comes." He went to her guard and said, "Give her over." He said, "I fear the government." Rabbi Meir said to him, "Take this potful of dinars; use half for bribes and keep half".... And the guard gave her to him.
>
> Eventually the matter became known to the palace.... They engraved the image of Rabbi Meir on the gates of Rome and said that whoever sees this face should bring him in. One day the Romans saw him and ran after him. He ran away from them and entered a brothel. Some say he saw gentile food, dipped one finger in it, and licked another. Others say that Elijah appeared in the form of a prostitute and embraced him. They said, "If that were Rabbi Meir, he would never have done that." He arose and fled to Babylonia. Some say it was because of this matter, while others say it was because of the Beruria Incident. (Avoda Zara 17b–18b)

This long and complex story is composed of three acts: (1) Rabbi Ḥanania ben Teradyon's martyrdom, (2) Beruria's sister's forced prostitution and rescue by Rabbi Meir, and (3) Rabbi Meir's attempts to evade Roman capture and his ultimate escape to Babylonia. This is not the place to discuss the several plot twists, motifs, and structural parallels of this highly elaborate narrative (most notably, the intriguing parallel between Rabbi Meir and his sister-in-law, both of whom are trapped in a brothel and have to maintain their chastity while assuming the appearance of sin[50]). What is important, for our purpose, are the two mentions

50. On the broader implication of this parallel regarding the rabbinic analogy between Jews and women, see pp. 204–7.

of Beruria. The first, in the beginning of the second act, is Beruria sending Rabbi Meir to save her sister. *"It is a disgrace for me that my sister sits in a brothel,"* she says, in a statement which smacks of hubris; her sister is languishing in Roman sexual captivity, and all Beruria cares about is her own honor. The second, at the end of the third act, is *the Beruria Incident*. It is here that the phrase appears, ominous and unexplained, prompting Rashi to tell his terrible tale.

In sum, the Beruria emerging from all the narratives that can be legitimately taken into account (i.e., those in the Tosefta and Talmud, where her name is actually mentioned) is an extraordinarily talented woman who distinguishes herself in the male world of the beit midrash; repeatedly outperforms men and puts them to shame with her scholarship; and is arrogant, aggressive, and derisive in doing so. An overreacherix through and through.

Rashi's Elusive Source

Hence the answer to our first question must be yes: Beruria absolutely is the overreacherix Rashi's tale makes her out to be. The Beruria Incident, while not actually *in* the Talmud, is perfectly consistent with the Beruria *of* the Talmud. So consistent, in fact, that it has gone down in history as an inherent part of the Beruria corpus. We cannot think of Beruria today without thinking of the tragic ending Rashi gives her story.[51]

Which brings us to our second question: Where does Rashi get his damning Incident? To answer that, let us zoom in and look at it more closely.

---

51. According to Rachel Adler, Beruria was essentially a rabbinic thought experiment on the question "What if there were a woman who was just like us?" Beruria, she says, "is viewed as a threat, a competitor, an arrogant woman contemptuous of men and of rabbinic tradition. This negative pole of the rabbinic attitude toward Beruria, which culminates in the tale of her adultery and suicide, is filled with malignant power.... Rashi's story is thematically contiguous with the earlier portions of the Beruria legend.... The ugliness of this story haunts us precisely because it is credible." Rachel Adler, "The Virgin in the Brothel and Other Anomalies: Character and Context in the Legend of Beruriah," 29–104.

Close Reading

Act 1

Once Beruria mocked the words of the rabbis, "Women are flighty."

Rabbi Meir said to her, "By your life! You will ultimately admit to their words."

Act 2

He instructed one of his disciples to tempt her to transgression. The disciple entreated her for many days until she gave in to him.

Act 3

When the matter became known to her, she strangled herself, and Rabbi Meir fled because of the disgrace.

Act 1 – Scorn	*Home*	*Beruria, Rabbi Meir*
Act 2 – Seduction	*Home*	*Beruria, Disciple*
Act 3 – Suicide	*Home*	*Beruria, Rabbi Meir*

Although not as literarily rich or complex, the Beruria Incident reads rather like the stories of the Talmud; like them, it is a three-act drama, of condensed time and space, a limited cast of characters, and intense dramatic action. We can also see a number of similarities between the text and its context: the Avoda Zara account of Rabbi Meir's rescue of Beruria's sister. In both, Rabbi Meir stages a chastity test, a woman must resist seduction, and ultimate sexual scandal (caused by Rabbi Meir or the woman) forces Rabbi Meir to flee to Babylonia.

Yet none of this brings us any closer to discovering the origin of the Beruria Incident, which, as noted, is found nowhere before Rashi's explanation of the obscure phrase at the end of the Avoda Zara narrative. This is not the only instance where the Talmud mentions a tale without telling it, and Rashi obligingly fills in the gap. In other cases, however, we find earlier versions of Rashi's story, either in rabbinic or in post-rabbinic literature.[52] At times, Rashi himself tells us that he got his story from a "book of legends."[53] Yet here, we have nothing; there are no earlier versions of the Beruria Incident, and Rashi does not disclose his source. The provenance of the Beruria Incident remains a mystery.

Consequently, modern scholarship has made numerous attempts to identify the origin of Rashi's story. Let's review three of the leading theories.

I. Broad Context: A Rabbinic Seduction Story

> When Rashi relates this event, he connects Beruria's downfall to a saying of the sages on the nature of women ("women are light-headed") which is found in a totally different section of the Babylonian Talmud: Kiddushin 80b. Surprisingly, it is exactly in this part of the vast talmudic corpus that the story of the seduction of Rabbi Meir is found.... It is clear that the tradition found in Rashi relies on three distinct literary components. The first of these was an amoraic saying about the light-headed nature of women, followed by the Rabbi Meir seduction story. The second was another Beruria tradition in which she mocks a saying of the sages about the nature of women. This story, however, does not have a tragic ending.... The third component was a literary motif on feminine corruptibility: All women can be seduced, and it is just a question of the right amount of pressure. This well-known motif is found often in folklore, and documented already in Hellenistic

52. Rashi's "Incident of Baaya the Tax Collector" (Sanhedrin 44b), for example, is recounted in Y Ḥagiga 2:2, and his "Incident of Natan Detzutzita" (Sanhedrin 31b) appears in the 11th-century *Ḥibbur Yafeh MeHaYeshua*, 5:25. Surveying several cases where Rashi provides a full version of a narrative merely alluded to in the Talmud, Yirmiyahu Malchi concludes that these versions all "came to Rashi through tradition." Yirmiyahu Malchi, "On Incidents Referred to in the Talmud and Explained in Rashi and Other Sources," 2:163.
53. Taanit 8a, Sanhedrin 31b.

> literature. These three together are the ingredients from which the medieval Beruria legend was composed.[54]

According to this first theory by Tal Ilan, Rashi draws on three different sources for the Beruria Incident: (1) the rabbinic seduction story cycle in Kiddushin 80b–81b,[55] (2) the Eiruvin account of Beruria's mockery of the dictum "Do not converse too much with a woman," and (3) the folkloristic trope of women who are tested and found wanting.[56] Admittedly, the Incident does resemble the story in Eiruvin, which might explain the Scorn (Act 1), and there are several similarities to other temptation narratives, both in rabbinic and in world literature, which might explain the Seduction (Act 2). Yet the tragic ending of Suicide (Act 3) is, by Ilan's own admission, unaccounted for.

II. Broad Context: The Rav Papa Incident

> This incident is not the only personal story the Talmud mentions without explicating. In the last chapter of Tractate Pesaḥim ... [the Talmud refers to] "the Rav Papa Incident" (Pesaḥim 112b). What is the Rav Papa Incident? Here too, like in the case of the Beruria Incident, the Talmud does not elaborate. But unlike the Beruria Incident, about which we know nothing except what Rashi tells us, the Rav Papa Incident has an ancient geonic tradition, cited in numerous variants by medieval commentaries .... This is Rashi's version of the Rav Papa Incident:

54. Tal Ilan, "The Quest for the Historical Beruriah, Rachel, and Imma Shalom," 6.
55. See pp. 96–97.
56. "The tested woman plot is one of the great story machines of all time .... It has adapted to myth and to drama, to chronicle and to history, and to prose fiction from Hellenistic romance to the novel of psychological development .... The temptation of a married woman to commit adultery is particularly attractive .... In such stories the sexual test begins [with] a husband decid[ing] to woo her in disguise or convinc[ing] his most trusted friend to perform the test." Lois E. Bueler, *The Tested Woman Plot: Women's Choices, Men's Judgments, and the Shaping of Stories*, 1–85.

> There was an Aramaean woman who owed Rav Papa money, and he would enter her home every day to collect it. One day she strangled her son and put him on the bed, and when Rav Papa entered she said, "Sit until I get your money." And so he did. When she returned she said, "You have killed my son!" And he fled the country.
>
> A simple comparison between this story and the Beruria Incident shows a clear resemblance: Both stories are of a mysterious talmudic episode, referenced as "some say because of the incident of...," and open with a tale of a woman. Both describe a man who meets this woman frequently, both feature a death by strangling, and both end with the same outcome: the need to flee the land. The similarity is not just in the stories' motifs, but also in their respective structures: (1) "Once Beruria mocked" is analogous to "There was an Aramaean woman"; (2) "The disciple entreated her for many days" is analogous to "he would enter her home every day"; (3) "When the matter became known to her, she strangled herself" is analogous to "One day she strangled her son"; (4) "And Rabbi Meir fled" is analogous to "And he fled the country".... I believe such extensive parallelism cannot be a matter of chance. We cannot identify its cause with certainty, but we may surmise the following: There are, in the Talmud, two unexplained personal stories introduced as "some say"; one of these – the Rav Papa Incident – has an ancient geonic tradition, while the other – the Beruria Incident – does not. A desire to fill this gap arose, presumably leading to the creation of the Beruria Incident, which was heavily influenced by, and borrowed extensively from, the Rav Papa Incident.[57]

In this second theory, Eitam Henkin traces the source of the Beruria Incident to the equally obscure Rav Papa Incident – which, unlike the former, does appear prior to Rashi, and which he believes was used as its template. But while the structural parallels between the two narratives are undeniable, the Rav Papa Incident contains only one of the Beruria

57. Eitam Henkin, "The Mystery of the 'Beruria Incident': A Suggested Solution," 151–53.

Incident's three plot elements: the death (Act 3). The mockery (Act 1) and adultery (Act 2) do not feature in it at all.

III. Immediate Context: Beruria's Sister

> Although the story of Beruria's seduction and suicide is extant only in Rashi's authoritative 11th-century French commentary on the Babylonian Talmud, I think I can show how it was generated there.... Beruria had, according to the Talmud, a double, in fact a sister.... One sister becomes an exemplum of the proper behavior of a woman, because she had not studied Torah in accordance with Rabbi Eliezer and thus was not led into lewdness. The other sister dies a wanton, because she violated the taboo, submitted to temptation, and learned Torah. My theory is that Beruria's story is generated as the dark double of the story of her sister.... This point-for-point homology between the two narratives can be laid out as a series of structural oppositions:

The Sister	Beruria
Behaves light-mindedly (-)	Studies Torah (+)
Sent to brothel (-)	Marries scholar (+)
Passes Rabbi Meir's test (+)	Fails Rabbi Meir's test (-)
Rescued by miracle (+)	Commits suicide (-)....

> Taken together, the story of the two sisters forms one exemplum... a demonstration that there is an intrinsic and necessary connection between a scholarly woman and uncontrolled sexuality.[58]

A third theory, by Daniel Boyarin, locates the origin of the Beruria Incident in its immediate, rather than broad, context. For Boyarin, the Incident was created through an inversion of the story of Beruria's sister in Avoda Zara, illustrating the rabbis' preference for a flighty and ignorant woman who ultimately maintains her chastity, over one who

58. Boyarin, *Carnal Israel*, 190–91.

studies Torah and is therefore more readily seduced.[59] The theory, which casts the Beruria Incident as a sort of talmudic fan fiction, is compelling; the stories of Beruria and her sister are indeed an almost perfect mirror image of one another. Yet this theory, too, does not account for the Incident in its entirety, explaining the Seduction (Act 2) and Suicide (Act 3), but not, strictly speaking, the Scorn (Act 1).

Unreading the Beruria Incident

No theory, then, is quite sufficient in identifying the talmudic source of the Beruria Incident. But what if there is none? What if the Incident isn't based in the Talmud at all? As opposed to the other interpretations, which try and ground the Beruria Incident in the Talmud, I propose that we try to unyoke it, demonstrating that, for all of its apparent consistency, the Beruria Incident has nothing to do with the Beruria of the Talmud.

Immediate Context, Redux

First, we must return to the Incident's immediate context in Avoda Zara, beginning with Beruria's entrance in the second act:

> Beruria the wife of Rabbi Meir was the daughter of Rabbi Ḥanania ben Teradyon. She said to Rabbi Meir, "It is a disgrace for me that my sister sits in a brothel." He took a potful of dinars and went [to Rome].... And the guard gave her to him.
>
> Eventually the matter became known to the palace.... One day the Romans saw him and ran after him. He ran away from them and entered a brothel. Some say he saw gentile food, dipped one finger in it, and licked another. Others say that Elijah appeared in the form of a prostitute and embraced him. They said, "If that were Rabbi Meir, he would never have done that." He arose and fled to Babylonia. Some say it was because of this matter, while others say it was because of the Beruria Incident.

59. In the Avoda Zara account, Beruria's sister is described as strutting flirtatiously before the noblemen of Rome.

Rashi's Beruria Incident, as mentioned, is derived from the story's enigmatic final words, an alternative reason for Rabbi Meir's flight to Babylonia. *Some say it was because of this matter, while others say it was because of the Beruria Incident.* What is *this matter* to which *the Beruria Incident* is counterposed? The story seems to provide us with two possibilities: One, in the second act, is Rabbi Meir's rescue of his sister-in-law and consequent entanglement with the Roman authorities; the other, in the third act, is his attempt to throw off his pursuers by appearing to sin (eating non-kosher food or embracing a prostitute). Yet these, precisely, are the two possibilities mentioned in the story's final line! *Some say it was because of this matter,* the latter part of the story, where Rabbi Meir becomes a sinner in the eyes of his fellow Jews and must escape the shame, *while others say it was because of the Beruria Incident,* the former part of the story, set into motion by Beruria, which turns Rabbi Meir into a fugitive from Roman rule.[60] The story is thus self-contained; we don't need Rashi's tale to understand it. The real Beruria Incident is right here under our very noses.[61]

In fact, so extraneous is Rashi's tale to the story in Avoda Zara, that one mainstream geonic tradition denies its existence altogether. Rabbi Nissim Gaon, an important commentator who lived one generation before Rashi, interprets the story's penultimate sentence, *He arose and fled to Babylonia,* as "He went, took his wife and all his possessions, and moved to Iraq." Rabbi Meir managed to escape the Romans, and he and his wife immigrated to Babylonia; the end.[62] Rashi's Beruria Incident, according to Rabbi Nissim, never even happened.

---

60. In this, the Beruria Incident is not unlike the Destruction story cycle, which begins with "Jerusalem was destroyed because of Kamtza and Bar Kamtza" (p. 68), although the Kamtza—Bar Kamtza confusion merely instigates the action and doesn't play an important part in it at all.

61. The point is made, traditionally, by Rabbi Yehuda ben Kalonymus, *Seder Yiḥusei Tannaim VeAmoraim,* s.v. "Beruria"; and in contemporary scholarship, by Henkin, "The Mystery of the 'Beruria Incident,'" 155–58; and Dalia Hoshen, *Beruriah the Tannait: A Theological Reading of a Female Mishnaic Scholar,* 71.

62. Rabbi Nissim Gaon, *Ḥibbur Yafeh MeHaYeshua,* 5:11. Avraham Grossman argues that this interpretation by Rabbi Nissim, who bases much of his writings on earlier Babylonian traditions, is to be preferred to Rashi's unsourced tale. Avraham Grossman, *Pious and Rebellious: Jewish Women in Europe in the Middle Ages,* 271.

Historical Context: Rashi Reassessed

Having unstitched Rashi's tale from its talmudic context, let us continue to unravel it. If the absence of the Beruria Incident in all sources prior to Rashi were not strange enough, even more suspicious is its absence in all sources *after* Rashi, as well. None of the commentators who lived during and immediately after Rashi, who frequently refer to him in their commentaries, ever once mention the Incident, despite its highly unorthodox nature and the many things about it that require explanation (this silence is particularly telling in the case of the Tosafot, a collection of commentaries by Rashi's successors, who completely ignore the Incident, although one of their primary concerns is explaining difficulties in Rashi, and although just one page before the Incident they discuss the permissibility of committing suicide[63]). The first mention of the Beruria Incident subsequent to Rashi is in the 14th-century work *Menorat HaMaor*, written some two hundred years after the former's death.[64]

What are we to make of this glaring omission? To answer that, we must understand the historical conditions of the reproduction of text in the Middle Ages. Up until the invention of the printing press, manuscripts were, of course, copied by hand, and subject to a variety of scribal errors. One common type of error occurred when someone studying from a manuscript would add a comment in the margins or between the lines, and the scribe, unable to distinguish between the two, would copy the comment as part of the body text. Such erroneous insertions were rampant in medieval manuscripts; the Talmud itself isn't free of them. Rashi notes several instances of fragments miscopied into the talmudic text.[65] Subsequent commentators point to similar insertions made in Rashi's commentary, which they attribute to "an errant student writing in the manuscript."[66]

63. Tosafot, Avoda Zara 18a; instead of the proximate Beruria Incident, the Tosafot cite a story from Gittin 57b as their prooftext in the matter.

64. Rabbi Isaac Aboab, *Menorat HaMaor*, 1:2:3.

65. Rashi, Shabbat 71b, Shevuot 3b, Keritot 4a.

66. Rabbi Yoel Sirkis, *Hagahot HaBaḥ*, Moed Katan 19a (see also Avoda Zara 66a). "The wide dissemination of [Rashi's] talmudic commentary hastened the introduction of numerous annotations and editorial changes, and differing versions of the commentary were in the hands even of early sages.... How did these differing versions come to be? Several scholars... believe that we are dealing with later additions, written

All this – the foreignness of the Beruria Incident to rabbinic values, its superfluity to the Avoda Zara narrative, the occurrence of scribal errors in Rashi – leads to the following conclusion: The Beruria Incident isn't a real Rashi. It is what is known as a pseudo-Rashi, a later comment mistakenly copied into Rashi and misattributed to him.[67]

Beruria's Nemesis

So not only is the Beruria Incident not grounded in the Talmud, it is also not based on any of the authoritative rabbinic traditions Rashi draws upon in his commentary. It is, by all evidence, a piece of popular folklore, a medieval legend of the type that was sometimes erroneously inserted into the commentaries of the time.[68]

Where did such a legend come from?

I'd like to suggest it came, precisely, from the archetype of the overreacherix. From the belief that a female taking up a male role must be guilty of hubris and must come to nemesis; that a woman who transgresses the boundaries of her gender will inevitably be brought down by the very femininity she sought to surpass; that the fate of someone like Beruria cannot be any different to the fate of Cleopatra or Messalina or Pope Joan (the latter an extremely popular tale at the time the Incident first emerged). "Anyone who teaches his daughter Torah teaches her licentiousness," warned Rabbi Eliezer, and Jews in the Middle Ages believed him. Beruria, the woman Torah scholar, had to fall.

---

as marginal notes and then inserted into the commentary." Grossman, *Rashi*, 142. That the only surviving manuscript of Rashi's commentary to Tractate Avoda Zara is dated to the early 14th century (around the time of the Incident's first appearance in *Menorat HaMaor*) lends itself to the plausibility of the manuscript's corruption in the two centuries after Rashi's death.

67. See Naomi Cohen, "Bruria in the Bavli and in Rashi 'Avodah Zarah' 18B," 30; Henkin, "The Mystery of the 'Beruria Incident,'" 146–49; Hoshen, *Beruriah the Tannait*, 72–73. Henkin's essay, combining the breadth of the yeshiva with the depth of academic scholarship, was particularly influential in the composition of this section. His tragic loss in 2015 deprived the world of Talmud of one of its brightest rising stars.

68. Dalia Hoshen discusses the proliferation of "folk legends attributed to [the rabbis], which were eventually revealed as medieval products situated outside the talmudic literature." Hoshen, *Beruriah the Tannait*, 70.

There was just one problem: Beruria does not fall. In all of the talmudic stories of Beruria, nemesis is nowhere to be found. So a legend arose, not unlike the smear campaigns directed against other powerful women in history, wherein Beruria falls into scandal and is mortally punished for her overreaching. And in a cruel twist of fate, the legend was mistakenly added into Rashi, destroying Beruria's legacy forever.

Hence, because the Beruria Incident is completely extraneous to the Beruria of the Talmud, because it is neither talmudic nor rabbinic nor in any way canonically Jewish, I propose that we strike it from the record. Like the non-talmudic stories of Rabbi Ḥanania ben Teradyon's daughter or Rabbi Meir's wife, the Incident is not a legitimate Beruria narrative, and cannot be read as part of her corpus. In previous chapters we had tried to reread the heroine's story; in this case, we must try and unread it. The Beruria Incident must be removed from consideration.

A Woman in a Man's World: Beruria Revisioned

Our next step is to try and revision the Beruria of the Talmud, without the giant shadow cast by Rashi's Incident. To this end, I'd like to turn to a firsthand account of a 21st-century overreacherix. If in centuries past it was the throne room and the battlefield, the theater and the study hall that were considered an exclusive male domain, today it is the executive boardroom:

> When I entered the workforce, I figured if sexism still existed, I would just prove it wrong. I would do my job and do it well. What I didn't know at the time was that… success has often been contingent upon a woman not speaking out but fitting in, or more colloquially, being "one of the guys." The first women to enter corporate America dressed in manly suits with button-down shirts. One veteran banking executive told me that she wore her hair in a bun for ten years because she did not want anyone to notice she was a woman. While styles have relaxed, women still worry about sticking out too much. I know an engineer at a tech start-up who removes her earrings before going to work so

> coworkers won't be reminded that she is – *shhh!* – not a man.... I started noticing how often employees were judged not by their objective performance, but by the subjective standard of how well they fit in. Given that the summer outing at McKinsey was a deep-sea fishing trip and most company dinners ended with whiskey sipping and cigar smoking, I sometimes struggled to pass the "fitting in" test. One night, encouraged by the male partners, I puffed away on a cigar – just one of the guys. Except that the smoking nauseated me and I reeked of cigar smoke for days. If that was fitting in, I stuck out.[69]

Fitting in, says tech executive Sheryl Sandberg, is the ultimate requirement for a woman in a man's world. It is also, paradoxically, the ultimate liability. Businesswomen today might not have to disguise themselves as men like the overreacherixes of yore, but they do have to adopt stereotypically masculine traits: competitiveness, assertiveness, dominance. Yet these very qualities, celebrated in a man, are stigmatized in a woman. As evidence, the 2003 Heidi/Howard experiment, in which business school students were asked to assess two identical profiles of venture capitalists – one male, one female. The male, Howard, was judged to be powerful and assertive, whereas the female, Heidi, was deemed arrogant and aggressive:

> By focusing on her career and taking a calculated approach to amassing power, Heidi violated our stereotypical expectations of women. Yet by behaving in the exact same manner, Howard lived up to our stereotypical expectations of men. The end result? Liked him, disliked her.... I have seen this dynamic play out over and over. When a woman excels at her job, both male and female coworkers will remark that she may be accomplishing a lot but is "not as well-liked by her peers." She is probably also "too aggressive," "not a team player," "a bit political," "can't be trusted," or "difficult".... When a woman acts forcefully or competitively, she's deviating from expected behavior. If a woman pushes to get

69. Sheryl Sandberg, *Lean In: Women, Work, and the Will to Lead*, 142–43.

> the job done, if she's highly competent, if she focuses on results rather than on pleasing others, she's acting like a man. And if she acts like a man, people dislike her.[70]

A woman in a traditional male role, it seems, cannot win. If she simply wants, like Sandberg, to "do [her] job and do it well," she must be at least as dominant and forceful as the men around her. But if she is as dominant and forceful as the men around her, she is branded as "too aggressive." For a woman in a man's world, the stigma of hubris is unavoidable.

Which begs the question: What if the women historically branded as overreacherixes – those audacious, aggressive, arrogant women – weren't overreacherixes at all? What if they were women merely trying to fit in? Women whose love for business or politics or art or Torah made them long to be part of a man's world?

With this question in mind, let us return to the talmudic portrayal of Beruria.

(i)

> Rabbi Simlai came before Rabbi Yoḥanan. He said to him, "Let the master teach me the Book of Genealogies".... He said to him, "We teach this book neither to Lodites nor to Nehardeans, and certainly not to you, who are from Lod and whose residence is in Nehardea." Rabbi Simlai pressed him, and he consented. Rabbi Simlai said to him, "Let the master teach me the book in three months." Rabbi Yoḥanan took a clod of earth, threw it at him, and said, "If Beruria, the wife of Rabbi Meir, the daughter of Rabbi Ḥanania ben Teradyon, learned three hundred traditions in a day from three hundred rabbis, and even so did not fulfill her responsibility in three years – how can you say in three months?"

Note that no one, in the Rabbi Simlai story, is excluded from the beit midrash because of who they are; not the uncouth Nehardeans, not the ignorant Lodites (Rabbi Yoḥanan, when all is said and done,

70. Ibid., 39–41.

agrees to teach Rabbi Simlai), not even – contrary to Rabbi Eliezer's edict – women. But you must be willing to work hard. The only thing that will get you removed from the beit midrash is laziness. This is not so much a description of Beruria's scholarly excellence as it is of her unbelievable grit, the supreme effort she put into her learning. Here is a woman who has spent her every hour in study, learning as much Torah as she could from as many rabbis as would teach her. A woman who knows that to merit a place in the beit midrash she can't just be as good as her male peers – she has to be better.

(ii)

> There were certain thugs in Rabbi Meir's neighborhood who used to trouble him greatly. He prayed that they should die. Beruria his wife said to him, "What is the reason for your opinion? Is it because it is written, 'Let sins cease'?... Cast your eyes to the end of the verse: 'And they are wicked no more.' Since sins will cease, they will be wicked no more. So pray that they repent and be wicked no more." He prayed for them, and they repented.
>
> A certain heretic said to Beruria, "It is written, 'Sing, barren woman, who did not bear.' Because she did not bear, she should sing?" She said to him, "Fool! Cast your eyes to the end of the verse, where it is written, 'For the children of the desolate woman will be more than the children of her that married, said the Lord.'"

Given her dedication to her studies, it is not surprising that Beruria ends up running circles around the men with whom she argues. But what about her hubris, of which we have identified several instances, beginning with her calling the heretic a *fool* here? Viewed in context, we find that Beruria is only doing what the men around her do all the time; "fool" is a common insult in the world of the rabbis, frequently thrown out in response to bad scholarship.[71] Beruria is simply fitting

71. Shabbat 121b, Eiruvin 101a, Bava Batra 115b, Ḥullin 87a.

in, and her behavior should not be regarded as any more derisive just because she's a woman.

(iii)

> Rabbi Yosei the Galilean was walking along the road. He met Beruria. He said to her, "By which road shall we go to Lod?" She said to him, "Galilean fool! Did not the rabbis say, 'Do not converse too much with a woman'? You should have said, 'By which to Lod?'"
>
> Beruria found a certain disciple who was reciting his lesson in a whisper. She kicked him and said to him, "Is it not written, 'Ordered in all and secure'? If it is ordered in your 248 limbs, it will be secure, and if not, it will not be secure."

In this case, too, Beruria's aggressive behavior, both verbally and physically, is in no way unique. "Galilean fool" is mentioned earlier in the sugya (Eiruvin 53b) as a popular slur directed against Galileans and their bumbling speech; similarly, kicking – like pushing or hurling clods of earth – was a standard form of rabbinic rebuke.[72] Beruria is behaving like the typical Torah scholar she is. And perhaps what so upsets her (in the second story) is the sight of a disciple not making the most of his learning opportunity, the same opportunity she had to work so hard for.

Yet it is her mockery (in the first story), of Rabbi Yosei in particular, and of the rabbinic dictum in general, that is the most incriminating; it's this mockery that provides the basis, as we've seen, for the mockery (of another rabbinic dictum) in the Beruria Incident. But what if it isn't mockery at all? What if Beruria is saying, sincerely and without a hint of sarcasm, "Please don't talk to me too much"?

Beruria is a woman in a man's world. She knows this puts her in a precarious position. She knows the stigma that attaches itself to a learned woman, the accusations of hubris, the charges of promiscuity. It is the latter, specifically, that is of great concern. "Anyone who teaches his daughter Torah teaches her licentiousness," after all. Beruria knows she

72. Shabbat 31a, 156a, Pesaḥim 62b (above), Rosh Hashana 25a, Shevuot 18b, 30b.

must be extremely careful, steering clear of anything that might come across as in any way immodest. She cannot afford to be seen speaking to a man on the highway.[73]

(iv)

> Beruria the wife of Rabbi Meir was the daughter of Rabbi Ḥanania ben Teradyon. She said to Rabbi Meir, "It is a disgrace for me that my sister sits in a brothel."

The same sense of caution might explain the opening of the second act of the Avoda Zara narrative (which we now know to be the real Beruria Incident). "My entire life," says Beruria to Rabbi Meir, "I've fought the stigma of licentiousness, guarding myself against any charge of impropriety. I've spent my days surrounded by men, and have never spoken to any of them except to learn or teach Torah. I've worked harder than any man has to, and been as chaste as any woman should. I can't have my sister living in a Roman harem; it will ruin me. Please bring her home, and save the reputation I've worked so hard to protect."

The Moral of the Story: The Danger of Stigma

Let us, then, save the reputation Beruria worked so hard to protect. In our primary reading, we had determined that Beruria was an overreacherix, based on the threefold definition of the archetype as (1) a woman who takes up a male role, (2) is guilty of hubris, and (3) comes to nemesis. Yet by unreading the Beruria Incident, we have eliminated the nemesis from Beruria's story. And by revisioning the Beruria of the Talmud, we find there is no hubris in it either. Hence Beruria (the Beruria portrayed in the sources that can legitimately be read as part of her corpus) is *not* an overreacherix. There is no derision imputed to her, no fall in her fate. If in previous chapters we've seen the Talmud invoking anti-feminine archetypes in order to deconstruct them, here the archetype isn't invoked

73. For the highway as a place prone to sexual immorality, see Sukka 52a, Kiddushin 81a, Avoda Zara 17a.

at all. Beruria is simply a woman devoted to her Torah; a woman who has thrown herself into her studies, knowing that as a female scholar she has more to prove; a woman doing her utmost to earn her place in the beit midrash, while remaining, as Caesar's wife, above suspicion.

And earn it she does. Nowhere in the Talmud (once we remove the destructive influence of the Beruria Incident) do we find any trace of criticism directed at Beruria. The rabbis of the Talmud, far from accusing Beruria of derision or arrogance or promiscuity, seem to have nothing but high regard for her. They accept her into their ranks, and don't even mind when they are repeatedly defeated by her.

In this, the rabbis are far more noble than so many of us. The most tolerant among us, who most readily accept the Other into our midst, still cannot bear to be outdone by them. So we stigmatize, slapping on a label designed to keep them in their place. A powerful woman is promiscuous; a political adversary has got to be unscrupulous; a wealthy foreigner must have cheated his way to the top. Such stigmas destroy reputations, they ruin lives. They all but destroyed Beruria's legacy. But if the rabbis were able to get past their stigma, were able to acknowledge the superiority of a learned woman without labeling her licentious, we ought to be able to do so, as well. As opposed to the Mishna, which blots out Beruria's name for the sake of modesty, and the medieval legend, which sullies it with charges of immodesty, the rabbis of the Talmud treat Beruria without sanction or stigma – simply as one of their own.

Ima Shalom
The Angel in the House

The Archetype: All the Honor of the King's Daughter Is Within

> She was intensely sympathetic. She was immensely charming. She was utterly unselfish. She excelled in the difficult arts of family life. She sacrificed herself daily.... Above all – I need not say it – she was pure. Her purity was supposed to be her chief beauty – her blushes, her great grace. In those days – the last of Queen Victoria – every house had its angel.[1]

Contrary to the other five, our sixth and final archetype is not damning or derogatory of women. Quite the opposite; the angel in the house is the idealized image of a woman as the perfect wife, mother, and homemaker.[2] Coined in the 19th century (in a poem by Coventry Patmore

1. Virginia Woolf, "Professions for Women," 237.
2. This does not, however, make it any less oppressive. Throughout history, two principal strategies were deployed in the subordination of women: one was to denigrate them, the other was to praise them to the sky. "To convince woman... [to] maintain her traditional place... she was identified with everything that was beautiful and holy." Barbara Welter, "The Cult of True Womanhood: 1820–1860," 174.

by the same name), the archetype is based on the Victorian doctrine of separate spheres: the divide between the male domain of the public, the civic, and the political, and the female domain of the private, the domestic, and the familial. It was the man who went out into the world, to fight and to conquer, to profit and rule, while the woman remained at home to tend to the house and children. Although systematically articulated only after the Industrial Revolution, and the consequent removal of the workplace from the home, the doctrine of separate spheres can be traced all the way back to the beginning of time.

In the first chapter of Genesis, Adam and Eve are created with a common purpose. "Be fruitful and multiply," God blesses the first couple, "fill the earth, and subdue it" (Gen. 1:28). Two chapters later, they sin and are punished, their joint blessing severed into two distinct curses: Adam is condemned to the "hard labor… of the field," whereas Eve is cursed with the "hard labor [of] childbearing" (Gen. 3:16–18). This division of labor persists throughout the Bible, perhaps most explicitly in the psalmist's description of the pious man and his family: "You shall enjoy the fruit of your labors… and you shall prosper. Your wife shall be like a fruitful vine in the innermost parts of your house; your sons, like olive plants around your table" (Ps. 128:2–3).

That the woman's rightful place is in "the innermost parts of [the] house" becomes, for the rabbis, a matter of marital law. According to the Mishna, a man may divorce his wife if she "goes out of her house with her head uncovered, spins wool in the marketplace, and speaks with every man" (M Ketubot 7:6).[3] The marketplace, a rabbinic metonymy for the great outdoors, is a site of decadence and danger – certainly no place for an honorable woman. "A man must conquer his wife so she does not go out into the marketplace," says the midrash, "since if she goes out into the marketplace she succumbs to sin" (Genesis Rabba 8:12).[4]

3. In a parallel passage in the Tosefta, it is not only permissible to divorce a wife for such transgressions; it is required (T Sotah 5:9).
4. This restriction, Miriam Peskowitz points out, was not uniquely rabbinic, and could be found in many other cultures of classical Antiquity. It was also largely prescriptive, rather than descriptive; in actual fact, women in rabbinic times engaged in a variety of labors which necessitated a presence in the market. Miriam B. Peskowitz, *Spinning Fantasies: Rabbis, Gender and History*, 64, 148.

Keeping the woman indoors, the midrash continues, preserves not only her innocence, but her ignorance as well. "It is the way of a woman to sit inside her home, and the way of a man to go out to the marketplace and learn wisdom from others" (Genesis Rabba 18:1).

Yet it is not just the woman that the doctrine of separate spheres comes to protect, it is also the home at whose center she stands. The woman is the guardian of the house, mainstay of the family, source of stability and sanctity within the home. All depends on her, and all may rise and fall by her virtue:

> "All the honor of the king's daughter is within" (Ps. 45:14) – Rabbi Yosei says: When a woman keeps chastely within the house, she is fit to marry a high priest and raise up sons who will be high priests.... Said Rabbi Pinḥas HaKohen bar Ḥama: When she keeps chastely within the house, just as the altar atones, so does she atone for her house, as it is said, "Your wife shall be like a fruitful vine in the innermost parts of your house" (Ps. 128:3). (Tanḥuma Vayishlaḥ 6)

Cornelia Pointing to Her Children as Her Treasures,
Angelica Kauffman

A woman's greatest honor, according to the rabbis, is to stay at home.[5] For if she does, and conducts herself piously within her walls, then will her house ascend to the heights of holiness, with her husband and sons serving as high priests.[6] If, however, she betrays her sacred role of angel in the house, if she ventures out into the market and behaves promiscuously, her home and family will suffer for her sins:

5. This is a deliberate misreading of the Psalms 45 verse, which speaks of *kevuda*, household goods, not *kevoda*, honor.
6. The Jerusalem Talmud offers an example of precisely such a reward in the tale of Kimḥit, who is so careful to maintain her modesty even when indoors that all seven of her sons become high priests (Y Yoma 1:1).

> A wife who walks in the marketplace and speaks with every man… [who] goes outside the house or in public thoroughfares, she brings evil upon herself and her sons, who will be evil and suffer from physical defects…. She will never find contentment; because of her sinful behavior her sons will be lame, mute, and blind, feeble-minded or evil. (Tanna DeBei Eliyahu Rabba 18)

In fact, so central is the woman to the house in rabbinic thought that the two are often identified as one. "His house is his wife," says Rabbi Yehuda (M Yoma 1:1), and Rabbi Yosei concurs, "In all my days, I did not call my wife 'my wife'… rather, I called my wife 'my house'" (Shabbat 118b). Talmudic Aramaic takes this identification one step further, with the word for house, *deveitehu,* doubling as the word for wife.[7]

Moving from Jewish to Greek literature, we find the very same notion of a preordained division of labor. In his classic treatise on household management, the philosopher Xenophon relays a conversation between an Athenian farmer and his newlywed wife, outlining the latter's domestic duties:

> God made provision from the first by shaping, as it seems to me, the woman's nature for indoor and the man's for outdoor occupations. Man's body and soul He furnished with a greater capacity for enduring heat and cold, wayfaring and military marches…. While in creating the body of woman with less capacity for these things, God would seem to have imposed on her the indoor works; and knowing that He had implanted in the woman and imposed upon her the nurture of new-born babies, He endowed

7. See Berakhot 10a, 51b, Pesaḥim 62b, Yevamot 63a, Ketubot 65a, Kiddushin 81b, Avoda Zara 18a (these are just a handful of examples, drawn from the texts cited in this book; there are numerous others). "Rabbinic Judaism perceived the female body and female activities in domestic terms…. Rabbinic social policy preferred that all nubile women be married and that all married women be confined to supportive familial roles, where they could provide for their husband's needs and nurture children at the same time…. When a woman crossed the boundary from the internal to the public realm she potentially endangered not only herself, but the entire structure of rabbinic sexual politics." Baskin, *Midrashic Women,* 88.

> her with a larger share of affection for the new-born child... [and] a larger measure of timidity than He bestowed on man. Knowing further that he to whom the outdoor works belonged would need to defend them against malign attack, He endowed the man in turn with a larger share of courage.... In proportion as you come to be a better helpmate to myself and to the children, a better guardian of our home, so will your honor increase throughout the household as mistress, wife, and mother, daily more dearly prized.[8]

According to Xenophon's biological determinism, woman was created to be a homemaker. Physically weaker and emotionally more tender and timid, she is simply better suited for indoor tasks.

Christianity and Islam similarly champion woman's role as angel in the house, charging their female followers with modesty, piety, and obedience. "Teach the young women to be sober, to love their husbands, to love their children, to be discreet, chaste, keepers at home, good, obedient to their own husbands," the New Testament exhorts,[9] and the Quran, for its part, commands, "O wives of the prophet! You are not like any other women, if you observe piety.... Settle in your homes, and do not display yourselves... and obey God and His messenger."[10]

But it is not only religious and philosophical writings that promote the ideology of separate spheres; works of literature also dramatize it to great effect. The fairytale of "Snow White" presents a perfect image of this domestic ideal, with the dwarfs heigh-hoing their way to work every day, while Snow White stays behind to cook and clean and sew, a bluebird perched angelically on her shoulder. She is left with strict instructions to keep herself safely at home, and not let anyone in. For as soon as

Snow White, Walt Disney Studios

8. Xenophon, *The Oeconomicus*, ch. 7.
9. Titus 2:4–5.
10. Sura 33:32–33.

she does, allowing the outside (in the form of the Evil Queen) to come indoors, disaster strikes.

The reverse scenario is depicted in "The Lady of Shalott," Alfred Lord Tennyson's poem about a mysterious woman shut up in a tower, cursed so that she can never go out, can never even look out, into the world. "Like an angel," the Lady sits at her loom, singing and weaving, her view of the outdoors confined to the images reflected in the mirror at her side.[11] Until one day, taken by the sight of Sir Lancelot riding by, she gets up, looks out, and runs from the tower. At that moment, the curse takes hold; the mirror cracks, the weave flies from the loom, and the Lady of Shalott dies.

Herein is the cautionary tale of the angel in the house. If the separation of the spheres is somehow compromised, if the outside world invades the home, or the angel leaves the home to go outside, everything falls apart. Both angel and house are destroyed.

Such is the fate of the Jellyby household in Charles Dickens's *Bleak House*. The zealous Mrs. Jellyby is so busy with her charitable work on behalf of the natives of Borioboola-Gha in faraway Africa, she completely neglects her own family. The result of this abandonment of the home, the dereliction of domestic duty for the sake of civic responsibility, is a house in shambles; Mrs. Jellyby's rooms are "not only very untidy but very dirty," her husband is "miserable" and on the verge of bankruptcy, her children, wild and unkempt, are "in a devil of a state."[12] Charity, for the angel in the house, begins – and ends – at home.

Which brings us back to Coventry Patmore's "Angel in the House," the popular poem that gave the archetype its name. Singing the praises of his wife (called, fittingly, Honoria), the poet extols her dedication to her home, her docile and delicate temper, her good-natured submissiveness to him. Above all, he commends his wife

Windsor Castle in Modern Times, Sir Edwin Landseer

11. Alfred Lord Tennyson, "The Lady of Shalott," pt. 1.
12. Charles Dickens, *Bleak House*, chs. 4–5.

for knowing her place, and not venturing beyond her feminine sphere: "How wise in all she ought to know, / How ignorant of all beside!"[13]

The question of what a woman "ought to know" stood at the heart of the 19th-century debate over female education. In 1864, Victorian writer John Ruskin delivered a lecture entitled "Of Queens' Gardens," where he argued that women ought to be schooled in all the sciences necessary for the fulfillment of their role as helpmates to their husbands. Men and women, he explained, have different strengths, and complete one another: "Man's power is active, progressive, defensive.... His intellect is for speculation and invention, his energy for adventure, for war, and for conquest"; whereas woman's intellect is "for sweet ordering, arrangement, and decision." It therefore falls to the man to contend with the public sphere, defending his more sensitive wife against the harsh realities of business and politics and war:

> By her office, and place, [woman] is protected from all danger and temptation. The man, in his rough work in open world, must encounter all peril and trial... often he must be wounded, or subdued; often misled; and always hardened. But he guards the woman from all this; within his house, as ruled by her... need enter no danger, no temptation, no cause of error or offense. This is the true nature of home – it is the place of peace.[14]

The world outside the home is a dangerous place, full of difficulty and strife, from which the angel – and her house – must be guarded. Hence the need to maintain the boundary between the public and private domain.

One more area from which women must be protected, and which must be protected from them, is religion. Although Ruskin advocated for girls' education to be almost the same as that of boys, the one exception

13. Coventry Patmore, "The Angel in the House," 2.2.1. In this respect, the angel in the house is something of an inverse of the overreacherix (see previous chapter).
14. John Ruskin, "Of Queens' Gardens," *Sesame and Lilies*, 68.

he made was the study of theology, for which women are entirely unqualified and "where they can know least."[15]

Thirteen years after Ruskin gave his influential lecture, there appeared the anonymous poem "Woman's Rights." Written in response to the budding feminist movement, the poem outlines what it believes to be the true rights of women – to smile, to cheer, and to comfort:

The right to be a comforter, /
When other comforts fail;
The right to cheer the drooping heart, /
When troubles most assail....
The right to be a bright sunbeam, /
In high or lowly home;
The right to smile with loving gleam, /
And point the joys to come.
The right to fan the fevered brow, /
To ease the troubled mind,
And gently tell in accents low, /
"All those who seek shall find."
Such are the noblest woman's rights, /
The rights which God hath given,
The right to comfort man on earth /
And smooth his path to Heaven.[16]

Woman's Mission, Companion of Manhood, George Elgar Hicks

Central to the women's rights movement was the campaign for women's suffrage, which drew vociferous objections, among others, on the grounds of separate spheres. Women, detractors claimed, are content with their domestic lot, their higher calling as wives and mothers. They would be the first to reject the right to vote, a right which would allow the conflicts of the political arena to enter the home, defiling its sanctity and destabilizing its peace. In the words of Reverend John Milton Williams:

15. Ibid., 73.
16. M.C.M.R, "Woman's Rights."

> Home is the charmed spot of this world. Whatever affects it touches human interests in their most tender and vulnerable spot. Amid the excitements of political campaigns, which sometimes threaten the stability of society, it should be neutral ground, the quiet retreat from battles without. To carrying the strife of politics into the sacred enclosure... exposing women to the calumnies and shafts certain to follow, our intelligent wives and mothers will never give their consent.... Woman has no call to the ballot-box, but she has a sphere of her own, of amazing responsibility and importance. She is the divinely appointed guardian of the home.... She should more fully realize that her position as wife and mother, and angel of the home, is the holiest, most responsible, and queenlike assigned to mortals; and dismiss all ambition for anything higher, as there is nothing else here so high for mortals.[17]

Such arguments were pervasive in the late 19th and early 20th century, echoed by politicians from all countries and clerics of all religions. Writing in his capacity as chief rabbi of Jerusalem in 1920, Rabbi Abraham Isaac Kook warned that granting women the vote and enabling their participation in public debate would have a ruinous effect on *shalom bayit* (lit., peace within the home). "The home for us remains a dwelling place of holiness.... When we demand of the woman that she go out into the political public domain... [then] raging differences of opinion will destroy *shalom bayit*, and the rifts in the family will fracture the nation."[18]

Even well into the 20th century, when most women in the Western world were given the right to vote, the doctrine of separate spheres remained culturally dominant. Ads from the '30s, '40s, and '50s regularly featured women in an apron and heels, happily vacuuming the living room rug, enraptured at the sight of their new KitchenAid, or gazing adoringly at the turkey that came out just right. The joys of being a domestic goddess abound.

17. John Milton Williams, "Woman Suffrage," *Bibliotheca Sacra*, 50:7.
18. Rabbi Abraham Isaac Kook, "On Women's Voting."

The angel in the house, then, is the ideal wife and mother, homemaker and helpmate; modest and innocent, obedient and supportive, sensitive and emotional; restricted to the private sphere, excluded from all public, political, and religious debates; bastion of sanctity and virtue within the home. The peace of the house depends on the peace of the angel in it. Both must be protected from the dangers and strife of the outside world. As long as the angel remains safely inside, she is honored and the home is safe. But if the boundary between the public and the private is jeopardized, if the outdoors is allowed in or the indoors out, the angel and her house both fall.

With this, we turn to the Talmud's angel in the house, our sixth and final heroine – Ima Shalom.

Primary Reading: The Fallen Angel of Lod

Ima Shalom[19] comes to us in what is widely considered to be the most famous story of the Talmud: the oven of Akhnai. The story, about a legendary rabbinic debate which culminates with the rabbis declaring themselves final arbiters of the halakhic system, over and above God, has been told more times than probably any other in rabbinic literature.[20] It's been taught in every Jewish school, sermonized about in every synagogue, discussed in every yeshiva; it's been analyzed by talmudic commentators, halakhic decisors, legal scholars, and philosophers (from Maimonides to the Vilna Gaon to Abraham Joshua Heschel to Erich Fromm); it's been explored in hundreds of books, articles, and popular essays.[21] If the Destruction of the Second Temple is the foundational trauma of rabbinic culture, the oven of Akhnai is, in many ways, its founding myth.[22]

One day, so the story goes, a debate breaks out in the Yavneh beit midrash over the purity of a certain oven. Rabbi Eliezer ben Hyrcanus insists that it's pure; the rest of the rabbis are adamant it's not. Brilliant scholar that he is, Rabbi Eliezer marshals "all the arguments in the world" in defense of his position.[23] The rabbis reject them each in turn. His arguments exhausted, Rabbi Eliezer summons a string of miracles

19. Ima was a standard rabbinic honorific (equivalent to the modern "lady" or "madam"); Shalom (and its longer version, Shlomzion) was one of the two most popular female names in the late Second Temple and early rabbinic periods. Ilan, "Notes on the Distribution of Women's Names," 191–92.

20. "The Oven of Akhnai story [is] possibly the most frequently cited talmudic passage in modern literature." Suzanne L. Stone, "In Pursuit of the Counter-Text: The Turn to the Jewish Legal Model in Contemporary American Legal Theory," 828.

21. For a survey of the traditional commentary on the story, see Izhak Englard, "Majority Decision vs. Individual Truth: The Interpretations of the 'Oven of Akhnai,'" 137–52; for a comprehensive roundup of its many halakhic, legal, theological, and historical interpretations, see Nachman Levine, "The Oven of Achnai Re-Deconstructed," 27 n. 1.

22. See Chapter 3. I use "myth" in the sense, not of fiction, but of a narrative of fundamental cultural significance (on the historicity of the oven of Akhnai, see n. 54).

23. Rabbi Eliezer's scholarly prowess is the stuff of legends. According to his teacher, Rabbi Yoḥanan ben Zakkai, "If all the sages of Israel were on one scale of the balance and Rabbi Eliezer ben Hyrcanus on the other scale, he would outweigh them all" (M Avot 2:8; see also Song of Songs Zuta 3:8).

to make his case: a carob tree which uproots itself, a stream which flows backward, the walls of the beit midrash which start to tilt and very nearly fall. One by one, these too are rejected. Outdone, Rabbi Eliezer calls on God to back him up. A Heavenly Voice promptly announces that of course Rabbi Eliezer is right, Rabbi Eliezer is always right. Thereupon, Rabbi Yehoshua ben Ḥanania rises to his feet and proclaims, "It is not in Heaven"; the Torah has been given to humans to observe, and humans alone are responsible for it. Not all the arguments in the world, nor any miracles, not even God Himself can determine the law once a majority of rabbis have decided it. This declaration of rabbinic independence is accepted on high with good humor, as God, we are told, smilingly says, "My sons have defeated Me" (Bava Metzia 59b).

The story of the oven of Akhnai thus tells of the seminal moment in Jewish history when the rabbis overrule God, human interpretation replaces divine intervention, and reason triumphs over miracles; the moment when human beings take control of the halakhic system; when, centuries after Sinai, the Torah is ultimately brought down to earth.[24]

This, however, is only Act 1 of the Akhnai drama. Although the vast majority of interpretations don't read beyond this point, the story doesn't end here. Its next two acts, far more obscure and a lot less triumphant, describe the fallout of the debate and the cataclysmic events that follow. "On that day," the Talmud continues, "they brought every object that Rabbi Eliezer had ruled was pure and burned it, and they voted and banned him" (ibid.). Rabbi Eliezer is excommunicated and is plunged into a great grief, setting off a series of natural disasters that decimate the world's crops, scorch the earth, and nearly kill the Patriarch

24. In his classic work on halakha, which takes its name from our story, 20th-century philosopher Eliezer Berkovits writes: "The nature of the authority of the scholars found its boldest expression in a story told in the Talmud and known as... the 'Akhnai Oven'.... [It] is an insistence on the human share and responsibility in the interpretation and administration of the revealed Word of God.... It was inconceivable that every time a question arose or a problem presented itself, one should have to contact the heavenly authority for a decision. God Himself, in the act of revelation, handed the deciding authority to man." Eliezer Berkovits, *Not in Heaven: The Nature and Function of Jewish Law*, 70–71.

Rabban Gamliel.[25] But it is not until the fourth and final act of the oven of Akhnai that the story reaches its truly tragic end:

Scene 1

> Ima Shalom, the wife of Rabbi Eliezer, was the sister of Rabban Gamliel. After that event she never allowed him to fall on his face.

Scene 2

> One day it was the new moon, and a poor man came and stood at the door.

Scene 3

> By the time she had taken him out bread, she found Rabbi Eliezer had fallen on his face. She said, "Stand up. You have killed my brother."

Scene 4

> Meanwhile a shofar went out from the house of Rabban Gamliel.

Scene 5

> Rabbi Eliezer said to her, "How did you know?" She said to him, "I have this tradition from my father's house: All gates are locked, except for the gates of wronging." (Bava Metzia 59b)

Scene 1 – Routine	*Indoors*	*Ima Shalom, Rabbi Eliezer*
Scene 2 – Break in the Routine	*Outdoors*	*Poor Man*
Scene 3 – Climax	*Indoors*	*Ima Shalom, Rabbi Eliezer*
Scene 4 – Dénouement	*Outdoors*	*Rabban Gamliel*
Scene 5 – Epilogue	*Indoors*	*Ima Shalom, Rabbi Eliezer*

25. The destruction caused by the upsetting of an important rabbi is a common rabbinic motif (see, among others, Shabbat 33b, Moed Katan 25b, Bava Kama 117a, Bava Metzia 84a, Bava Batra 9b); "Rabban Shimon ben Gamliel said: Wherever it says that the rabbis set their eyes in anger upon a particular person, it causes either death or poverty" (Moed Katan 17b).

Scene 1 – Routine

Act 4 of the oven of Akhnai opens, again like many a rabbinic legend, with a routine about to be broken.[26] Entering the fray is Ima Shalom, *the wife (deveitehu) of Rabbi Eliezer,* the excommunicatee, and *the sister of Rabban Gamliel,* the excommunicator (while Rabban Gamliel doesn't appear to have instigated the ban, as patriarch he bears ministerial responsibility for it). True to her name (lit., Mother Peace), Ima Shalom tries desperately to keep the peace between the two men whose lives she connects.[27] Shut up in her Lod home[28] with her persona-non-grata husband, day after day, week after week, for months on end, perhaps even years (we're not told how long this routine actually lasts), Ima Shalom comforts Rabbi Eliezer in his solitude. She becomes his caregiver and sole companion, cheering his drooping heart and easing his troubled mind (as is her woman's right). She also never leaves her husband's side, lest he *fall on his face,* pour out his heart in prayer,[29] and endanger the life of her brother (who, recall, has nearly died once before). Maternal and peaceful, dedicated and supportive, she does all she can to protect her home from impending disaster. As a matter of routine, Ima Shalom is a perfect angel in the house.

Scene 2 – Break in the Routine

But routines, we know, are bound to be broken. *One day it was the new moon.* The narrative is transported outdoors; as opposed to the Ben Hyrcanuses' household, where time seems to stand still, and every day is just like the one before, outside is a new moon, a new month about to begin.[30] *And a poor man came and stood at the door.* Breaking the

---

26. See p. 95 n. 15.
27. On the historical reliability of Ima Shalom's family connections, see below, p. 179.
28. See M Yadayim 4:3 (below, p. 199), Sanhedrin 32b.
29. As mentioned (p. 104 n. 33), prayer in prostration is a spontaneous outpouring of one's deepest feelings.
30. It should be noted that the print edition, as well as most talmudic manuscripts, add the clause "and she mistook a full month for an incomplete one," implying that Ima Shalom went outside because she had mistakenly assumed that it was Rosh Chodesh and therefore Rabbi Eliezer would not be falling on his face. However, as Ari Elon convincingly shows, this is an erroneous insertion, which cannot be reconciled with the facts of the narrative; the text explicitly states that the day was indeed Rosh

monotony of their days, disturbing the fragile peace of their family, a stranger appears at Rabbi Eliezer and Ima Shalom's door. The outside threatens to penetrate the home.

Scene 3 – Climax

With the climax of Act 4, we are back inside with Ima Shalom and Rabbi Eliezer. Yet the dramatic scene features both a flashback to the previous scene, when Ima Shalom had apparently *taken out* some bread to give the poor man, and a flashforward to the next scene, when the blast of the shofar *[going] out* from Rabban Gamliel's household confirms Ima Shalom's premonition of her brother's death.[31] This spilling of Scenes 2 and 4 into Scene 3 enacts the outdoors' invasion of the indoors. The boundary between the public and the private has been compromised.

Furthermore, the act's taut sequence lends its events an air of immediate temporal and causal connection:[32] Ima Shalom leaves the house → Rabbi Eliezer falls on his face → Rabban Gamliel dies. The moment the angel in the house leaves her home, neglecting domestic duties for the sake of civic responsibility (in this case, the giving of charity), tragedy strikes. Just as Rav Kook had cautioned, once the woman goes out into the public domain, *shalom bayit* – the peace within the home, the peace Ima Shalom had struggled to maintain – is destroyed.

Scene 4 – Dénouement

The narrative moves outdoors once more, as the sound of a *shofar [going] out from the house of Rabban Gamliel* announces the patriarch's death.[33] In stark contrast to the *house* of Scene 1, denoting both wife

Chodesh and yet Rabbi Eliezer did fall on his face. Since prayer in prostration, Elon argues, was not part of the fixed daily prayer (as it is today), it would not be obviated by Rosh Chodesh. Elon, "The Symbolization of the Plot Components," 30–36.

31. Tellingly, the same Aramaic root indicates both Ima Shalom's going out of her house (*apika*, a verb used in most manuscript variants) and the shofar blast going out of Rabban Gamliel's house (*nafak*).

32. Synchronicity in rabbinic literature often suggests a causal relationship. Raveh, *Fragments of Being*, 85.

33. In rabbinic times it was customary to mark important public events by the blowing of a shofar; these events included Rosh Chodesh (Niddah 38a, Sanhedrin 41a), excommunication (Moed Katan 16a–17b, Sanhedrin 7b), and death (Moed Katan 27b,

and home – the private sphere Ima Shalom constitutes for, and shares with, Rabbi Eliezer – the *house* here is altogether public: the political and religious institution of the patriarchate.[34]

Scene 5 – Epilogue

Act 4 ends back indoors with a dialogue between Rabbi Eliezer and Ima Shalom, where the latter provides the act – and the Akhnai narrative at large – with its final resonant words: *All gates are locked, except for the gates of wronging.* God always listens to those who have been wronged by others, and is quick to redress their pain. This, says Ima Shalom, is a *tradition from [her] father's house,* alluding to the political office of the patriarchate, of which she is a daughter and to which she lays claim.[35] Moreover, in pronouncing the cause of Rabban Gamliel's death, Ima Shalom – who had abandoned the private for the public – ventures even further beyond her sphere, and dabbles in theology, a field entirely unsuited for women.

Hence the fourth act of the oven of Akhnai is, according to its primary reading, a typical angel-in-the-house cautionary tale. A loving wife devotes her life to her home, supporting her husband through a time of conflict, carefully guarding the peace within her walls. But one day she makes the fatal mistake of leaving the house, choosing the civic over the domestic, the political over the familial, and the public over the private. At that moment, everything collapses; strife enters the home, the angel

---

Ketubot 17a). Though the shofar in our story is in the strict sense an announcement of death, it carries with it the additional connotations of Rosh Chodesh and Rabbi Eliezer's excommunication. Elon, "The Symbolization of the Plot Components," 82–93.

34. The patriarch served as leader of the Jewish community in Israel, deriving his power from the hereditary nature of the position (which could be traced back to Hillel the Elder), as well as from recognition by the Roman Empire. Among his duties were the running of the courts, appointing community treasurers, supervising halakhic decision-making, maintaining relations with the diaspora, and representing the community to the Roman authorities. Urbach, *The Sages*, 535–37.

35. The patriarchate being a hereditary position, Ima Shalom is not only a sister of a patriarch, but a daughter of one too.

is fallen, the house is destroyed. The tragic death at the end of the Akhnai story is the result of the woman betraying her sacred domestic duty.

But, one last time, is this really the story the Talmud is telling?

Household Matters: Ima Shalom Revisioned

We begin our revisioning of Ima Shalom with the 20th-century critique of the doctrine of separate spheres. "The personal is political," argued feminist activists of the '60s and '70s. Woman's household duties, her restriction to the roles of wife and mother, are a matter of political import. The dichotomy between the private and the public is demonstrably false.[36]

Even more trenchant was the feminist criticism of the angel in the house. One of the most powerful attacks, Betty Freidan's *The Feminine Mystique,* details the archetype's devastating psychological effects on the 20th-century American housewife:

> The problem lay buried, unspoken, for many years in the minds of American women. It was a strange stirring, a sense of dissatisfaction, a yearning that women suffered.... Each suburban wife struggled with it alone. As she made the beds, shopped for groceries, matched slipcover material, ate peanut butter sandwiches with her children, chauffeured Cub Scouts and Brownies, lay beside her husband at night – she was afraid to ask even of herself the silent question – "Is this all?" For over fifteen years there was no word of this yearning in the millions of words written about women, for women, in all the columns, books, and articles by experts telling women their role was to seek fulfillment as wives and mothers.... They were taught to pity the neurotic, unfeminine, unhappy women who wanted to be poets or physicists or presidents. They learned that truly feminine women do not want careers, higher education, political rights.... The suburban housewife – she was the dream image of the young American woman

36. "Personal problems are political problems. There are no personal solutions at this time. There is only collective action for a collective solution." Carol Hanisch, "The Personal Is Political," 85.

> and the envy, it was said, of women all over the world.... [But] sometimes a woman would say, "I feel empty somehow, incomplete." Or she would say, "I feel as if I don't exist." Sometimes she blotted out the feeling with a tranquilizer.... Sometimes, she went to a doctor with symptoms she could hardly describe: "A tired feeling. I get so angry with the children it scares me. I feel like crying without any reason." (A Cleveland doctor called it "the housewife's syndrome").... We can no longer ignore that voice within women that says: "I want something more than my husband and my children and my home."[37]

Behind the idealized image of the perfect wife and mother, says Freidan, is the terrible and gnawing emptiness of a woman who wants more out of life. She may be honored and glorified, the object of praise and the subject of poetry, but the angel in the house is often deeply unhappy.

Broad Context: Ima Shalom

With this deeper understanding of what it really means to be an angel in the house, let us try and revision the story of Ima Shalom, starting, as always, with the heroine's other appearances in rabbinic literature.

(i)

> Rabbi Eliezer had a certain disciple who issued a halakhic ruling in his presence. Said Rabbi Eliezer to his wife Ima Shalom, "I will be surprised if he lives out the week." And he did not live out the week. She said to him, "Are you a prophet?" He said to her, "I am not a prophet, nor the son of a prophet, but I have this tradition from my father's house: Anyone who issues a halakhic ruling in his teacher's presence is liable of death." (Eiruvin 63a)

This first talmudic mention of Ima Shalom is a reworking of an earlier narrative from the Sifra (Sifra Shemini, Mekhilta DeMiluim 33). The story features Ima Shalom as a mostly silent interlocutor of her husband, yet

37. Betty Freidan, *The Feminine Mystique*, 11–27.

it is noteworthy that Rabbi Eliezer chooses to share with her the goings-on of the beit midrash, bringing the politics of the rabbinic world into the home, allowing the outside in.[38] No less significant is Rabbi Eliezer's pronouncement of the reason for his disciple's death, engaging his wife in the same kind of crime-and-punishment theology that she had discussed with him at the end of the Akhnai narrative.[39]

(ii)

> They asked Ima Shalom, "Why are your children so beautiful?" She replied, "My husband does not converse with me at the beginning of the night, nor at the end of the night, but rather at midnight. And when he converses with me, he uncovers an inch and covers it again, and it is as if he were compelled by a demon. I asked him, 'What is the reason for this?' And he replied, 'So that I may not think of another woman, and my children be as bastards.'" (Nedarim 20a–b)

The second mention of Ima Shalom is part of an extended sugya on sexual ethics, in which the discussion oscillates between puritan and permissive views. At first, the story seems to be arguing for a more puritan

---

38. This exchange is even more striking given the fact that, in the earlier Sifra version, the first dialogue (*"I will be surprised if he lives out the week"*) is between Rabbi Eliezer and Ima Shalom, but the second one (*"Are you a prophet?"*) is between Rabbi Eliezer and his fellow rabbis. This creates a problem of continuity in the narrative; the question of whether Rabbi Eliezer is a prophet could only be asked by the person who had heard him prophesy the disciple's death. To solve this problem, the Bavli editors had to revise the story so that both dialogues featured the same interlocutor: either Ima Shalom (in the home) or the rabbis (in the beit midrash). Remarkably, they chose to edit Ima Shalom in, and the rabbis out.
39. In this sense, the two stories are mirror images of one another: In the Akhnai narrative, Ima Shalom predicts the death of Rabbi Eliezer's antagonist, is questioned by him, and quotes a tradition from her father's house; here, Rabbi Eliezer predicts the death of his antagonist, is questioned by Ima Shalom, and quotes a tradition from his father's house. This parallelism might explain why the talmudic editors made the choice to have both dialogues with Ima Shalom. It can also account for another change they made to the Sifra's original version, where Rabbi Eliezer says, "I have this tradition from my *rabbis*" (a far more plausible version, given Rabbi Eliezer's personal history; see below, pp. 198–99).

sexual ethic: the encounter between Ima Shalom and her (interestingly, unnamed) husband is prudish and perfunctory, at the dead of night[40] and almost fully clothed.[41] This, explains the husband, is to prevent his thinking of another woman and preserve the purity of conception.[42] Within the context of the sugya, however, the story is cited as part of the permissive side of the argument, since it demonstrates that one is allowed to talk during intercourse, euphemistically described as *convers[ing]* (the dialogue between Ima Shalom and her husband is understood to have taken place during the act itself).

Here, too, Ima Shalom seems entirely passive, submissive, modest – a perfect angel in the house (whose good conduct is rewarded with a beautiful family[43]). Until, that is, we note that the discursive context for Ima Shalom's private midnight dialogue with her husband is a very public dialogue with unnamed questioners – presumably rabbis – who are interested in the secret of her children's good looks.[44] In this story-around-a-story, Ima Shalom goes from passive interlocutor to active narrator, boldly sharing intimate details of the bedroom with other people, allowing the inside out. Furthermore, in identifying the

40. "Rabbi Eliezer says: The night consists of three watches … and in the third watch … a wife converses with her husband" (Berakhot 3a).
41. Elsewhere, it must be said, the rabbis denounce the practice of clothed intercourse, deeming it to be a violation of the marriage contract (which requires "closeness of the flesh"), and mandating that any man who wishes to treat his wife this way must divorce her with full payment of the contract (Ketubot 48a).
42. "According to talmudic morality, thinking of another person while having intercourse with one's spouse is accounted as a kind of virtual adultery. The theme of the importance of sexual partners having no images of another person at the time of intercourse is emphasized again and again in rabbinic literature." Boyarin, *Carnal Israel*, 213.
43. Underlying the sugya throughout is the assumption that a child's physical and mental makeup is determined by the sexual conduct during the moment of conception. Preceding the story is an argument (later dismissed by the sugya) that a child's physical defects are caused by improper physical behavior during sex (Nedarim 20a); following the story is a claim that its moral flaws are caused by immoral sexual behavior, i.e., intercourse without proper emotional intimacy (Nedarim 20b).
44. There is no explanation as to why it is Ima Shalom, rather than her husband, who is asked the question; one possibility (if we are to read this story as occurring after the oven of Akhnai) is that Rabbi Eliezer had already been excommunicated.

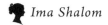

cause of her children's beauty, we find Ima Shalom once again engaged in theological matters, this time of a positive kind (merit and reward).

(iii)

> Ima Shalom, the wife of Rabbi Eliezer, was the sister of Rabban Gamliel. There was a philosopher in their neighborhood who had cultivated a reputation for not accepting bribes. They wanted to fool him. She brought him a golden lamp, came before him, and said, "I want a share in the patriarch's estate." He said to them, "Divide it." Said Rabban Gamliel to him, "It is written in our Torah, 'Where there is a son, a daughter does not inherit.'" He replied, "Since the day you were exiled from your land, the Torah of Moses has been taken away and the Evangelion given in its place, wherein it is written, 'A son and a daughter shall inherit alike.'" The next day, Rabban Gamliel brought him a Libyan donkey. Said he to them, "I have cast my eyes to the end of the Evangelion, wherein it is written, 'I come not to take away from the Torah of Moses, I come not to add to the Torah of Moses.' And there it is written, 'Where there is a son, a daughter does not inherit.'" Said she to him, "Let your light shine forth like a lamp." Said Rabban Gamliel, "A donkey came and overturned the lamp." (Shabbat 116a–b)

This last talmudic appearance of Ima Shalom opens with the same dual relationship mentioned in the Akhnai story. *Ima Shalom, the wife of Rabbi Eliezer, was the sister of Rabban Gamliel.* As opposed to the reference to her marriage to Rabbi Eliezer, which dates back to the Sifra and is therefore more credible,[45] Ima Shalom's fraternal relationship with Rabban Gamliel is found only in the Babylonian Talmud, raising the suspicion that this is one more fictitious family connection created to link two great rabbis with one another.[46]

---

45. A 3rd-century text of Israeli provenance, the Sifra is historically and geographically closer to Ima Shalom; see p. 133 n. 32.
46. See p. 133 n. 34.

Be that as it may, in the Bavli Rabban Gamliel and Ima Shalom are consistently presented as brother and sister. In this story, the two team up to expose the corruptibility of a local Christian judge.[47] They appear at his tribunal, pretending to be locked in a legal battle over their late father's estate.[48] Ima Shalom bribes the judge, who accordingly finds in her favor, awarding her a share of the patriarch's inheritance. When Rabban Gamliel protests that this is contrary to biblical law, the judge counters with the classic Christian claim that the old Mosaic law has been superseded by the new Christian Gospel, which decrees that daughters do inherit.[49] The next day, Rabban Gamliel outbribes his sister, and the judge reverses his ruling, saying that he has *cast [his] eyes to the end* of the

47. That "philosopher," a general term for a rabbinic adversary (Genesis Rabba 11:6, 20:4, Y Beitza 2:5, Avoda Zara 54b), is used in this context to mean a Christian becomes evident as the story progresses.

48. The question of whether daughters inherit is a point of conflict between Jewish and Christian law. According to the biblical verse referred to in the story (Num. 27:8), daughters do not inherit their fathers if there are sons in the family. Rabbinic law, however, dictates that daughters be granted maintenance out of their father's estate (M Ketubot 4:6, see also 4:11, 13:3; in this respect, daughters are comparable to widows who do not inherit but are similarly maintained, see p. 36). Moreover, rabbinic law goes to great lengths to enhance a woman's ability to amass wealth through the halakhic instruments of the dowry (through which a woman inherits a portion of her father's assets; M Ketubot 6:2–7) and the marriage contract (through which a woman inherits a portion of her husband's assets; M Ketubot 1:2–5). It also allows for fathers and husbands to endow their daughters and wives with a share of their wealth through gifts given prior to death (M Bava Batra 8:5, Bava Batra 128b). "While still adhering to the letter of the biblical law, [the rabbis], in essence, transformed it. They did not alter it to the extent that women inherited equally with men. But they did award a woman a sizable portion of her father's wealth and they made it possible for him to choose to give her any amount he wanted.... This area, more than marriage, divorce, or ritual, is one in which the rabbis felt women deserve to be given more rights than the Torah allows." Hauptman, *Rereading the Rabbis*, 177–92. Christian law, by contrast, grants daughters a share of their father's estate even when there are sons in the family. Holger Zellentin, *Rabbinic Parodies of Jewish and Christian Literature*, 154.

49. The derogatory rabbinic term for the Christian Gospel, playing on the original Greek *euangelion*, is *avon gilyon* – lit., scroll of sin (for the anti-Christian polemical tendencies of the Talmud, see p. 99).

Gospel,[50] where Jesus famously declares, *"I come not to take away from the Torah of Moses"*; this is an almost direct quotation of Jesus' Sermon on the Mount, which poses a major challenge to Christian theology, as it seemingly contradicts its supersessionist claim.[51] The original biblical law therefore stands, and Rabban Gamliel should inherit all. Ima Shalom, in a thinly veiled allusion to her bribe, implores the judge, *"Let your light shine forth like a lamp,"* to which Rabban Gamliel, unveiling the plot entirely, replies, *"A donkey came and overturned the lamp."*

As opposed to the previous, more ambivalent sources, this story describes Ima Shalom as an unequivocally public figure. She is out of the house, openly appearing in a court of law, demanding a share of her father's estate – thereby once more laying claim (even if just feigned) to the patriarchate. She does not shy away from conflict, and unabashedly takes part in both political matters, exposing the bribe-taking of the Christian judge, and theological debates, exposing the contradiction at the heart of Christianity.

The Ima Shalom portrayed in these sources is far from a typical housewife. Born to power, politically involved, religiously polemical, and publicly vocal, she is not – nor has she ever been – an angel in the house.

With this portrayal in mind, let's return to the story of the oven of Akhnai.

Immediate Context: The Oven of Akhnai, Take II

Although for most of its history, the Akhnai narrative was read only as far as its first act, and explored strictly in terms of its theological, halakhic, and jurisprudential significance, in recent decades it's been suggested that this is not at all the main thrust of the story. While *"It is*

50. The phrase is all but identical to the one used by Beruria in her argument with the heretic in Berakhot 10a (p. 137); interestingly, in both cases, a woman debates an opponent of rabbinic Judaism, implicitly defending the latter's position toward its women.
51. "Do not think that I have come to abolish the law or the prophets. I have come not to abolish them but to fulfill them" (Matthew 5:17; the previous verse, "Let your light so shine before men," is similarly invoked in our story).

not in Heaven" can be said to be the focus of the Yerushalmi version of the story (Y Moed Katan 3:1), the Bavli's account – read in its entirety, and within its context – appears to be far less about the drama between man and God and far more about the conflict between man and man.[52] Accordingly, criticism of the oven of Akhnai has shifted its emphasis from the theological to the ethical.

Let us, then, cast our eyes to the end of the story, reading it all the way through, and firmly within the context of its sugya.[53]

The Sugya – The Gates of Wronging

> Rabbi Yoḥanan says in the name of Rabbi Shimon ben Yoḥai: Wronging with words [*onaat devarim*] is a greater transgression than monetary wronging, since with the former it is written, "You shall fear God" (Lev. 25:17), and with the latter it is not written, "You shall fear God." And Rabbi Eleazar says: This one affects his person, while that one affects his possessions. Rabbi Shmuel bar Naḥmani said: For this one restitution is possible, while for that one restitution is impossible.
>
> It was taught before Rav Naḥman bar Yitzḥak: Anyone who shames another in public, it is as if he sheds his blood.... Rabbi Yoḥanan said in the name of Rabbi Shimon ben Yoḥai: It is better for a person to cast himself into a fiery furnace, rather than shame another in public....
>
> Rav said: A man should always be careful about wronging his wife [*onaat ishto*], for since her tears are frequent, punishment for her wronging is close at hand. Rabbi Eleazar said: Since the day the Temple was destroyed, the gates of prayer have been locked, as it

52. For these two central aspects of rabbinic storytelling, see p. xiv.

53. "Most interpretations of the story... take the scene out of its narrative context.... Such decontextualized readings run the risk of misinterpretation." Rubenstein, *Talmudic Stories*, 34. The following section draws heavily on Rubenstein's careful and contextual reading of the Akhnai narrative.

> is written, "Though I plead and cry out, He shuts out my prayer" (Lam. 3:8). Yet though the gates of prayer have been locked, the gates of tears have not been locked, for it is written, "Hear my prayer, O Lord, and give ear to my cry, keep not silent at my tears" (Ps. 39:13). And Rav said: Any man who follows his wife's counsel will descend into Hell, as it is written, "But there was none like Aḥab [who did give himself over to do that which was evil in the sight of the Lord, incited by his wife Jezebel]" (I Kings 21:25). Rav Papa objected to Abaye: But don't people say, "If your wife is short, bend down and whisper to her"? There is no difficulty: One refers to worldly matters, the other to household matters. Another version: One refers to heavenly matters, the other to worldly matters. Rav Ḥisda said: All gates are locked, except for the gates of wronging [*onaa*].... Rav Ḥelbo said: A man should always be careful of his wife's honor, since blessing is found in a man's home only on account of his wife, as it is written, "And he treated Abram well for her sake" (Gen. 12:16). And so did Rava say to the townspeople of Meḥoza: Honor your wives, that you may be enriched. (Bava Metzia 58b–59a)

The story of the oven of Akhnai is prefaced by an ethical discussion of the gravity of *onaa* (lit., wronging) – the pain, humiliation, and emotional distress people cause one another. Such wronging is considered far worse than other kinds of harm; it is deeply personal, can never be undone, and ought to be avoided at all costs. Victims of *onaa*, warns Rav Ḥisda, will always be heard and directly avenged by God, for though *all gates are locked*, the gates of wronging remain forever open. This is the background against which the Akhnai narrative must be read.

Act 1 – The Debate

> We learned elsewhere: If he cut an oven into segments and placed sand between the segments, Rabbi Eliezer rules that it is pure and the rabbis rule that it is impure. And this is the oven of Akhnai. What is Akhnai [lit., snake]? Rav Yehuda said Shmuel said: Since they surrounded it with words as a snake and ruled it impure. It was

> taught: On that day, Rabbi Eliezer argued all the arguments in the world, but they did not receive them from him. He said to them, "If the law is as I say, let the carob prove it." The carob uprooted itself from its place and went one hundred cubits, and some say four hundred cubits. They said to him, "We do not bring proof from the carob." The carob returned to its place. He said to them, "If the law is as I say, let the stream prove it." The water turned backward. They said to him, "We do not bring proof from a stream." The water returned to its place. He said to them, "If the law is as I say, let the walls of the beit midrash prove it." The walls of the beit midrash inclined to fall. Rabbi Yehoshua rebuked them, saying, "If scholars defeat each other in law, what is it to you?" It was taught: They did not fall because of the honor of Rabbi Yehoshua, and they did not stand because of the honor of Rabbi Eliezer, and they are still inclining and standing. He said to them, "If the law is as I say, let the Heavens prove it." A Heavenly Voice went forth and said, "What is it to you with Rabbi Eliezer, since the law is like him in every place?" Rabbi Yehoshua stood up on his feet and said, "It is not in Heaven" (Deut. 30:12). What is "It is not in Heaven"? Rabbi Yirmiah said, "We do not listen to a Heavenly Voice, since You already gave us the Torah on Mount Sinai and it is written there, 'Incline after the majority'" (Ex. 23:2). Rabbi Natan came upon Elijah. He said to him, "What was the Holy One doing at that time?" He said to him, "He smiled and said, 'My sons have defeated Me, My sons have defeated Me.'" (Bava Metzia 59a–b)

The founding myth of rabbinic culture begins, quite incongruously, with the most mundane of halakhic debates: an argument over the purity of an oven, broken into pieces and cemented back together with sand. The debate is mentioned as early as the Mishna (M Kelim 5:10) and then again in the Tosefta, where it is cited as the reason that "disagreements multiplied in Israel" (T Eduyot 2:1).[54] How does a pedestrian dispute

54. These mentions in earlier legal texts (to which the opening phrase "*We learned elsewhere*" refers) lend themselves to the assumption that the Akhnai legend is based on a historical occurrence (see p. 133 n. 31).

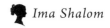

over a simple clay oven become the pivotal moment of rabbinic history? To answer that, we must take a closer look at the world of Yavneh.

Historical Context: Yavneh and Its Sages

The story of the oven of Akhnai takes place during the early years of the beit midrash of Yavneh. Founded by Rabbi Yoḥanan ben Zakkai and his two disciples, Rabbi Eliezer ben Hyrcanus and Rabbi Yehoshua ben Ḥanania, after their escape from Jerusalem,[55] Yavneh became the cradle of rabbinic civilization, the place where the first generations of rabbis worked out their rules of halakhic debate and decision-making. Coming to terms with the loss of the Second Temple, the dissolution of the Jerusalem High Court, and the consequent rise in Jewish division and sectarianism, the rabbis of Yavneh struggled to construct a unified halakhic system that would keep Judaism alive and the Jewish people together in wake of the Destruction.[56] The various tensions, the pull and tug of rabbinic ideologies that marked this initial period coalesced around two main factions in the beit midrash. On the one hand was Rabbi Eliezer ben Hyrcanus (otherwise known as "Rabbi Eliezer the Great"), famous for his staunch dedication to his studies and his perfect retention of everything he learned.[57] He was also an uncompromising traditionalist; after the upheaval of the Destruction, Rabbi Eliezer held fast to his received traditions, desperate to conserve halakha as it was, unwilling to let anything change. On the other hand was Rabbi

55. See p. 79.
56. "'At first there was no dispute in Israel' (T Ḥagiga 2:9). How did disputes begin? According to one view in the Tosefta, disputes were avoided by the adjudication of the great court which sat in the Temple precincts and determined either by vote or by tradition the status of all doubtful matters. In this view, when the great court was destroyed in 70, disputes could no longer be resolved in an orderly way and proliferated.... The essential problem of the Yavnean period [was] the creation of the society which would tolerate, even foster, disputes and discussions but which could nonetheless maintain order." Shaye J.D. Cohen, "The Significance of Yavneh: Pharisees, Rabbis, and the End of Jewish Sectarianism," 48–50.
57. Rabbi Eliezer was the first one in the beit midrash each morning, and the last one out each night (Sukka 28a). Rabbi Yoḥanan ben Zakkai called him "a plastered well which does not lose a drop" (M Avot 2:8; see also Avot DeRabbi Natan 25).

Yehoshua ben Ḥanania, veteran and most venerable of the sages.[58] Rabbi Yehoshua was a firm believer in creative interpretation, a champion of innovation within the beit midrash; if Jewish life has changed so drastically, he contended, Jewish law must be similarly revised to adapt to the new reality. It is between these two ideological poles – Rabbi Eliezer's traditionalism and Rabbi Yehoshua's innovation – that the drama of Akhnai plays itself out.[59]

Thus we find the sages of Yavneh, engaged in a heated debate over the purity of an oven destroyed and reconstructed.[60] *And this is the oven of Akhnai.* Although in its earlier mentions in the Mishna and Tosefta, Akhnai appears to refer to the oven's owner, in the Bavli the name is understood as the Aramaic word for snake, *since they surrounded it with words as a snake.* This opening image of a serpent's chokehold, together with the allusion to the previously discussed offense of *wronging with words,* are an ominous foreshadowing of things to come.

The debate begins with Rabbi Eliezer positioning himself against the rabbinic consensus, declaring that the oven is pure. *On that day, [he] argued all the arguments in the world, but they did not receive them from him.* Rabbi Eliezer persistently offers one argument after another for his

58. His mother would bring him to the synagogue as a baby, so that his learning could begin in the cradle (Y Yevamot 1:6).

59. The conflict between these two rabbis is best exemplified by their respective mottos: Rabbi Eliezer's repeatedly stated, "I never said anything that I did not hear from my teacher" (Sukka 28a; see also Berakhot 27b, Yoma 66b), while Rabbi Yehoshua was known for saying, "There cannot be a beit midrash without innovation" (Ḥagiga 3a).

60. There is perhaps some symbolism here: According to the Mishna, only objects contract impurity – non-objects cannot become impure (M Kelim 2:1). The question at hand is whether an oven, once broken, can ever be put back together again so that it regains its original object status and is subject to impurity. Rabbi Eliezer holds that it can't be, and therefore *rules that it is pure.* In his traditionalist view, what has been destroyed can never be reconstructed; at most, one can try and hold onto the remnants of the past. By contrast, the rabbis, following Rabbi Yehoshua's ideology of innovation, believe that if the oven's segments are reassembled, it does go back to being the object it once was, and accordingly *rule that it is impure.* Hence their attempt to pick up the broken pieces of Jewish life and put them back together again at Yavneh.

ruling, and the rabbis, just as persistently, reject them.[61] Having argued the matter to death, and failed to convince his fellow rabbis, Rabbi Eliezer turns to a less conventional mode of dispute: *"If the law is as I say, let the carob prove it."* The carob tree uproots itself and ambles one hundred cubits (and some say four hundred cubits) from its place. The rabbis, however, are unimpressed: *"We do not bring proof from the carob."* We have already established our rules for halakhic decision-making, and they do not include carob trees. The carob returns and reroots itself. Rabbi Eliezer does not back down: *"If the law is as I say, let the stream prove it."* The waters start flowing in the opposite direction. The rabbis, equally dismissive, retort: *"We do not bring proof from a stream."* The waters resume their natural course. Undeterred, Rabbi Eliezer makes a third attempt: *"If the law is as I say, let the walls of the beit midrash prove it."* The walls begin to cave, threatening to bring down the beit midrash. Rabbi Yehoshua, leader and spokesman for the rabbis, scolds the walls that this is none of their affair: *"If scholars defeat each other in law, what is it to you?"* The walls stop falling, but (unlike the tree and stream) they do not return to their former position. They remain at a tilt, in deference to the honor of both Rabbi Yehoshua and Rabbi Eliezer, *and they are still inclining.* Caught in the conflict between its two founding fathers, the beit midrash teeters on the brink.

Oblivious to the precariousness of the situation, Rabbi Eliezer goes for the jugular: *"If the law is as I say, let the Heavens prove it."* The rabbis might ignore proofs from trees, rivers, even the beit midrash, but they cannot dismiss the Lawgiver Himself. *"What is it to you with Rabbi Eliezer,"* a Heavenly Voice resounds, *"since the law is like him in every place?"* God endorses Rabbi Eliezer's halakhic ruling. The oven of Akhnai is pure. Case closed.

Not, however, for the rabbis of Yavneh. A defiant Rabbi Yehoshua *[stands] up on his feet* and declares: *"It is not in Heaven."* The Torah has been

61. Devora Steinmetz notes that even though, in this particular instance, "there is nothing... that suggests that Rabbi Eliezer is working with a received tradition," it is nonetheless plausible that "Rabbi Eliezer's passionate determination to prove what he knows to be the correct ruling... [and] the use of Q-B-L [receive] to describe the sages' rejection of Rabbi Eliezer's argument evoke the common association of Rabbi Eliezer with received tradition." Steinmetz, "Agada Unbound," 313–17.

brought down from Heaven and given over to human interpretation. It is rabbinic reason and debate that determine the law, not divine intervention, certainly in a post-Temple world, when such intervention is ever less likely. *"We do not listen to a Heavenly Voice,"* Rabbi Yirmiah explains in a later editorial comment, *"since You already gave us the Torah on Mount Sinai and it is written there, 'Incline after the majority.'"* With the Torah now on earth, the only way to decide its meaning is majority rule, especially after the loss of the centralized authority of the Jerusalem High Court.

The prooftexts cited by Rabbi Yehoshua and Rabbi Yirmiah are themselves telling. "It is not in Heaven" and "Incline after the majority" mean something completely different in their respective biblical contexts.[62] The rabbis' deliberate decontextualization enacts the transfer of authority from the Divine Author of the verses to their human readers. The meaning of "It is not in Heaven" is no longer set in Heaven, just as the meaning of "Incline after the majority" is now determined by the majority.[63]

Yet these blatant misreadings are welcomed by God, who seems only too pleased with the assertion of rabbinic authority. *"My sons have defeated Me,"* He says with paternal pride, happy to let the rabbis take the Torah from Him and assume responsibility for its interpretation.

So far, groundbreaking and momentous and full of pathos, is the famous Act 1 of the oven of Akhnai. But, as we've seen, the story goes on, with the triumph of *"It is not in Heaven"* and *"My sons have defeated Me"* unraveling into terrible tragedy.

Act 2 – Excommunication

> On that day, they brought every object that Rabbi Eliezer had ruled was pure and burned it, and they voted and banned him. They said, "Who will go and inform him?" Rabbi Akiva said to them, "I will

62. The first verse refers to the practicability of the Torah ("This command that I give you today is certainly not too difficult or beyond your reach, it is not in Heaven"; Deut. 30:11–12), the second – to the injunction *not* to follow the majority when giving testimony in court ("Do not bear witness in a dispute that inclines after the majority, so as to pervert justice"; Ex. 23:2).
63. See Daniel Boyarin, *Intertextuality and the Reading of Midrash*, 34–36.

> go and inform him, lest a man who is not fitting goes and informs him and destroys the whole world." What did Rabbi Akiva do? He dressed in black and wrapped himself in black and took off his shoes and went and sat before Rabbi Eliezer at a distance of four cubits, and his eyes streamed with tears. Rabbi Eliezer said to him, "Akiva, why is this day different from other days?" He said to him, "It seems to me that your colleagues are distancing themselves from you." His eyes too streamed with tears, and he took off his shoes and fell and sat upon the ground. (Bava Metzia 59b)

The shift, from rabbinic authority to rabbinic authoritarianism, is immediate. *On that day,* the Talmud continues, repeating the fateful phrase which had opened Act 1, everything Rabbi Eliezer had ever declared pure is piled up and burned, and he himself is excommunicated. As opposed to the walls of the beit midrash, which had merely *incline[d] after the majority,* neither standing nor falling, the rabbis seek to quash the minority entirely, banishing Rabbi Eliezer from the beit midrash. Exactly what it was that got Rabbi Eliezer banned is a matter of scholarly disagreement. Some critics believe it was his insistence on adhering to received tradition in a reality which required halakhic innovation;[64] others maintain that it was his rejection of the principle of majority rule;[65] still others say it was his invocation of miracles in the face of reasoned

---

64. "The dispute about the oven was the climax of a long-drawn-out struggle waged between Rabbi Eliezer against the sages and the school of the Nasi. The issue between them was, in general, based upon the conflict between the early halakha, transmitted through the old tradition (which Rabbi Eliezer regarded as an essential element), and the later halakha, which was based also on theoretical argument and exegesis, as sources of equal value with oral tradition, in order to be able to meet such current difficulties and legal problems as might arise from time to time." Yitzhak D. Gilat, *R. Eliezer ben Hyrcanus: A Scholar Outcast,* 483–84.
65. "When the sages came to Yavneh and were worried about what would happen in the future to the words of the Torah ... they adopted the principle of 'the rule is according to the majority'.... Because Rabbi Eliezer refused to accept the rule ... [he] was put under a ban." Judah Goldin, "On the Account of the Banning of R. Eliezer ben Hyrqanus: An Analysis and Proposal," 92–97.

debate.[66] Whatever the cause, it is clear that Rabbi Eliezer refused to follow the rules of the halakhic game, the only rules which would allow for the survival and integrity of Jewish law after the Destruction. Clinging to tradition in a radically changing world, opposing the majority when unity was desperately needed, calling on divine intervention in a post-Temple reality – any one of these would render the rabbinic attempt to reconstruct Judaism at Yavneh null and void. The beit midrash, whose walls Rabbi Eliezer had sent reeling, really would collapse.

And so, concerned for their fledgling halakhic system, the rabbis decide to excommunicate Rabbi Eliezer. Rabbi Akiva, his disciple and friend, is sent to him to break the news. The drama narrows from the momentous to the intimate, as Yavneh and the rabbis and the future of halakha all fade into the background, and we're left with Rabbi Akiva sitting on the ground before Rabbi Eliezer, keeping a distance of four cubits, barefoot and in black in sympathy with his excommunicated teacher (the Talmud considers excommunication to be a form of social death, and many of its rituals are patterned after those of mourning[67]). Rabbi Eliezer, still unaware of the turmoil he has caused at Yavneh, doesn't understand. *"It seems to me,"* says Rabbi Akiva gently, *"that your colleagues are distancing themselves from you."* Rabbi Eliezer breaks down crying, removes his shoes, and falls to the ground in mourning. His fellow rabbis have wronged him, have slighted his honor, and Rabbi Eliezer's pain – just as Rabbi Akiva had feared – is about to *destroy the whole world.*

Act 3 – Devastation

> The world was smitten in one-third of the wheat, one-third of the olives, and one-half of the barley. And some say that also

66. "[The story] decidedly favors the orderly procedures of legal adjudication above the nonrational intrusions of miracles and Heavenly Voices in the academies of Torah studies. Allowing for such supernatural intrusions would undermine the central role of study and rational debate in the development and elaboration of the law." David Hartman, *A Living Covenant: The Innovative Spirit in Traditional Judaism*, 33.

67. "What is the ban (*shamta*)? There is death there (*sham mita*)" (Moed Katan 17a). Significantly, the laws of excommunication and mourning are discussed in tandem, with the sugya repeatedly stating: "There is a similar law for the excommunicatee and the mourner" (Moed Katan 13a–15b).

> the dough in the hands of women swelled up. It was taught: The destruction was so great on that day that also every place that Rabbi Eliezer fixed his gaze was immediately burned. And also Rabban Gamliel was on a ship. A wave of the sea stood to drown him. He said, "It seems to me that this is because of the son of Hyrcanus." He stood up on his feet and said, "Master of the Universe, it is known to You that I acted not for my honor, nor for the honor of my father's house, but for Your honor, so that disagreements do not multiply in Israel." The sea immediately rested from its raging. (Bava Metzia 59b)

With Act 3 the drama broadens once more, revealing the devastating effects of Rabbi Eliezer's excommunication. *On that day,* says the Talmud yet again, the world is struck by a series of cataclysms: crops are ruined, dough is spoiled, fires flare wherever Rabbi Eliezer sets his eyes. Rabbi Eliezer has been the victim of *onaa,* and God's revenge, as the sugya had foretold, is close at hand. The narrative establishes several parallels between the crime of wronging and its punishment: The rejection of Rabbi Eliezer's three miracles is avenged by three natural disasters. The miracles' progression from the natural (carob, stream) to the man-made (the walls of the beit midrash) is mirrored in the disasters' spread from nature (crops) to culture (dough). And the rabbis' burning of *every object that Rabbi Eliezer had ruled was pure* is punished by the fires set to *every place that Rabbi Eliezer fixed his gaze.*

The parallelism extends to the second half of Act 3, where we encounter Rabban Gamliel aboard a ship. The previously dismissed divine intervention, the Heavenly Voice defied by Rabbi Yehoshua's *"It is not in Heaven,"* returns in the form of a deadly storm threatening to drown the patriarch. Like Rabbi Yehoshua, Rabban Gamliel *[stands] up on his feet* and proclaims the principle by which he acted: *"So that disagreements do not multiply in Israel."*[68] Rabbi Eliezer was excommunicated not because of insubordination to Rabban Gamliel or the patriarchate, but in order to preserve halakhic unity among the people. Like Rabbi Yehoshua, Rabban Gamliel believes that personal conviction and

68. The principle harkens back to the Tosefta's comment that because of the oven of Akhnai "disagreements multiplied in Israel."

honor must be disregarded when the survival of halakha is at stake. And, like with Rabbi Yehoshua, God accepts the truth of this principle, and retreats. Rabban Gamliel's life, for now at least, is spared.

Act 4 – Death

> Ima Shalom, the wife of Rabbi Eliezer, was the sister of Rabban Gamliel. After that event she never allowed him to fall on his face. One day it was the new moon, and a poor man came and stood at the door.
> By the time she had taken him out bread, she found Rabbi Eliezer had fallen on his face. She said, "Stand up. You have killed my brother."
> Meanwhile a shofar went out from the house of Rabban Gamliel. Rabbi Eliezer said to her, "How did you know?" She said to him, "I have this tradition from my father's house: All gates are locked, except for the gates of wronging." (Bava Metzia 59b)

Act 4 takes us back to Ima Shalom and the death of the brother she tried so hard to protect. The absence of the act from the Yerushalmi version of the Akhnai story, and its transition to Aramaic (when the first three acts had been in Hebrew), imply that this is a later, Babylonian addition. Significantly, Ima Shalom's dramatic concluding statement – *"All gates are locked, except for the gates of wronging [onaa]"* – returns the story to Hebrew, echoing Rav Ḥisda's pronouncement from the preceding sugya. Ima Shalom, keeper of the peace, is the ultimate mediator: Within the broad context of the Bavli, she is a literary character used to connect Rabbi Eliezer and Rabban Gamliel; within the immediate context of the sugya, she links the story back to the preceding discussion; and within the story itself, she tries to intercede between her feuding husband and brother.[69]

69. This is not the only case in the Talmud of a woman struggling to mediate between the two men in her life; Queen Shlomzion, caught between her husband King Yannai and her brother Rabbi Shimon ben Shataḥ (Berakhot 48a), and Rabbi Yoḥanan's sister, caught between her brother and her husband Reish Lakish (Bava Metzia 84a), are two other examples of this talmudic motif.

Moreover, just as Act 3 mirrors Act 1, Acts 2 and 4 neatly reflect one another. We are once again back in an intimate space. Rabbi Akiva's support of Rabbi Eliezer is taken up by Ima Shalom, who similarly attempts to ease his distress. Rabbi Eliezer's falling to the ground in tears in Act 2 is repeated in his *fall[ing] on his face* and crying out in prayer here. And Rabbi Akiva's announcement of Rabbi Eliezer's social death is echoed in Ima Shalom's announcement of her brother's actual death. Rabbi Eliezer's pain, which has caused so much devastation already, exacts its ultimate price. Rabban Gamliel may have done what he did to save the halakhic system, but he pays for it with his life.

Having read the oven of Akhnai in its entirety, we may now chart the narrative's general structure, with its manifold parallels and contrasts:

	Act 1: The Debate	**Act 3: Devastation**
Sphere	Public	Public
Setting	Outdoors (carob, stream)	Outdoors (crops, sea)
Characters	Rabbi Yehoshua, Rabbi Eliezer (sage vs. sage; conflict)	Rabbi Eliezer, Rabban Gamliel (sage vs. sage; conflict)
Plot	(i) Three miracles of nature	(i) Three natural disasters
	(ii) Divine intervention (Heavenly Voice)	(ii) Divine intervention (storm)
	(iii) Rejection by Rabbi Yehoshua who *[stands] up on his feet* and recites a religious principle (*"It is not in Heaven"*)	(iii) Rejection by Rabban Gamliel who *[stands] up on his feet* and recites a political principle (*"So that disagreements do not multiply"*)
Outcome	Principle preserves the halakhic system	Principle preserves the halakhic system

	Act 2: Excommunication	Act 4: Death
Sphere	Private	Private
Setting	Indoors[70]	Indoors
Characters	Rabbi Eliezer, Rabbi Akiva (sage and friend; support)	Rabbi Eliezer, Ima Shalom (sage and wife; support)
Plot	(i) Dialogue	(iii) Rabbi Eliezer *[falls] on his face* and prays
	(ii) Rabbi Akiva announces social death	(ii) Ima Shalom announces death
	(iii) Rabbi Eliezer *[falls]… upon the ground* and cries	(i) Dialogue
Outcome	Pain causes devastation	Pain causes death

Read both horizontally and vertically, the chart reveals the magnificent structural artistry of the Akhnai narrative: Act 3 mirrors Act 1, Act 4 mirrors Act 2, and the two pairs are almost perfect negative images of one another.[71] This structure, coupled with the context of *onaa*, points to the complex relationship posited by the story between the political (represented in Acts 1 and 3) and the personal (represented in Acts 2 and 4). If the personal is political, as the feminists of the 1960s proclaimed, the

70. The formulation "fell and sat upon the ground" in Act 3 is only ever used within the context of indoor spaces (see Menaḥot 32b, 44a).

71. Note the series of opposites that distinguish the top and bottom halves of the chart: public/private, outdoors/indoors, conflict/support, divine intervention/human dialogue, standing/falling, abstract principles/personal pain.

political is often deeply personal. The oven of Akhnai is not, contrary to how it is almost universally understood, a story of a halakhic debate, a dispute between traditionalism and innovation, God and man, a great sage and majority rule. The oven of Akhnai is a story about what happens when a halakhic debate turns ugly. When a clash of religious values deteriorates into personal shaming. When in the name of political principles, great pain is inflicted. The rabbis might have been anxious to preserve the integrity of the halakhic system, and justifiably so, but in their anxiety they impose on Rabbi Eliezer a punishment disproportionate in its cruelty. They ban him from the beit midrash, and the declaration of independence at the beginning of the story rapidly gives way to the destruction at its end. The truest of principles, the story seems to say, the most sacred of values, do not justify the wronging of another person. God may be happy to let His sons defeat Him, but He will not forgive them for destroying one another.

Banned from the Company of All Men: The Oven of Akhnai, Take III

Thus far the ethical reading of the story. As opposed to the majority of interpretations, which regard only the religious and political aspects of the oven of Akhnai, just as Rabbi Yehoshua and Rabban Gamliel had done (and to the same detriment), the ethical reading takes the personal into account as well.[72] Yet I submit there is one more dimension to the story. If recent readings have shifted their focus from the man—God relationship to the man—man relationship, I propose to take it one step further and ask: What is the role of the man—woman relationship in the founding myth of the oven of Akhnai?

72. "[The story] focuses less on legal controversy than its aftermath, the interpersonal relationships, emotional harm, and verbal wrong.... If there is nothing more rabbinic than argumentation and debate, there is nothing more human than to feel pain at rejection and disgrace.... The story warns that the human element must not be overlooked. Feelings of shame and humiliation matter, and must not be ignored in the name of legal considerations." Rubenstein, *Talmudic Stories*, 47–48.

For there is something else lurking behind the story's elaborate structure. The binary opposites that govern the horizontal division of the narrative – Acts 1 and 3, in contrast with Acts 2 and 4 – bear a striking resemblance to the doctrine of separate spheres; public and private, outdoors and indoors, conflict and support, general principles and individual emotion – these are precisely the differences between the male domain of the outside world and the female domain of the home. Underlying the Akhnai narrative, then, are the same conceptual distinctions of separate spheres, the basis for the archetype of the angel in the house.

The connection to the archetype is redoubled when we look back at the preceding sugya, which contains no fewer than three references to the angel in the house:

In describing the extreme pain caused by *onaa,* the Talmud places a special emphasis on the wronging of one's wife. *Rav said: A man should always be careful about wronging his wife, for since her tears are frequent, punishment for her wronging is close at hand.* Women are particularly susceptible to *onaa* because they are more quickly moved to tears, says Rav, evoking the image of the angel in the house as a delicate, highly emotional creature who must be protected by her man.

The sugya then moves to a debate about the expediency of consulting one's wife. Is it, as Rav Papa argues, a necessary measure of consideration or, per Rav, a dangerous road to Hell? The debate is resolved by distinguishing between two types of issues: *worldly matters,* in which a wife should not be consulted, and *household matters,* in which she should. Herein is a classic expression of separate spheres ideology, put forth, centuries before the Victorians, by the editors of the Talmud; women ought to be fully involved in questions of hearth and home, but completely excluded from the public square. Alternatively, the editors posit a distinction between *worldly matters* and *heavenly matters;* even if women are to be included in the worldly sphere of politics, they must be kept out of the heavenly sphere of religion.

Finally, Rav's edict against the wronging of women is recast toward the end of the sugya (just before the story of Akhnai) in Rav Ḥelbo's positive command that women be honored by their husbands, *since blessing is found in a man's home only on account of his wife,* followed by Rava's instruction to the townspeople of Meḥoza: *Honor your wives, that you may be enriched*. The angel in the house is conjured up once more, as the idealized and honored wife who is the guardian of the home, source of its stability and prosperity.

The background to the oven of Akhnai is thus fraught with angels in houses. And the structure of the story itself, we've seen, is organized around the dichotomy of separate spheres. Which begs the question: Who is the angel in the house of the Akhnai narrative? We've already determined that Ima Shalom is no angel. Wherefore, then, the archetypal description of woman as emotional and easily upset, mainstay of prosperity, respected in private, rejected from the public? To whom does it refer?

The answer, I'd like to claim, is Rabbi Eliezer ben Hyrcanus. The image of the domesticated woman set up in the preceding sugya finds a perfect corollary in the character of the excommunicated rabbi. What we have here is a gender reversal of this highly gendered archetype.

If the sugya said, *Honor your wives, that you may be enriched*, it is Rabbi Eliezer who, when honored, was the source of prosperity and plenty. The moment his honor is slighted and he is placed under a ban, the crops are smitten and the world descends into poverty (it may well have been this poverty that brought the poor man to the Ben Hyrcanuses' door).

Second, if the sugya maintained that women ought to be included in all *household matters*, but excluded from *worldly* and *heavenly matters*, it is Rabbi Eliezer who is cruelly rejected from the public domains of religion and politics and restricted to his home. Excommunication, in early rabbinic times, consisted mainly of banishment from the beit midrash, the locus of religious and political life.[73] Rabbi Eliezer is expelled from the communal study of Torah, barred from halakhic debate and decision-making, his previously dominant voice no longer heard at Yavneh.[74] He

73. "One who is banned may not read a passage of Scripture to others nor may others read it to him; he may not teach Torah to others nor may others teach him" (Semaḥot 5:12). See Gideon Libson, "Excommunication and Banning in the Mishnaic and Talmudic Period," 108.

74. After his excommunication, Rabbi Eliezer's halakhic traditions were essentially expunged from the beit midrash (Niddah 7b). In some cases, the tradition was maintained but cited in the name of another rabbi, so that it would not be attributed to Rabbi Eliezer (Sifrei Deuteronomy 188, Y Moed Katan 3:1). In this, Rabbi Eliezer

is forced to stay home, cut off from his rabbinic colleagues in a ban that will last until the end of his days.[75] Ironically, the same Rabbi Eliezer who decreed that "anyone who teaches his daughter Torah teaches her licentiousness" (M Sotah 3:4) ends up as far removed from the beit midrash as the women he had sought to exclude.[76]

And if the sugya described women as easily moved to tears, it is Rabbi Eliezer who breaks down and cries when Rabbi Akiva informs him of the excommunication. It is Rabbi Eliezer who cries, time and again, whenever he finds himself separated from the world of Torah.

Broad Context: Rabbi Eliezer

(i)

> There was an incident with Rabbi Eliezer ben Hyrcanus, whose father had plowmen who would plow the soft soil, while he plowed the rocky soil. He sat and wept. His father said to him, "Why do you weep? Are you upset that you are plowing the rocky soil? Now, go and plow the soft soil." He sat on the soft soil and wept. His father said, "Why do you weep? Are you upset that you are plowing the soft soil?" He said, "No." "So why do you weep?" He said, "Because I want to learn Torah." His father said, "But you

---

is not unlike the female scholar Beruria, whose name was similarly erased from her law (see p. 130).

75. Elsewhere, the Talmud recounts the heartrending scene of Rabbi Eliezer's death: "When Rabbi Eliezer took ill, Rabbi Akiva and his colleagues came to visit him.... They entered and sat before him at a distance of four cubits. Rabbi Eliezer said to them, 'Why have you come?' They said to him, 'We have come to learn Torah.' He said to them, 'And why have you not come until now?' They said to him, 'We did not have time'.... He raised his two arms and placed them on his heart and said, 'Woe to you, my two arms, as they are like two Torah scrolls that are now being rolled up. I have learned much Torah, and I have taught much Torah.... I can teach three hundred laws with regard to a snow-white leprous mark, but no one has ever asked me about them'.... They asked him, 'What is the law with regard to a shoe that is on a model?' Rabbi Eliezer said to them, 'It is pure,' and his soul left him in purity. Rabbi Yehoshua stood on his feet and said, 'The ban is rescinded, the ban is rescinded'" (Sanhedrin 68a).

76. See p. 119. For similar objections by Rabbi Eliezer to women's study of Torah, see Y Sotah 3:4, Yoma 66b.

> are twenty-eight years old, and you want to learn Torah? Rather, marry a woman and she will bear you sons, and you will send them to school." He went for two weeks without tasting a thing, until Elijah appeared to him and said, "Ben Hyrcanus, why do you weep?" He said, "Because I want to learn Torah." Said Elijah, "If you want to learn Torah, go up to Jerusalem to Rabban Yoḥanan ben Zakkai." He arose and went to Rabban Yoḥanan ben Zakkai. He sat and wept. Rabban Yoḥanan said, "Why do you weep?" Said he, "Because I want to learn Torah." (Pirkei DeRabbi Eliezer 1)

Rabbi Eliezer's origin story depicts him as a latecomer to the beit midrash, son of a non-rabbinic farmer family who was brought up to till the land. Yet Rabbi Eliezer refuses to accept the destiny to which he was born. Just as in the Akhnai narrative, he sits on the ground and cries, longing to learn. Angel in the house that he is, he is told to seek fulfillment in the religious achievements of his sons. And still, he weeps. Rabbi Eliezer yearns for Torah.

(ii)

> When Rabbi Yosei ben Durmaskit visited Rabbi Eliezer in Lod, he said to him, "What new thing did you have in the beit midrash today?" He said to him, "Their votes were counted and they decided that Ammon and Moab must give tithe for the poor in the seventh year." Rabbi Eliezer wept and said, "'The counsel of the Lord is with them that fear Him, and His covenant to make them know it' (Ps. 25:14). Go and tell them: Don't worry about your voting. I received a tradition from Rabbi Yoḥanan ben Zakkai who heard it from his teacher, and his teacher from his teacher, and so back to a law given to Moses at Sinai, that Ammon and Moab must give tithe for the poor in the seventh year." (M Yadayim 4:3)

This scene from the Mishna, generally understood to have taken place after the excommunication, has Rabbi Eliezer confined to his home in Lod. With him and his traditionalist views barred from Yavneh, Rabbi Eliezer must rely on his disciple Rabbi Yosei for news of the goings-on of the beit midrash. Upon hearing that the rabbis, through reasoned debate and a majority vote, have arrived at the same halakhic conclusion for which he already had a tradition, Rabbi Eliezer once again bursts into tears. The pain of his absence from the beit midrash is unbearable. His life, without Torah, is empty. And Yavneh itself is poorer for it.

Hence it is Rabbi Eliezer, not Ima Shalom, who is the real angel in the house of the oven of Akhnai.[77] The tragedy of Akhnai is not, as we had originally thought, the result of the woman's foray from the private to the public, but rather of the man's banishment from the public to the private!

The implications of this gender reversal are radical. In identifying Rabbi Eliezer with the angel in the house, and his confinement to the private sphere as the source of his *onaa,* there is an unspoken acknowledgment of the deprivation that is the lot of women everywhere. The text establishes Rabbi Eliezer as the woman of the Akhnai story at the very same time as it elicits our sympathy for his excommunication from the beit midrash, the distress it causes, the tears it makes him shed. This sympathy cannot but be projected back onto the story's context, onto the women for whom Rabbi Eliezer stands; the women whose exclusion from the world of Torah is just as cruel, its effects just as devastating. The Talmud may not say so explicitly, but the analogy is clear: Women are in a constant state of excommunication.

"A woman is covered up like a mourner, banned from the company of all men, and confined within a prison" (Eiruvin 100b). Here, for those for whom the Akhnai analogy was a little too subtle, is a

77. While nearly all analyses ignore this gendered aspect of the narrative, one notable exception is Charlotte Fonrobert, whose sensitive reading addresses "the thread of gender, which the editors carefully wove into the fabric of the sugya and therefore the talmudic framing of the story." Fonrobert notes the application of Rav's statement about the tearfulness of women to Rabbi Eliezer, but ultimately concludes that "it is not so much that the editors focus on Rabbi Eliezer's feminization" and moves on to discuss the husband—wife relationship as a metaphor for the beit midrash. I argue, quite to the contrary, that it is precisely the feminization of Rabbi Eliezer that is the main focus of the story. Charlotte E. Fonrobert, "When the Rabbi Weeps: On Reading Gender in Talmudic Aggadah," 57–71.

rabbinic admission in black and white: Women are permanently punished, banned, and imprisoned within their homes. And though Rashi glosses the passage with the verse "All the honor of the king's daughter is within," attempting (in true angel-in-the-house fashion) to idealize this fate, the original authors of the passage recognize just how harsh it is.[78] Rashi may regard the imprisonment indoors as a source of honor, but for rabbis of the Talmud, it is the cause of *onaa*.

Thus does the story of the oven of Akhnai subvert the archetype of the angel in the house. As opposed to previous texts we've read, it does so not by breaking the archetype down, but rather by upholding it and simply reversing its referent. If Beruria was a rabbinic thought experiment on what if a woman were just like a man,[79] the Akhnai narrative is a rabbinic thought experiment on what if a man were treated just like a woman. If a man, cast in the role of angel in the house, finds his rejection from the beit midrash deeply painful – a pain that devastates him and nearly destroys the world – then, we must assume, this is true for all angels in all houses. Herein is an acknowledgement, no less revolutionary for its being implicit, of the misery of those who are kept out of the world of Torah. The misery of women whose angelic image masks the unhappiness of their confinement indoors; whose uncontested authority in matters of the household is supposed to make up for their absence from the public sphere; whose idealization as bastions of peace and purity is meant to conceal the emptiness of their days. Such is a misery which, according to Ima Shalom, God will always hear, and which He will be quick to redress.

78. The passage is part of a list of Eve's punishments following the sin of the Tree of Knowledge. "This tradition presents women's inferior social condition as an integral part of the natural order of the world; it does not, however, make any effort to justify it.... The text uses a sympathetic rhetoric of pain, misery, and isolation by linking women's condition to that of prisoners and mourners, without any attempt at excuses." Ishay Rosen-Zvi, "Misogyny and Its Discontents," 220–21.

79. See p. 141 n. 51.

The Moral of the Story: The Danger of Exclusion

We are never so well-intentioned as when we exclude the Other. It's for their own good, we reason, it's to protect them, and anyway, they wouldn't want to take part even if they could. Or we tell ourselves it's to preserve the system, which would never survive if they were to be included. Or we say it is God's will, that the division is something He preordained. And though there may be some situations that call for separation, there are many more that don't. For exclusion doesn't just wrong the Others excluded. It also wrongs us, who are deprived of the good those Others might bring. And, the Akhnai story teaches, it wrongs God, who will swiftly answer their prayers. The Others may have all gates locked to them, but the gates of wronging remain forever open.

Conclusion

Today, thank God, women are no longer locked out of the world of Torah. Together with many non-rabbinic Others, they have taken their place in the beit midrash. The democratization of the study of Talmud, coupled with the newfound appreciation of aggada's literary properties and its subversive nature,[1] have resulted in the stories of the Talmud being read as they have never been read before. If we cast our eyes to the end of these stories (at least, their end thus far), we will find a history of tales revisioned and redeemed, a history to which this book proposes to add another small piece. The six named talmudic heroines, traditionally read as one-dimensional, anti-feminine archetypes, now appear in all their complicated glory; they are not perfect (as no human, and certainly no talmudic character, is), but they are strong, resourceful women, contending with their difficult circumstances with fortitude and with grace. The heroines of the Talmud have been redeemed and, as rabbinic stories tell more of their creators than of their characters, the rabbis have been redeemed along with them.[2]

---

1. See pp. xxii–xxiii.
2. See p. xxi. I repeat my opening caveat that the rabbis are far from consistent in their feminism (as they are far from consistent in all things), and that alongside these

She Who Was Downtrodden: The Feminized Jew

The question remains: How is it that the rabbis, who lived in an era so pervaded by patriarchal thought, when women were considered so foreign and inferior – so Other – how is it that the rabbis were able to display such acute sensitivity toward women as they do in our stories?

One answer, I believe, lies in the paradoxical fact that women, for the rabbis, were not only the paradigmatic Other – they were also the symbolic Self.

The sugya preceding the Akhnai myth predicated womanhood on being (1) tender and timid, (2) politically powerless, and (3) an indoor creature. This threefold definition holds true not just for Rabbi Eliezer of the Akhnai narrative – but also for his entire rabbinic class. "Torah scholars," says the Talmud, "are similar to women, yet act mightily like men" (Yoma 71a). As opposed to the other men of their world – the Roman soldiers, the Israelite farmers, the Babylonian servants – the rabbis had no military might, no physical prowess, no pugilistic aggression. They may *act mightily like men* when it comes to their scholarship,[3] but in all other things, the rabbis are *similar to women* – timid and docile and delicate.[4]

The rabbis were also indoor creatures, permanent dwellers of the beit midrash. Jacob, "a homely man, sitting in tents" (Gen. 25:27), is

moments of proto-feminist understanding are many moments of patriarchal prejudice. And yet, in their stories of the named heroines of the Talmud, the rabbis time and again deconstruct anti-feminine archetypes, in a manner so consistent it cannot but be deliberate, a product of their carefully crafted storytelling.

3. Indeed, when we find rabbis behaving violently it is almost always within the context of scholarly debate or halakhic dispute (see, for example, p. 155 n. 72).
4. According to Daniel Boyarin, "the image of the ideal male as nonaggressive, not strong, not physically active is a positive product of the self-fashioning of rabbinic masculinity.... The behaviors that the rabbis portray as ideal for themselves... are often stigmatized as 'female,' and the rabbis seem sometimes to have been willing and able to take that representation in and transvalue it into a positive self-representation as female or femminized [sic]." Boyarin, *Unheroic Conduct*, 81–99. It must be noted, however, that for Boyarin the feminization of the rabbis makes them, in places, less sensitive to actual women – whereas I am claiming the opposite.

portrayed in the midrash as a proto-rabbinic figure, spending all his days within the yeshiva walls (Genesis Rabba 63:10).[5] The rabbis themselves are compared to "a bride [who] keeps herself secluded all the time she is in her father's home" (Derekh Eretz Zuta 7:2), as confined to the house of study as women were to the house.

Finally, the rabbis – for all of their authority in religious matters and internal Jewish affairs – possessed no real political power vis-à-vis other nations. Theirs was a world born of the Destruction, a world of statelessness, exile, and subordination. With no national sovereignty, the rabbis were to their Roman and Persian rulers what women were to men: repressed and restricted, financially dependent and politically dispossessed (Rabbi Meir, recall, was just as vulnerable to Roman violence hiding in his brothel as his sister-in-law was in hers[6]). The rabbis knew what it meant to be dominated and defenseless; hence their uncanny ability to identify with women.

Yet it was not just themselves that the rabbis compared to women – it was all Jews. Rabbinic Judaism, created by men in a patriarchal world, nevertheless saw itself in the image and likeness of women. The Talmud ascribes to the Jewish people the typical feminine virtues of being "compassionate, humble, and kind" (Y Kiddushin 4:1); the midrash speaks with praise of "the tents of Torah within which Israel dwell" (Lekaḥ Tov 38:9); and in several instances, the rabbis equate the pain and powerlessness of Jewish life after the Destruction with the pain and powerlessness of womanhood:

> Why is Israel likened to a female? Just as a female receives a burden and discharges it, receives a burden and discharges it… so Israel are enslaved and delivered, enslaved and delivered… their pains are like the pains of a female in childbirth…. [Said Israel,]

5. See also Berakhot 63b and Shabbat 83b; this is in contrast with Esau, "a man of the outdoors" (Gen. 25:27), regarded by the midrash as a proto-Roman.
6. According to Rachel Adler, the talmudic incident of Rabbi Meir's escape from the Romans is "an attempt by the sages to draw an analogy between their own experience of marginality and stigma in an often hostile empire, and women's vulnerability and powerlessness under patriarchal institutions." Adler, "The Virgin in the Brothel," 103.

> "I am she who was shrouded and downtrodden in the shadow of kingdoms." (Song of Songs Rabba 1:5–2:1)[7]

Subjugated among the nations, Jews were, for the rabbis, the women of the ancient world.[8] And, like women, they would have to bear their burden with fortitude and strength. Little wonder, then, that the rabbis told stories of heroines doing precisely that.

The feminization of Jews did not begin with the rabbis. The Bible regularly refers to the People of Israel – a small, and subsequently defeated, nation – as "daughter,"[9] "maiden,"[10] and "widow."[11] These feminine metaphors, connoting vulnerability and submission, deeply influenced the rabbis, and went on to form an essential part of Jewish self-perception for over two thousand years of exile. The Jew of the diaspora, studious and physically delicate, and the Judaism of the diaspora, politically disempowered and centered in the home, were seen as distinctly female. Medieval talmudists described their kind as "humble and feeble" and "honor[ed] when dwelling in their houses."[12] Kabbalistic writings repeatedly used women as a symbol for the People of Israel.[13] And modern Jewish thinkers characterized their religion as "having the most

7. See also Song of Songs Rabba 1:9, 4:12. Not for nothing is the figure of the fallen noblewoman a recurring rabbinic metaphor for the fall of Jerusalem (see p. 62 n. 14).
8. "The condition of Israel among the nations: feminine Israel, masculine nations.... The Judaism set forth by rabbinic literature and normative from antiquity to our time – derive[s] entirely from men... but these are men who identify with the virtues they see in women, and who put forth a religious system that means to feminize Israel." Jacob Neusner, *Androgynous Judaism: Masculine and Feminine in the Dual Torah*, viii.
9. Is. 22:4, 52:2; Jer. 4:31, 6:26, 8:21–23; Lam. 2:1, 3:48, 4:3.
10. Is. 37:22; Jer. 14:17, 18:13; Amos 5:2; Lam. 2:13.
11. Is. 54:4; Lam. 1:1. "The biblical view understood that women were powerless and subordinate without being inferior. This insight had enormous implications for the way Israel viewed itself... [and its] destiny." Tikva Frymer-Kensky, *Reading the Women of the Bible*, xvi–vii.
12. Rashi, Yoma 71a; HaMeiri, ad loc.
13. Zohar 1:196b; Zohar Ḥadash 1:98b, 2:48a.

tender and soft... the female aspects of humanity" and "the triumph of the 'feminine' over the 'masculine.'"[14]

At the same time, the analogy between Jews and women was adopted by antisemites throughout history – from the church father's reference to Jews as "effeminates,"[15] through the medieval myth of Jewish male menstruation,[16] to Nazi comparisons of Jewish and female inferiority (in relation to the Aryan man).[17] But if feminization was invoked by antisemites as a sign of weakness, the Jews themselves considered it a mark of strength. Their enemies may have denigrated them as women, but for the rabbis and their heirs, it was a point of pride.

Reading the Text, Regarding the Other, Redux

The second explanation for the rabbis' proto-feminist empathy is that women, as mentioned, were the ultimate Other, and it is through their stories that the rabbis articulated their ethics of otherness. If the rabbis were able to see women as fully fledged human beings who ought to be regarded as such, it is because they wished for all Others to be treated this way.

Which brings me to my final question: If what I am saying is true, and the moral lessons posited in this book are indeed the moral lessons the rabbis wanted us to learn, why did they go to such lengths to conceal them? Why not give them to us upfront? Why must we go through the intricate process of close and contextual reading to uncover what these stories really mean?

14. Adolf Jellinek, *Predigten*, 3:94; Rabbi Samson Raphael Hirsch, *Jeschurun*, 4:182.
15. John Chrysostom, *Against the Jews*, ch. 2.
16. "[The Jews] are unwarlike and weak even as women, and it is said that they have a flux of blood every month. God has smitten them in their hinder parts, and put them to perpetual opprobrium." Jacques de Vitry, *History of the East*, ch. 82.
17. Otto Weininger, the Austrian philosopher of Jewish descent whose self-hating views were espoused by the Nazis, argued that "the Jew, like the woman, is wanting in personality; his failure to grasp the idea of true society is due to his lack of a free intelligible ego.... Greatness is absent from the nature of the woman and the Jew." Otto Weininger, *Sex and Character*, ch. 13.

The answer, I submit, is that the rabbis wanted us to know, firsthand, how easy it is to misread, to misunderstand, to come away with the wrong idea. By constructing their stories to be deliberately misleading, the rabbis force us, the readers, to commit the very moral errors the stories come to warn us against. Like Ulla, we dismissed Yalta the first time we read her story. Like the people of Meḥoza, we projected onto Ḥoma the first time we read hers. We instrumentalized, we stigmatized, we excluded. We were no better in our primary readings than the people in the heroines' own world, and we misread them just as badly. By the time we had revisioned each story, and realized the extent of our error, we discovered how prone we are to misinterpretation, and how important it is to try and avoid it – in reading, as in life.[18]

How, then, do we avoid misinterpretation? We follow the reading rules of aggada, the same rules we used to revision our stories: (1) Close reading – We must take into account every detail, look closely at what's been said, listen carefully to the silences. We must be sensitive. (2) Contextual reading – We must consider the bigger picture, realize there might be other circumstances of which we are unaware. We must be humble. (3) Reading hypotheses – We must put ourselves in another person's shoes, try to see things from their perspective. We must be empathetic.

Herein is perhaps the most ingenious feature of rabbinic storytelling, a stunning coming together of form and content. The moral lessons of these stories are inculcated in us by the same reading practices used to decipher them. Aggada doesn't just teach us to be more moral; the very act of reading it makes us so.

And this, for me, is the ultimate lesson of the stories of the heroines of the Talmud. Far more than the rabbinic attitude toward marriage or sexuality or what it means to be a woman in the world, these stories come to show us how apt we are to misinterpret, and how dangerous such misinterpretation can be for the Other. They force us, in the process of their own revisioning, to look below the surface. And they shape

18. "In many aggadic narratives the heroes are disguised… and then revealed… the revelation invoking a profound human truth. This attests to the belief of the storytellers, and the rabbis in general, that tangible reality is generally a façade, and that man's role is to reveal the truth behind it." Fraenkel, *The Aggadic Narrative*, 132.

us, their readers, to be more sensitive, more humble, more empathetic. To be more moral.

In reading, as in life.

Bibliography

Yalta

Adler, Rachel. *Engendering Judaism: An Inclusive Theology and Ethics.* Philadelphia: The Jewish Publication Society, 1998.

Baskin, Judith R. *Midrashic Women: Formations of the Feminine in Rabbinic Literature.* Hanover and London: Brandeis University Press, 2002.

Fonrobert, Charlotte E. *Menstrual Purity: Rabbinic and Christian Reconstructions of Biblical Gender.* Stanford: Stanford University Press, 2002.

Hevroni, Ido. "Yalta – The Third Rib: Redaction and Meaning in Bavli Berakhot, Chapter 7." *Hebrew Union College Annual* 91 (2020): 1–52.

Ilan, Tal. *Integrating Women into Second Temple History.* Tübingen: Mohr Siebeck, 1999.

———. *Mine and Yours Are Hers: Retrieving Women's History from Rabbinic Literature.* Leiden: Brill, 1997.

Kosman, Admiel. *Women's Tractate: Wisdom, Love, Faithfulness, Passion, Beauty, Sex, Holiness.* Jerusalem: Keter, 2005 [Hebrew].

Or, Tamara, ed. *Massekhet Betsah: A Feminist Commentary on the Babylonian Talmud*. Tübingen: Mohr Siebeck, 2010.
Valler, Shulamit. *Women in Jewish Society in the Talmudic Period*. Tel Aviv: Hakibbutz Hameuchad, 2000 [Hebrew].

Ḥoma

Baskin, Judith R. *Midrashic Women: Formations of the Feminine in Rabbinic Literature*. Hanover and London: Brandeis University Press, 2002.
Calderon, Ruth. *A Bride for One Night: Talmudic Tales*. Translated by Ilana Kurshan. Philadelphia: The Jewish Publication Society, 2014.
Friedman, Mordechai A. "Tamar, a Symbol of Life: The 'Killer Wife' Superstition in the Bible and Jewish Tradition." *Association for Jewish Studies Review* 15:1 (1990): 23–61.
Hauptman, Judith. *Rereading the Rabbis: A Woman's Voice*. Boulder: Westview Press, 1998.
Ilan, Tal. *Integrating Women into Second Temple History*. Tübingen: Mohr Siebeck, 1999.
———. *Mine and Yours Are Hers: Retrieving Women's History from Rabbinic Literature*. Leiden: Brill, 1997.
Kosman, Admiel. *Women's Tractate: Wisdom, Love, Faithfulness, Passion, Beauty, Sex, Holiness*. Jerusalem: Keter, 2005 [Hebrew].
Raveh, Inbar. *Fragments of Being: Stories of the Sages – Literary Structures and Worldview*. Or Yehuda: Kinneret, Zmora-Bitan, Dvir, 2008 [Hebrew].
Rosen-Zvi, Ishay. "The Evil Inclination, Sexuality, and Forbidden Cohabitations: A Chapter in Talmudic Anthropology." *Theory and Criticism* 14 (1999): 55–84 [Hebrew].
Valler, Shulamit. *Women and Womanhood in the Stories of the Babylonian Talmud*. Tel Aviv: Hakibbutz Hameuchad, 1993 [Hebrew].

Marta

Cohen, Naomi G. "The Theological Stratum of the Martha b. Boethus Tradition." *The Harvard Theological Review* 69:1–2 (1976): 187–95.

Ilan, Tal. *Mine and Yours Are Hers: Retrieving Women's History from Rabbinic Literature.* Leiden: Brill, 1997.

Mandel, Paul. "Tales of the Destruction of the Temple: Between the Land of Israel and Babylonia." *Center and Diaspora: The Land of Israel and the Diaspora in the Second Temple, Mishna and Talmud Periods.* Edited by Isaiah M. Gafni et al. Jerusalem: The Zalman Shazar Center for Jewish History, 2004 [Hebrew].

Meir, Ofra. *The Poetics of Rabbinic Stories.* Tel Aviv: Sifriat Poalim, 1993 [Hebrew].

Rubenstein, Jeffrey L. *Talmudic Stories: Narrative Art, Composition, and Culture.* Baltimore: Johns Hopkins University Press, 1999.

Valler, Shulamit. *Women and Womanhood in the Stories of the Babylonian Talmud.* Tel Aviv: Hakibbutz Hameuchad, 1993 [Hebrew].

———. *Women in Jewish Society in the Talmudic Period.* Tel Aviv: Hakibbutz Hameuchad, 2000 [Hebrew].

Watts Belser, Julia. *Rabbinic Tales of Destruction: Gender, Sex, and Disability in the Ruins of Jerusalem.* Oxford: Oxford University Press, 2018.

Yisraeli-Taran, Anat. *Legends of the Destruction.* Tel Aviv: Hakibbutz Hameuchad, 1997 [Hebrew].

Ḥeruta

Calderon, Ruth. *A Bride for One Night: Talmudic Tales.* Translated by Ilana Kurshan. Philadelphia: The Jewish Publication Society, 2014.

Elon, Ari. "The Symbolization of the Plot Components in the Talmudic Story." Master's thesis, The Hebrew University of Jerusalem, 1982 [Hebrew].

Fraenkel, Jonah. *The Aggadic Narrative: Harmony of Form and Content.* Tel Aviv: Hakibbutz Hameuchad, 2001 [Hebrew].

Hevroni, Ido. "An Arrow in Satan's Eye: Contexts and Meaning in a Polemical Talmudic Story." PhD thesis, Bar-Ilan University, 2005 [Hebrew].

Ilan, Tal. *Silencing the Queen: The Literary Histories of Shelamzion and Other Jewish Women*. Tübingen: Mohr Siebeck, 2006.

Kiel, Yishai. *Sexuality in the Babylonian Talmud: Christian and Sasanian Contexts in Late Antiquity*. New York: Cambridge University Press, 2016.

Kosman, Admiel. *Women's Tractate: Wisdom, Love, Faithfulness, Passion, Beauty, Sex, Holiness*. Jerusalem: Keter, 2005 [Hebrew].

Naeh, Shlomo. "Freedom and Celibacy: A Talmudic Variation on Tales of Temptation and Fall in Genesis and Its Syrian Background." *The Book of Genesis in Jewish and Oriental Christian Interpretation*. Edited by Judith Frishman and Lucas Van Rompay. Leuven: Traditio Exegetica Graeca, 1997.

Rosen-Zvi, Ishay. "The Evil Inclination, Sexuality, and Forbidden Cohabitations: A Chapter in Talmudic Anthropology." *Theory and Criticism* 14 (1999): 55–84 [Hebrew].

Rubenstein, Jeffrey L. *The Land of Truth: Talmud Tales, Timeless Teachings*. Philadelphia: The Jewish Publication Society, 2018.

Schremer, Adiel. "Marriage, Sexuality, and Holiness: The Anti-Ascetic Legacy of Talmudic Judaism." *Gender Relationships in Marriage and Out*. Edited by R.T. Blau. New York: Yeshiva University Press, 2007.

Stein, Dina. "Let the 'People' Go? The 'Folk' and their 'Lore' as Tropes in the Reconstruction of Rabbinic Culture." *Prooftexts* 29:2 (2009): 206–41.

Valler, Shulamit. *Women in Jewish Society in the Talmudic Period*. Tel Aviv: Hakibbutz Hameuchad, 2000 [Hebrew].

Beruria

Adler, Rachel. "The Virgin in the Brothel and Other Anomalies: Character and Context in the Legend of Beruriah." *Tikkun* 3 (1988): 28–32, 102–5.

Bacon, Brenda S. "How Shall We Tell the Story of Beruriah's End?" *Nashim: A Journal of Jewish Women's Studies & Gender Issues* 5 (2002): 231–39.

Baskin, Judith R. *Midrashic Women: Formations of the Feminine in Rabbinic Literature*. Hanover and London: Brandeis University Press, 2002.

Boyarin, Daniel. *Carnal Israel: Reading Sex in Talmudic Culture*. Berkeley: University of California Press, 1993.

———. "Diachrony vs. Synchrony: 'The Legend of Beruria.'" *Jerusalem Studies in Jewish Folklore* 11–12 (1990): 7–17 [Hebrew].

Brown, Iris. "Forgotten and Revived: The Bruria Episode in Contemporary Orthodox Discourse." *Daat: A Journal of Jewish Philosophy & Kabbalah* 83 (2017): 407–22 [Hebrew].

Calderon, Ruth. *A Bride for One Night: Talmudic Tales*. Translated by Ilana Kurshan. Philadelphia: The Jewish Publication Society, 2014.

Cohen, Naomi G. "Bruria in the Bavli and in Rashi 'Avodah Zarah' 18B." *Tradition* 48 (2015): 29–40.

Drori, Itamar. "The Beruriah Incident: Tradition of Exclusion as a Presence of Ethical Principles." *PaRDeS: Zeitschrift der Vereinigung für Jüdische Studien* 20 (2014): 99–116.

Goodblatt, David. "The Beruriah Traditions." *Journal of Jewish Studies* 26 (1975): 68–85.

Grossman, Avraham. *Pious and Rebellious: Jewish Women in Europe in the Middle Ages*. Jerusalem: The Zalman Shazar Center for Jewish History, 2001 [Hebrew].

Hartman, Tova, and Charlie Buckholtz. "'Beruriah Said Well': The Many Lives (and Deaths) of a Talmudic Social Critic." *Prooftexts* 31 (2011): 181–209.

Henkin, Eitam. "The Mystery of the 'Beruria Incident': A Suggested Solution." *Akdamot* 21 (2008): 140–59 [Hebrew].

Hoshen, Dalia. *Beruriah the Tannait: A Theological Reading of a Female Mishnaic Scholar*. Lanham, MD: University Press of America, 2007.

Ilan, Tal. *Integrating Women into Second Temple History*. Tübingen: Mohr Siebeck, 1999.

———. *Mine and Yours Are Hers: Retrieving Women's History from Rabbinic Literature*. Leiden: Brill, 1997.

———. "The Quest for the Historical Beruriah, Rachel, and Imma Shalom." *Association for Jewish Studies Review* 22:1 (1997): 1–17.

Monnickendam, Yifat. "Bruria as a Contradictory Analogy to Rabbi Meir." *Derech Aggadah* 2 (1999): 37–63 [Hebrew].

Ozick, Cynthia. "Notes toward Finding the Right Question (A Vindication of the Rights of Jewish Women)." *Lilith* 6 (1979): 19–29.

Shenhar, Aliza. "The Figure of Rabbi Meir and Its Literary Characterization in the Legends." *Heqer Veiyun: Studies in Judaism*. Edited by Efrat Carmon. Haifa: Haifa University Press, 1976 [Hebrew].

Simon-Shoshan, Moshe. "The Death of Beruriah and Its Afterlife: A Reevaluation of the Provenance and Significance of Ma'aseh de-Beruriah." *Jewish Quarterly Review* 110:3 (2020): 383–411.

Ima Shalom

Boyarin, Daniel. *Carnal Israel: Reading Sex in Talmudic Culture*. Berkeley: University of California Press, 1993.

Elon, Ari. "The Symbolization of the Plot Components in the Talmudic Story." Master's thesis, The Hebrew University of Jerusalem, 1982 [Hebrew].

Fonrobert, Charlotte E. "When the Rabbi Weeps: On Reading Gender in Talmudic Aggadah." *Nashim: A Journal of Jewish Women's Studies & Gender Issues* 4 (2001): 56–83.

Ilan, Tal. *Mine and Yours Are Hers: Retrieving Women's History from Rabbinic Literature*. Leiden: Brill, 1997.

———. "The Quest for the Historical Beruriah, Rachel, and Imma Shalom." *Association for Jewish Studies Review* 22:1 (1997): 1–17.

Levine, Nachman. "The Oven of Achnai Re-Deconstructed." *Hebrew Studies* 45 (2004): 27–47.

Raveh, Inbar. *Fragments of Being: Stories of the Sages – Literary Structures and Worldview*. Or Yehuda: Kinneret, Zmora-Bitan, Dvir, 2008 [Hebrew].

Rubenstein, Jeffrey L. *Talmudic Stories: Narrative Art, Composition, and Culture*. Baltimore: Johns Hopkins University Press, 1999.

Sobolev-Mandelbaum, Liat. "Immah Shalom: The Controversial Role Model." *Women in Judaism: A Multidisciplinary e-Journal* 14:2 (2017): 1–20.

Steinmetz, Devora. "Agada Unbound: Inter-Agadic Characterization of the Sages in the Bavli and Implications for Reading Agada." *Creation and Composition: The Contribution of the Bavli Redactors.* Edited by Jeffrey L. Rubenstein. Tübingen: Mohr Siebeck, 2005.

Stone, Suzanne L. "In Pursuit of the Counter-Text: The Turn to the Jewish Legal Model in Contemporary American Legal Theory." *Harvard Law Review* 106:4 (1993): 813–94.

Valler, Shulamit. *Women in Jewish Society in the Talmudic Period.* Tel Aviv: Hakibbutz Hameuchad, 2000 [Hebrew].

General

Abarbanell, Nitza. *Eve and Lilith.* Ramat Gan: Bar-Ilan University Press, 1994 [Hebrew].

Adler, Rachel. *Engendering Judaism: An Inclusive Theology and Ethics.* Philadelphia: The Jewish Publication Society, 1998.

———. "The Jew Who Wasn't There: Halacha and the Jewish Woman." *Response: A Contemporary Jewish Review* 18 (1973): 77–82.

———. "The Virgin in the Brothel and Other Anomalies: Character and Context in the Legend of Beruriah." *Tikkun* 3 (1988): 28–32, 102–5.

Alexander, E. Shanks. "The Impact of Feminism on Rabbinic Studies." *Jews and Gender: The Challenge to Hierarchy.* Edited by Jonathan Frankel. Oxford: Oxford University Press, 2000.

———. "The Orality of Rabbinic Writings." *The Cambridge Companion to the Talmud and Rabbinic Literature.* Edited by Charlotte E. Fonrobert and Martin S. Jaffee. Cambridge: Cambridge University Press, 2007.

Appleton Aguiar, Sarah. *The Bitch Is Back: Wicked Women in Literature.* Carbondale, IL: Southern Illinois University Press, 2001.

Archer, Léonie J. *Her Price Is Beyond Rubies: The Jewish Woman in Graeco-Roman Palestine.* Sheffield: Sheffield Academic Press, 1990.

———. "The Virgin and the Harlot in the Writings of Formative Judaism." *History Workshop Journal* 24 (1987): 1–16.

Baader, Benjamin Maria. *Gender, Judaism, and Bourgeois Culture in Germany, 1800–1870.* Bloomington and Indianapolis: Indiana University Press, 2006.

Bacon, Brenda S. "How Shall We Tell the Story of Beruriah's End?" *Nashim: A Journal of Jewish Women's Studies & Gender Issues* 5 (2002): 231–39.

Baer, Yitzhak. *Israel Among the Nations: An Essay on the History of the Period of the Second Temple and the Mishna and on the Foundations of the Halacha and Jewish Religion*. Jerusalem: The Bialik Institute, 1955 [Hebrew].

———. "Jerusalem in the Times of the Great Revolt." *Zion* 36 (1971): 127–90 [Hebrew].

Baker, Cynthia M. *Rebuilding the House of Israel: Architectures of Gender in Jewish Antiquity*. Stanford: Stanford University Press, 2002.

Bar-Ilan, Meir. *Some Jewish Women in Antiquity*. Atlanta: Brown Judaic Studies, 1998.

Baskin, Judith R. *Midrashic Women: Formations of the Feminine in Rabbinic Literature*. Hanover and London: Brandeis University Press, 2002.

Baudrillard, Jean. *The Transparency of Evil: Essays on Extreme Phenomena*. Translated by James Benedict. London: Verso, 1993.

Beard, Mary. *Women & Power: A Manifesto*. London: Profile Books, 2017.

Beattie, James. "Essay on Laughter and Ludicrous Composition." *Essays*. 3rd ed. London: Dilly, 1779.

Beauvoir, Simone de. *The Second Sex*. Translated by H.M. Parshley. Patna: Scientific Book Company, 1960.

Beer, Moshe. *The Babylonian Amoraim: Aspects of Economic Life*. Ramat Gan: Bar-Ilan University Press, 1974 [Hebrew].

Berkovits, Eliezer. *Not in Heaven: The Nature and Function of Jewish Law*. Jerusalem: Shalem Press, 2010.

Bernau, Anke. *Virgins: A Cultural History*. London: Granta Books, 2007.

Biale, David. *Eros and the Jews: From Biblical Israel to Contemporary America*. New York: BasicBooks, 1992.

Biale, Rachel. *Women and Jewish Law: The Essential Texts, Their History, and Their Relevance for Today*. New York: Schocken Books, 1995.

Bialik, H.N., and Y.N. Ravnitzky, eds. *The Book of Legends*. Tel Aviv: Dvir, 1987 [Hebrew].

Boyarin, Daniel. *Carnal Israel: Reading Sex in Talmudic Culture*. Berkeley: University of California Press, 1993.

———. "Diachrony vs. Synchrony: 'The Legend of Beruria.'" *Jerusalem Studies in Jewish Folklore* 11–12 (1990): 7–17 [Hebrew].

———. "Friends Without Benefits; or, Academic Love." *Sex in Antiquity: Exploring Gender and Sexuality in the Ancient World.* Edited by Mark Masterson et al. London: Routledge, 2015.

———. "Hellenism in Jewish Babylonia." *The Cambridge Companion to the Talmud and Rabbinic Literature.* Edited by Charlotte E. Fonrobert and Martin S. Jaffee. Cambridge: Cambridge University Press, 2007.

———. "Homotopia: The Feminized Jewish Man and the Lives of Women in Late Antiquity." *Differences: A Journal of Feminist Cultural Studies* 7:2 (1995): 41–81.

———. *Intertextuality and the Reading of Midrash.* Bloomington and Indianapolis: Indiana University Press, 1990.

———. *Unheroic Conduct: The Rise of Heterosexuality and the Invention of the Jewish Man.* Berkeley: University of California Press, 1997.

Brand, Yehoshua. *Ceramics in Talmudic Literature.* Jerusalem: Mossad Harav Kook, 1953 [Hebrew].

Brown, Iris. "Forgotten and Revived: The Bruria Episode in Contemporary Orthodox Discourse." *Daat: A Journal of Jewish Philosophy & Kabbalah* 83 (2017): 407–22 [Hebrew].

Bueler, Lois E. *The Tested Woman Plot: Women's Choices, Men's Judgments, and the Shaping of Stories.* Columbus: Ohio State University Press, 2001.

Calderon, Ruth. *A Bride for One Night: Talmudic Tales.* Translated by Ilana Kurshan. Philadelphia: The Jewish Publication Society, 2014.

Cavanagh, Sheila T. *Wanton Eyes and Chaste Desires: Female Sexuality in the Faerie Queene.* Bloomington and Indianapolis: Indiana University Press, 1994.

Clark, Elizabeth A. "Ideology, History, and the Construction of 'Woman' in Late Ancient Christianity." *Journal of Early Christian Studies* 2 (1984): 155–84.

Cohen, Naomi G. "Bruria in the Bavli and in Rashi 'Avodah Zarah' 18B." *Tradition* 48 (2015): 29–40.

———. "The Theological Stratum of the Martha b. Boethus Tradition." *The Harvard Theological Review* 69:1–2 (1976): 187–95.

Cohen, Shaye J.D. "The Significance of Yavneh: Pharisees, Rabbis, and the End of Jewish Sectarianism." *Hebrew Union College Annual* 55 (1984): 27–53.

———. *Why Aren't Jewish Women Circumcised? Gender and Covenant in Judaism*. Berkeley: University of California Press, 2003.

Douglas, Susan. *Where the Girls Are: Growing Up Female in the Mass Media*. New York: Three Rivers Press, 1995.

Drori, Itamar. "The Beruriah Incident: Tradition of Exclusion as a Presence of Ethical Principles." *PaRDeS: Zeitschrift der Vereinigung für Jüdische Studien* 20 (2014): 99–116.

Eilberg-Schwartz, Howard. *God's Phallus and Other Problems for Men in Monotheism*. Boston: Beacon, 1994.

Elbaum, Jacob. *Medieval Perspectives on Aggadah and Midrash*. Jerusalem: The Bialik Institute, 2000 [Hebrew].

Elman, Yaakov. "Middle Persian Culture and Babylonian Sages: Accommodation and Resistance in the Shaping of Rabbinic Legal Tradition." *The Cambridge Companion to the Talmud and Rabbinic Literature*. Edited by Charlotte E. Fonrobert and Martin S. Jaffee. Cambridge: Cambridge University Press, 2007.

Elon, Ari. "The Symbolization of the Plot Components in the Talmudic Story." Master's thesis, The Hebrew University of Jerusalem, 1982 [Hebrew].

Englard, Izhak. "Majority Decision vs. Individual Truth: The Interpretations of the 'Oven of Akhnai.'" *Tradition* 15:1–2 (1975): 137–52.

Fonrobert, Charlotte E. *Menstrual Purity: Rabbinic and Christian Reconstructions of Biblical Gender*. Stanford: Stanford University Press, 2002.

———. "Regulating the Human Body: Rabbinic Legal Discourse and the Making of Jewish Gender." *The Cambridge Companion to the Talmud and Rabbinic Literature*. Edited by Charlotte E. Fonrobert and Martin S. Jaffee. Cambridge: Cambridge University Press, 2007.

———. "When the Rabbi Weeps: On Reading Gender in Talmudic Aggadah." *Nashim: A Journal of Jewish Women's Studies & Gender Issues* 4 (2001): 56–83.

Fraenkel, Jonah. *The Aggadic Narrative: Harmony of Form and Content.* Tel Aviv: Hakibbutz Hameuchad, 2001 [Hebrew].

———. "Hermeneutic Problems in the Study of Aggadic Narrative." *Tarbiz* 47 (1978): 139–72 [Hebrew].

———. *Studies in the Spiritual World of Aggadic Narrative.* Tel Aviv: Hakibbutz Hameuchad, 1981 [Hebrew].

Freidan, Betty. *The Feminine Mystique.* New York: Dell Publishing, 1963.

Freud, Sigmund. "On the Universal Tendency of Debasement in the Sphere of Love." *The Standard Edition of the Complete Psychological Works.* Edited and translated by James Strachey. Vol. 11. London: The Hogarth Press, 1957.

Friedman, Mordechai A. "Tamar, a Symbol of Life: The 'Killer Wife' Superstition in the Bible and Jewish Tradition." *Association for Jewish Studies Review* 15:1 (1990): 23–61.

Frye, Northrop. *Anatomy of Criticism: Four Essays.* Princeton: Princeton University Press, 1957.

Frymer-Kensky, Tikva. *Reading the Women of the Bible.* New York: Schocken Books, 2002.

Gafni, Isaiah M. "The Institution of Marriage in Rabbinic Times." *The Jewish Family: Metaphor and Memory.* Edited by David M. Kraemer. New York: Oxford University Press, 1989.

———. "Rabbinic Historiography and Representations of the Past." *The Cambridge Companion to the Talmud and Rabbinic Literature.* Edited by Charlotte E. Fonrobert and Martin S. Jaffee. Cambridge: Cambridge University Press, 2007.

Gerhardsson, Birger. *Memory and Manuscript: Oral Tradition and Written Transmission in Rabbinic Judaism and Early Christianity.* Grand Rapids: William B. Eerdmans Publishing Company, 1998.

Gilat, Yitzhak D. *R. Eliezer ben Hyrcanus: A Scholar Outcast.* Ramat Gan: Bar-Ilan University Press, 1984.

Goldin, Judah. "On the Account of the Banning of R. Eliezer ben Hyrqanus: An Analysis and Proposal." *The Journal of the Ancient Near Eastern Society* 16–17 (1984–85): 85–97.

Goodblatt, David. "The Beruriah Traditions." *Journal of Jewish Studies* 26 (1975): 68–85.

Green, William S. "What's in a Name? The Problematics of Rabbinic Biography." *Approaches to Ancient Judaism: Theory and Practice*. Edited by William S. Green. Missoula, MT: Scholars Press, 1987.

Grossman, Avraham. *Pious and Rebellious: Jewish Women in Europe in the Middle Ages*. Jerusalem: The Zalman Shazar Center for Jewish History, 2001 [Hebrew].

———. *Rashi*. Translated by Joel Linsider. Liverpool: Littman Library of Jewish Civilization, 2012.

Halberstam, Chaya. "Encircling the Law: The Legal Boundaries of Rabbinic Judaism." *Jewish Studies Quarterly* 16:4 (2009): 396–424.

Hanisch, Carol. "The Personal Is Political." *Notes from the Second Year*. Edited by Shulamith Firestone. New York: Radical Feminism, 1970.

Hartman, David. *A Living Covenant: The Innovative Spirit in Traditional Judaism*. Woodstock, VT: Jewish Lights, 1997.

Hartman, Tova, and Charlie Buckholtz. "'Beruriah Said Well': The Many Lives (and Deaths) of a Talmudic Social Critic." *Prooftexts* 31 (2011): 181–209.

Hasan-Rokem, Galit. *Tales of the Neighborhood*. Berkeley: University of California Press, 2003.

———. *Web of Life: Folklore and Midrash in Rabbinic Literature*. Translated by Batya Stein. Stanford: Stanford University Press, 2000.

Hauptman, Judith. "Feminist Perspectives on Jewish Studies: Rabbinics." *Feminist Perspectives in Jewish Studies*. Edited by Lynn Davidman and Shelley Tanenbaum. New Haven: Yale University Press, 1995.

———. "Images of Women in the Talmud." *Religion and Sexism: Images of Woman in the Jewish and Christian Traditions*. Edited by Rosemary Radford Ruether. New York: Simon and Schuster, 1974.

———. *Rereading the Rabbis: A Woman's Voice*. Boulder: Westview Press, 1998.

———. "Women Reading Talmud." *Lift Up Your Voice: Women's Voices and Feminist Interpretation in Jewish Studies*. Edited by Rina Levine-Melammed. Tel Aviv: Yediot Books, 2001 [Hebrew].

Hayes, Christine. "The 'Other' in Rabbinic Literature." *The Cambridge Companion to the Talmud and Rabbinic Literature*. Edited by Charlotte E. Fonrobert and Martin S. Jaffee. Cambridge: Cambridge University Press, 2007.

Heinz, Evelyn J., and John J. Teunissen. "Culture and the Humanities: The Archetypal Approach." *Jungian Literary Criticism*. Edited by Richard P. Sugg. Evanston: Northwestern University Press, 1992.

Hengel, Martin. *The Zealots: Investigations into the Jewish Freedom Movement in the Period from Herod 1 until 70 Ad.* Edinburgh: T. & T. Clark, 1989.

Henkin, Eitam. "The Mystery of the 'Beruria Incident': A Suggested Solution." *Akdamot* 21 (2008): 140–59 [Hebrew].

Herford, R. Travers. *Christianity in the Talmud and Midrash*. London: Williams & Norgate, 1903.

Herr, M.D. "The Conception of History Among the Sages." *Studies in Jewish History in the Mishna and Talmud Period*. Edited by Isaiah M. Gafni. Jerusalem: The Zalman Shazar Center for Jewish History, 1994 [Hebrew].

———. "Marriage from a Socio-Economic Perspective According to the Halakhah." *Families of Israel: The Jewish Conception of the Family*. Jerusalem: Ministry of Education and Culture, 1976 [Hebrew].

Hevroni, Ido. "An Arrow in Satan's Eye: Contexts and Meaning in a Polemical Talmudic Story." PhD thesis, Bar-Ilan University, 2005 [Hebrew].

———. "Yalta – The Third Rib: Redaction and Meaning in Bavli Berakhot, Chapter 7." *Hebrew Union College Annual* 91 (2020): 1–52.

Hoshen, Dalia. *Beruriah the Tannait: A Theological Reading of a Female Mishnaic Scholar*. Lanham, MD: University Press of America, 2007.

Ilan, Tal. *Integrating Women into Second Temple History*. Tübingen: Mohr Siebeck, 1999.

———. *Jewish Women in Greco-Roman Palestine: An Inquiry into Image and Status*. Tübingen: Mohr Siebeck, 2020.

———. *Mine and Yours Are Hers: Retrieving Women's History from Rabbinic Literature*. Leiden: Brill, 1997.

———. "Notes on the Distribution of Women's Names in Palestine in the Second Temple and Mishnaic Period." *Journal of Jewish Studies* 40 (1989): 186–200.

———. "The Quest for the Historical Beruriah, Rachel, and Imma Shalom." *Association for Jewish Studies Review* 22:1 (1997): 1–17.

———. "Rabbinic Literature and Women's Studies." *Lift Up Your Voice: Women's Voices and Feminist Interpretation in Jewish Studies*. Edited by Rina Levine-Melammed. Tel Aviv: Yediot Books, 2001 [Hebrew].

———. *Silencing the Queen: The Literary Histories of Shelamzion and Other Jewish Women*. Tübingen: Mohr Siebeck, 2006.

Jaffee, Martin S. "Rabbinic Authorship as a Collective Enterprise." *The Cambridge Companion to the Talmud and Rabbinic Literature*. Edited by Charlotte E. Fonrobert and Martin S. Jaffee. Cambridge: Cambridge University Press, 2007.

Jung, C.G. "Fundamental Questions of Psychotherapy." *Collected Works of C.G. Jung*. Translated by R.F.G. Hull. Vol. 16. New York: Bollingen Foundation, 1954.

Jütte, Robert. *The Jewish Body: A History*. Translated by Elizabeth Bredeck. Philadelphia: University of Pennsylvania Press, 2021.

Kalmin, Richard. *Sages, Stories, Authors, and Editors in Rabbinic Babylonia*. Atlanta: Brown Judaic Studies, 1994.

Kaplow, Susi. "Getting Angry." *Radical Feminism*. Edited by Anne Koedt et al. New York: Quadrangle Books, 1973.

Kiel, Yishai. *Sexuality in the Babylonian Talmud: Christian and Sasanian Contexts in Late Antiquity*. New York: Cambridge University Press, 2016.

Kiperwasser, Reuven. "Narrative Bricolage and Cultural Hybrids in Rabbinic Babylonia: On the Narratives of Seduction and the Topos of Light." *The Aggada of the Bavli and Its Cultural World*. Edited by Geoffrey Herman and Jeffrey L. Rubenstein. Providence: Brown Judaic Studies, 2018.

———. "Wives of Commoners and the Masculinity of the Rabbis: Jokes, Serious Matters, and Migrating Traditions." *Journal for the Study of Judaism in the Persian, Hellenistic, and Roman Period* 48:3 (2017): 418–45.

Kolodny, Annette. "Dancing Through the Minefield: Some Observations on the Theory, Practice, and Politics of a Feminist Literary Criticism." *Feminisms: An Anthology of Literary Theory and*

Criticism. Edited by Robyn R. Warhol and Diane Price Herndl. New Brunswick, NJ: Rutgers University Press, 1997.

Kosman, Admiel. *Gender and Dialogue in the Rabbinic Prism*. Boston and Berlin: De Gruyter, 2012.

———. *Women's Tractate: Wisdom, Love, Faithfulness, Passion, Beauty, Sex, Holiness*. Jerusalem: Keter, 2005 [Hebrew].

Kotnik, Vlado. "The Idea of Prima Donna: The History of a Very Special Opera's Institution." *International Review of the Aesthetics and Sociology of Music* 47:2 (2016): 237–87.

Kraemer, Ross S. "Jewish Women in the Diaspora World of Late Antiquity." *Jewish Women in Historical Perspective*. Edited by Judith R. Baskin. Detroit: Wayne State University Press, 1991.

Labovitz, Gail. "'Even Your Mother and Your Mother's Mother': Rabbinic Literature on Women's Usage of Cosmetics." *Nashim: A Journal of Jewish Women's Studies & Gender Issues* 23 (2012): 12–34.

Lau, Binyamin. *The Sages: Character, Context & Creativity*. Translated by Ilana Kurshan. Vols. 1–4. Jerusalem: Maggid Books, 2010–15.

Levin, Harry. *The Overreacher: A Study of Christopher Marlowe*. Cambridge, MA: Harvard University Press, 1952.

Levinas, Emmanuel. *Totality and Infinity: An Essay on Exteriority*. Translated by Alphonso Lingis. Dordrecht: Kluwer Academic Publishers, 1991.

Levine, Nachman. "The Oven of Achnai Re-Deconstructed." *Hebrew Studies* 45 (2004): 27–47.

Levinson, Joshua. "Bodies and Bo(a)rders: Emerging Fictions of Identity in Late Antiquity." *The Harvard Theological Review* 93:4 (2000): 343–72.

———. "Cultural Androgyny in Rabbinic Literature." *From Athens to Jerusalem: Medicine in Hellenized Jewish Lore and in Early Christian Literature*. Edited by Samuel Kottek and Manfred Horstmanshoff. Rotterdam: Erasmus, 2000.

———. "From Parable to Invention: The Development of Fiction as a Cultural Category." *Higayon L'Yona: New Aspects in the Study of Midrash, Aggadah and Piyut*. Edited by Joshua Levinson et al. Jerusalem: Magnes, 2006 [Hebrew].

Libson, Gideon. "Excommunication and Banning in the Mishnaic and Talmudic Period." Master's thesis, The Hebrew University of Jerusalem, 1973 [Hebrew].

Malchi, Yirmiyahu. "On Incidents Referred to in the Talmud and Explained in Rashi and Other Sources." *Ma'aseh Sippur: Studies in Jewish Narrative*. Edited by A. Lipsker and R. Kushelevsky. Ramat Gan: Bar-Ilan University Press, 2009 [Hebrew].

Mandel, Paul. "Tales of the Destruction of the Temple: Between the Land of Israel and Babylonia." *Center and Diaspora: The Land of Israel and the Diaspora in the Second Temple, Mishna and Talmud Periods*. Edited by Isaiah M. Gafni et al. Jerusalem: The Zalman Shazar Center for Jewish History, 2004 [Hebrew].

Mayerhofer, Kerstin. "Inferiority Embodied: The 'Men-struating' Jew and Pre-Modern Notions of Identity and Difference." *Comprehending Antisemitism through the Ages: A Historical Perspective*. Edited by Armin Lange et al. Vol. 3. Boston and Berlin: De Gruyter, 2021.

McAuley, Mairéad. *Reproducing Rome: Motherhood in Virgil, Ovid, Seneca, and Statius*. Oxford: Oxford University Press, 2016.

Meir, Ofra. "The Influence of the Redactional Process on the Worldview of Aggadic Stories." *Tura* 3 (1994): 67–84 [Hebrew].

———. *The Poetics of Rabbinic Stories*. Tel Aviv: Sifriat Poalim, 1993 [Hebrew].

Monnickendam, Yifat. "Bruria as a Contradictory Analogy to Rabbi Meir." *Derech Aggadah* 2 (1999): 37–63 [Hebrew].

Mor, Sagit. "The Status of Female Captives on Their Return to the Jewish Community in the Talmudic Literature." *Jewish Studies* 42 (2004): 107–18 [Hebrew].

Naeh, Shlomo. "Freedom and Celibacy: A Talmudic Variation on Tales of Temptation and Fall in Genesis and Its Syrian Background." *The Book of Genesis in Jewish and Oriental Christian Interpretation*. Edited by Judith Frishman and Lucas Van Rompay. Leuven: Traditio Exegetica Graeca, 1997.

Neusner, Jacob. *Androgynous Judaism: Masculine and Feminine in the Dual Torah*. Eugene, OR: Wipf and Stock, 1993.

———. *Development of a Legend: Studies on the Traditions Concerning Yohanan ben Zakkai*. Leiden: Brill, 1970.

———. *How the Rabbis Liberated Women*. Atlanta: Scholars Press, 1998.

———. *Judaism in the Matrix of Christianity*. Philadelphia: Fortress Press, 1986.

———. *Method and Meaning in Ancient Judaism*. Atlanta: Brown Judaic Studies, 1979.

Or, Tamara, ed. *Massekhet Betsah: A Feminist Commentary on the Babylonian Talmud*. Tübingen: Mohr Siebeck, 2010.

Ozick, Cynthia. "Notes toward Finding the Right Question (A Vindication of the Rights of Jewish Women)." *Lilith* 6 (1979): 19–29.

Peskowitz, Miriam B. *Spinning Fantasies: Rabbis, Gender and History*. Berkeley: University of California Press, 1997.

Place, Janey. "Women in Film Noir." *Women in Film Noir*. Edited by E. Ann Kaplan. London: British Film Institute, 1998.

Pomeroy, Sarah B. *Goddesses, Whores, Wives, & Slaves: Women in Classical Antiquity*. London: Pimlico, 1994.

Raveh, Inbar. *Feminist Rereadings of Rabbinic Literature*. Translated by Kaeren Fish. Waltham, MA: Brandeis University Press, 2014.

———. *Fragments of Being: Stories of the Sages – Literary Structures and Worldview*. Or Yehuda: Kinneret, Zmora-Bitan, Dvir, 2008 [Hebrew].

Reilly, Kevin. *The West and the World: A History of Civilization from the Ancient World to 1700*. Princeton: Markus Weiner Publishers, 1989.

Rogers, Katharine M. *The Troublesome Helpmate: A History of Misogyny in Literature*. Seattle: University of Washington Press, 1966.

Rosen-Zvi, Ishay. *Demonic Desires: Yetzer Hara and the Problem of Evil in Late Antiquity*. Philadelphia: University of Pennsylvania Press, 2011.

———. "The Evil Inclination, Sexuality, and Forbidden Cohabitations: A Chapter in Talmudic Anthropology." *Theory and Criticism* 14 (1999): 55–84 [Hebrew].

———. "Misogyny and Its Discontents." *Prooftexts* 25 (2005): 217–27.

Rubenstein, Jeffrey L. *The Culture of the Babylonian Talmud*. Baltimore: Johns Hopkins University Press, 2003.

———. *The Land of Truth: Talmud Tales, Timeless Teachings*. Philadelphia: The Jewish Publication Society, 2018.

———. "Social and Institutional Settings of Rabbinic Literature." *The Cambridge Companion to the Talmud and Rabbinic Literature*. Edited by Charlotte E. Fonrobert and Martin S. Jaffe. Cambridge: Cambridge University Press, 2007.

———. *Talmudic Stories: Narrative Art, Composition, and Culture*. Baltimore: Johns Hopkins University Press, 1999.

Rudlin, John. *Commedia Dell'arte: An Actor's Handbook*. London: Routledge, 1994.

Ruether, Rosemary Radford. "Judaism and Christianity: Two Fourth-Century Religions." *Studies in Religion* 2 (1972): 1–10.

Russ, Joanna. "What Can a Heroine Do? Or Why Women Can't Write." *Images of Women in Fiction: Feminist Perspectives*. Edited by Susan Koppelman. Cornillon: Bowling Green University Press, 1972.

Safrai, Chana. "Beauty, Beautification, and Cosmetics: Social Control and Halacha in Talmudic Times." *Jewish Legal Writings by Women*. Edited by Micah D. Halpern and Chana Safrai. Jerusalem: Urim, 1998.

———. "Expectations and Prediction for Women's and Gender Studies in Rabbinic Literature." *Lift Up Your Voice: Women's Voices and Feminist Interpretation in Jewish Studies*. Edited by Rina Levine-Melammed. Tel Aviv: Yediot Books, 2001 [Hebrew].

Safrai, Shmuel. "New Inquiries into the Status and Activities of Rabban Yohanan ben Zakkai After the Destruction." *Memorial Volume for Gedalyahu Alon*. Edited by M. Dorman et al. Tel Aviv: Hakibbutz Hameuchad, 1970 [Hebrew].

———. "Tales of the Sages in the Palestinian Tradition and the Babylonian Talmud." *Scripta Hierosolymitana* 22 (1971): 209–32.

Sandberg, Sheryl. *Lean In: Women, Work, and the Will to Lead*. New York: Knopf, 2013.

Satlow, Michael L. "Jewish Construction of Nakedness in Late Antiquity." *Journal of Biblical Literature* 116 (1997): 429–54.

———. "Male and Female, Did They Create It? Gender and the Judaism of the Sages." *Continuity and Renewal: Jews and Judaism in Byzantine-Christian Palestine*. Edited by Lee I. Levine. Jerusalem: Yad Ben-Zvi Press, 2004 [Hebrew].

———. *Tasting the Dish: Rabbinic Rhetoric of Sexuality*. Atlanta: Scholars Press, 1995.

———. "'Try to Be a Man': The Rabbinic Construction of Masculinity." *The Harvard Theological Review* 89:1 (1996): 19–40.

Schremer, Adiel. "Marriage, Sexuality, and Holiness: The Anti-Ascetic Legacy of Talmudic Judaism." *Gender Relationships in Marriage and Out*. Edited by R.T. Blau. New York: Yeshiva University Press, 2007.

Schwartz, Daniel R. "More on 'Zechariah ben Avkules: Humility or Zealotry?'" *Zion* 53:3 (1988): 313–16 [Hebrew].

Schwartz, Seth. "The Political Geography of Rabbinic Texts." *The Cambridge Companion to the Talmud and Rabbinic Literature*. Edited by Charlotte E. Fonrobert and Martin S. Jaffee. Cambridge: Cambridge University Press, 2007.

Segal, Eliezer. "Law as Allegory? An Unnoticed Literary Device in Talmudic Narratives." *Prooftexts* 8:2 (1988): 245–56.

Shenhar, Aliza. "The Figure of Rabbi Meir and Its Literary Characterization in the Legends." *Heqer Veiyun: Studies in Judaism*. Edited by Efrat Carmon. Haifa: Haifa University Press, 1976 [Hebrew].

Simon-Shoshan, Moshe. "The Death of Beruriah and Its Afterlife: A Reevaluation of the Provenance and Significance of Ma'aseh de-Beruriah." *Jewish Quarterly Review* 110:3 (2020): 383–411.

———. "A Doorway of Their Own: Female Ethos in Dialogue in the Talmuds." *Nashim: A Journal of Jewish Women's Studies & Gender Issues* 35 (2019): 97–127.

Sobolev-Mandelbaum, Liat. "Immah Shalom: The Controversial Role Model." *Women in Judaism: A Multidisciplinary e-Journal* 14:2 (2017): 1–20.

Sperber, Daniel. *Roman Palestine 200–400: Money and Prices*. 2nd ed. Ramat Gan: Bar-Ilan University Press, 1991.

Stein, Dina. "Folklore Elements in Late Midrash: A Folkloristic Perspective on Pirkei de Rabbi Eliezer." PhD thesis, Hebrew University of Jerusalem, 1998 [Hebrew].

———. "Let the 'People' Go? The 'Folk' and their 'Lore' as Tropes in the Reconstruction of Rabbinic Culture." *Prooftexts* 29:2 (2009): 206–41.

Steinmetz, Devora. "Agada Unbound: Inter-Agadic Characterization of the Sages in the Bavli and Implications for Reading Agada." *Creation and Composition: The Contribution of the Bavli Redactors*. Edited by Jeffrey L. Rubenstein. Tübingen: Mohr Siebeck, 2005.

Stern, David. "The Captive Woman: Hellenization, Greco-Roman Erotic Narrative, and Rabbinic Literature." *Poetics Today* 19:1 (1998): 91–127.

Stone, Suzanne L. "In Pursuit of the Counter-Text: The Turn to the Jewish Legal Model in Contemporary American Legal Theory," *Harvard Law Review* 106:4 (1993): 813–94.

Strack, Hermann L., and Günter Stemberger. *Introduction to the Talmud and Midrash*. Translated by Markus Bockmuehl. Minneapolis: Fortress Press, 1996.

Tylor, Edward B. "On a Method of Investigating the Development of Institutions, Applied to Laws of Marriage and Descent." *Journal of the Anthropological Institute of Great Britain and Ireland* 18 (1889): 245–72.

Tzuberi, Christiane. "'And the Woman Is a High-Priest': From the Temple to the Kitchen, From the Laws of Ritual Im/Purity to the Laws of Kashrut." Introduction to *Seder Qodashim: A Feminist Commentary on the Babylonian Talmud*. Edited by Tal Ilan et al. Tübingen: Mohr Siebeck, 2012.

Urbach, Ephraim E. *The Sages: Their Concepts and Beliefs*. Jerusalem: Magnes Press, 1975 [Hebrew].

Valler, Shulamit. *Women and Womanhood in the Stories of the Babylonian Talmud*. Tel Aviv: Hakibbutz Hameuchad, 1993 [Hebrew].

———. *Women in Jewish Society in the Talmudic Period*. Tel Aviv: Hakibbutz Hameuchad, 2000 [Hebrew].

Visotzky, Burton L. "Midrash Mishle: A Critical Edition." PhD thesis, The Jewish Theological Seminary of America, 1983.

———. "Overturning the Lamp." *Journal of Jewish Studies* 38 (1987): 75–83.

Walker, Steven F. *Jung and Jungians on Myth*. London: Routledge, 2002.

Watts Belser, Julia. *Rabbinic Tales of Destruction: Gender, Sex, and Disability in the Ruins of Jerusalem*. Oxford: Oxford University Press, 2018.

Wegner, Judith R. *Chattel or Person? The Status of Women in the Mishnah*. Oxford: Oxford University Press, 1988.

———. "The Image and Status of Women in Classical Rabbinic Judaism." *Jewish Women in Historical Perspective*. Edited by Judith R. Baskin. Detroit: Wayne State University Press, 1998.

Welter, Barbara. "The Cult of True Womanhood: 1820–1860." *American Quarterly* 18:2 (1966): 151–74.

Wimpfheimer, Barry S. *The Talmud: A Biography*. Princeton: Princeton University Press, 2018.

Woolf, Virginia. *A Room of One's Own*. London: Hogarth Press, 1929.

———. "Professions for Women." *The Death of the Moth and Other Essays*. New York: Harcourt, 1974.

Yassif, Eli. *The Hebrew Folktale: History, Genre, Meaning*. Jerusalem: The Bialik Institute, 1994 [Hebrew].

Yisraeli-Taran, Anat. *Legends of the Destruction*. Tel Aviv: Hakibbutz Hameuchad, 1997 [Hebrew].

Yuval, Israel Jacob. *Two Nations in Your Womb: Perceptions of Jews and Christians in Late Antiquity and the Middle Ages*. Berkeley: University of California Press, 2008.

Zeitlin, Froma I. *Playing the Other: Gender and Society in Classical Greek Literature*. Chicago: University of Chicago Press, 1996.

Zellentin, Holger. *Rabbinic Parodies of Jewish and Christian Literature*. Tübingen: Mohr Siebeck, 2011.

General Index

Source Index

Bible

Mishna

Tosefta

Jerusalem Talmud

Babylonian Talmud

Minor Tractates

Midrash

Image Credits

p. 2: 1866, Public Domain, attribution: Dr. Jorgen
p. 3: 1607, Public Domain, Web Gallery of Art
p. 5: 2013, Shakespear's Globe Theater © Alastair Muir
p. 6: 1921, Public Domain, attribution: Janneman
p. 7: 1847, Public Domain, attribution: Bensin
p. 25: 18th–early 19th centuries, Public Domain, attribution: Vincent Steenberg
p. 27: 1886, Public Domain, attribution: Shuishouyue
p. 29: c. 1888, Public Domain, attribution: Androstachys
p. 30: Doodko/Shutterstock
p. 31: Pictorial Press Ltd/Alamy Stock Photo, modified from original
p. 53: 19th cent, Public Domain, attribution: Tiberioclaudio99
p. 54: 1767–1768, Public Domain, attribution: Themadchopper
p. 55: 1845, Public Domain, attribution: A1AA1A
p. 56: United Archives GmbH/Alamy Stock Photo
p. 57: Photo 12/Alamy Stock Photo
p. 88: Left – © Ann Ronan Picture Library/London/Great Britain/HIP/Art Resource, NY. Right – Undated, Public Domain, attribution: Micione
p. 89: Above left and right – 1900, Gustave Doré, Public Domain, attributions: 1677venzel gottorpskij and IPork. Below left and right – Ballet Company National Opera of Ukraine, modified from original
p. 90: Left – United Archives GmbH/Alamy Stock Photo. Right – Allstar Picture Ltd/Alamy Stock Photo

p. 91: Right – 1960, By Dell Publishing, 1960. Photograph by Jacques Lowe. *Modern Screen*, Public Domain, attribution: Mutter Erde. Left – ScreenProd/Photononstop/Alamy Stock Photos.

p. 118: Jozef Sedmak/Alamy Stock Photos

p. 120: Above – 1860–1882, Donated to Wikimedia Commons as part of a project by the National Gallery of Art. CC0. Attribution: Brwz. Below – 1911, Public Domain, attribution: Shakko

p. 123: 1791, Public Domain, attribution: copyfraud

p. 125: Album/Alamy Stock Photo

p. 161: c. 1785, Public Domain, attribution: RomanHistorian

p. 163: Moviestore Collection Ltd/Alamy Stock Photo

p. 164: 1841–1843, Public Domain, BotMultichillT

p. 166: *Woman's Mission: Companion of Manhood*, 1863, George Elgar Hicks, Photo: Tate

p. 168: Upper left – © Hamilton Beach Brands Inc. Upper right and lower left – Patti McConville/Alamy Stock Photo. Lower right – Neil Baylis/Alamy Stock Photo

About the Author

Gila Fine is a lecturer of rabbinic literature at the Pardes Institute of Jewish Studies, exploring the tales of the Talmud through philosophy, literary criticism, psychoanalysis, and pop-culture. She serves on the faculties of the Nachshon Project, Amudim Seminary, the Tikvah Scholars Program, and the London School of Jewish Studies, and has taught thousands of students at conferences, campuses, and communities across the Jewish world. As editor in chief of Maggid Books, Gila edited and published over a hundred titles of contemporary Jewish thought, including several bestsellers and eight National Jewish Book Award winners. Her work has been featured in the BBC, *Haaretz, The Jerusalem Post, The Jerusalem Report, Tradition, Jewish News,* and *The Jewish Chronicle* (which selected her as one of the ten most influential Brits in Israel). *Haaretz* has called her "a young woman on her way to becoming one of the more outstanding Jewish thinkers of the next generation."

The fonts used in this book are from the Arno family

Maggid Books
The best of contemporary Jewish thought from
Koren Publishers Jerusalem Ltd.